REA

DO NOT REMOVE
CARDS FROM POCKET

Funny Women

Also by Mary Unterbrink

Jazz Women at the Keyboard (McFarland, 1983)
Manatees, Gentle Giants in Peril (1984)

Funny Women
American Comediennes, 1860–1985

by

Mary Unterbrink

McFarland & Company, Inc., Publishers
Jefferson, North Carolina, and London

Library of Congress Cataloguing-in-Publication Data

Unterbrink, Mary, 1937–
Funny women.

Bibliography: p. 229.
Includes index.
1. Women comedians — United States — Biography.
2. American wit and humor — History and criticism.
I. Title.
PN2285.U57   1987   792.7′028′088042   85-43595

ISBN 0-89950-226-1 (acid-free natural paper)

Printed in the United States of America.

McFarland   Box 611   Jefferson NC   28640

To my family

Acknowledgments

Many people contributed to the writing of this book and I am grateful to all of them for their friendship and support. My husband, Larry, participated in the research all through the many months of compiling the material and writing the manuscript. For ongoing editorial and research assistance, and for the generous loan of books and comedy recordings from their collections, I thank Rosemary Jones, Barbara Contardi, Reid Austin, Dixie Engesser, Carolyn Wells, Gail Stocker, Martha Moffett, Jack Higgins, Isaac Corkland, Martha Munzer, Charlotte Shaffman, John Ziegler, Lu Oliver, Harry Crease, Greta Silver, Emma Lobel, Barbara Dinerman, Dennis O'Donovan, Niki Fotopoulos and Elizabeth McNeil.

I am indebted to the comediennes themselves for sharing their anecdotes, biographical material and photographs. My thanks go especially to Phyllis Diller and Erma Bombeck for finding the time to be so helpful; also Carol Burnett, Geri Jewell, Minnie Pearl, Mary Gross, Diane Nichols, Monica Piper, Martha Raye, Emily Levine, Joan Rivers, Jane Anderson, and Dana Vance. Without them and all the other funny women, past and present, this book would not have been possible.

Table of Contents

List of Photographs

Preface

Egyptian paintings depicting slapstick humor have existed for over 5,000 years. The debate over what is funny, and who is funny, has probably been going on even longer. The ploys comic performers use to get laughs range from a feather-coaxed tickle to the big punch. Audiences respond with giggles, belly laughs, or the ultimate breakup of convulsive laughter which has them "rolling in the aisles." An absolute standard for comedy does not exist — the audience is the sole arbiter.

This collection of funny women is meant to be representative of the different eras and major trends of American show business. The entertainers I have chosen are as diverse as the genres of comedy which have developed over the years (mime, farce, burlesque, satire, situation comedy, to name just a few). The individual performer's humor may be verbal or unabashedly physical. She may be known for her repartee or her creation of a comedic character. Whatever her contribution, it carries her own individual stamp, and defies imitation. The successful comedienne establishes a special contact with her audiences which sets her apart and guarantees her staying power, while other performers often fade away.

Any effort to compile profiles of leading comediennes over the past eventful 125 years will inevitably result in certain performers being omitted. Perhaps they will be recognized in another work — there is definitely enough material for more books on this subject. The eclectic assemblage you find here was not hastily decided upon, for the term "comedienne" itself is not easily defined. The line between "comedy actress" and "comedienne" blurs even among the entertainers themselves. A woman comically delivering lines written by someone else may consider herself a comedienne, whereas another, who extemporaneously breaks up the audience, may insist she's acting.

A common thread uncovered during the research of this book is each woman's total belief in herself and her firm sense of commitment to her craft. These performers, writers, and directors share the marvelous gift of a comic spirit. They are intrinsically funny and possess an instinct for creating comedy. Because the careers of many of these women spanned several decades, they have overlapped different eras. Their profiles have been placed to correspond with the medium in which they either first became successful or in which they made their most significant contribution to American comedy.

It is hoped that this book conveys a sense of what women have been up to in comedy since the mid-1800s. Reading these pages should bring back memories of some of your favorite comediennes from the past and enhance your appreciation of today's funnier-than-ever funny women.

Introduction

Millions of television viewers watch as Joan Rivers strides onstage amid music and applause. The hottest comedienne of the eighties jabs a long red fingernail toward the studio audience and asks, "Can we talk?"

Joan belongs to a large sorority of funny women who have generated laughter throughout our country's history. Beginning in the 1870s, entertainers toured America on vaudeville circuits, bringing their humor and pathos to those who flocked to see them. Singers, dancers, skaters, acrobats, animal trainers, ventriloquists and comics traveled together from town to town, doing their routines in small theaters or on makeshift stages in town halls. During vaudeville's heyday, as many as 20,000 vaudeville performers traveled the circuit, sometimes performing six shows a day. Women were among the first vaudevillians as mothers, sisters, daughters in family acts, in husband-and-wife teams, as members of various partnerships and troupes, or performing solo. Though of another era, these women weren't much different from contemporary comediennes.

Lotta Crabtree, the toast of San Francisco during the Gold Rush days, was skillful at improvising. Irene Franklin's original satires on everyday events and her impersonations of ordinary women (instead of well-known subjects) parallel those performed by Lily Tomlin. Ruth Draper developed one of her monologues around a telephone conversation with an imaginary friend. Gay Nineties comedienne Trixie Friganza's self-effacing humor about her looks and weight was the prototype of material used by Phyllis Diller and Joan Rivers.

The Palace Theatre, vaudeville's mecca, opened in New York City in 1913. A dream common to all vaudevillians was to walk out on stage at the Palace. Many spent their entire lives pursuing that goal. When young American men left to fight in World War I a few years later, vaudeville provided brief respites for patrons worried about a world in turmoil. The Roaring Twenties began with Women's Suffrage and ended

1

in despair when the stock market crashed. Phyllis Diller maintains that in order to create good comedy, something must be wrong or out of kilter. Her theory certainly held true during the thirties and forties when the gaps between Americans' hopes and their fulfillment were never wider. If there was ever a need for humor to divert attention from people's misery, it was during the Depression. Comedy flourished as radio listeners tuned in their favorite shows. During World War II, comedy again helped to raise the morale of a nation whose sons were being sacrificed. (Radio fans have not forgotten the lift those broadcasts gave them. Records and cassettes of the routines of Burns and Allen, and "Fibber McGee and Molly" are still being sold.) Displaced vaudevillians worked again. Touring with the USO, they entertained fighting troops and personnel at armed forces installations during and after the conflict.

In the fifties, Americans were introduced to the innovative, mesmerizing effect of television which allowed us to see our favorite funny men and women in our own homes. The new medium propelled comediennes into the national limelight, making some of them world celebrities. (It's been said that Lucille Ball's face has been seen on this planet by more people, more often, than the face of any other person who has ever lived.)

Political satire became popular in the sixties, reflecting a country embroiled in civil rights issues and the protest movement over the Vietnam conflict. Clubs and concert stages became the major outlets for creative comedy minds. From the late seventies on, humor focused more on personal relationships, the sexual revolution and feminism.

From vaudeville to video, funny women evolved into a comedic national treasure. They came from diverse backgrounds and entered the comedy arena at different stages in life. Martha Raye was born in a charity ward of a hospital; Ruth Draper was the daughter of a well-to-do physician. Irene Franklin was carried on stage as an infant; Phyllis Diller, a housewife with five children, first stepped into the spotlight at the age of 37. Mabel Normand quit school at 13; Joan Rivers graduated Phi Beta Kappa from a prestigious college.

Some comediennes were born into show business families. Ray Dooley was the daughter of a circus clown, Gracie Allen's father was a clog-and-minstrel man, and Elaine May's father was an actor. Others, like Marie Dressler who left the comforts of home at 14, severed family ties to pursue a career.

A marriage often crumbled under the demands of maintaining a full-blown career, but performers Gracie Allen, Marian Jordan, Jean Carroll, Jane Ace, Minnie Pearl and Anne Meara were among those who worked out a way to combine the two.

After only a few years at the top, the thriving career of Totie Fields was cut short by her untimely death. In contrast, veterans such as Bea Lillie, Mae West, Sophie Tucker, Ruth Draper, Moms Mabley and Eve Arden continued to please their fans for four, five, or even six decades.

More than a century after the first nervous, perspiring vaudevillians walked onstage hoping to earn the laughter of an audience, the benefits of comedy are still being discovered. In 1979, the importance of laughter in combatting illness was documented in *An Anatomy of an Illness*. Author Norman Cousins revealed how laughter helped him recover from a usually fatal disease. Comedy films and records provided uplifting feelings which served as a conditioning agent and increased the value of his medical treatment. His book initiated studies of how laughter and positive emotions can help maintain good health and overcome disease.

Women have created their share of humor over the years, though they have not had an easy time presenting it to the public, because those making the hiring decisions and having final approval on materials have nearly always been male. The so-called "women's humor" was often easily dismissed as being irrelevant to a mass audience, even though women outnumber men in this country. It seems incongruous that women's observations about dating, sex, marriage and motherhood are labeled "women's humor" while the material men have performed for well over a century about dating, sex, marriage and fatherhood has never been labeled "men's humor."

With today's changing attitudes toward women, comediennes are making themselves heard in a world that has been economically, politically and psychologically dominated by men. The revolution in consciousness produces comedy with sensitivity and heightened awareness, serving as a catharsis for the performers themselves, as well as the women in their audiences. The feminine perspective is also appreciated by increasing numbers of men, who are reassessing their relationships with wives, lovers, mothers, daughters, and female coworkers and acquaintances.

More women than ever before are seeking a career in comedy, and the number of outlets for their talents is growing with the proliferation of comedy clubs, improvisational groups and talent showcases around the country. Not deterred by the fact that comedy is still widely considered a man's domain which few females are encouraged to enter, these funny women share their zany perceptions of American life.

Chapter One
The Early Days (1860–1930)

Life was hard for a woman performing on the American stage during the nineteenth century. Vaudeville, the national showcase for entertainers during the late 1800s and early 1900s, was especially grueling. If the early vaudevillian didn't have an agent, she had to answer ads in show business trade journals to find work. She auditioned, and if she got the job, she often performed as many as six shows a day in halls and theaters at stops along the circuit. She traveled with a troupe of other entertainers across the country in trains which were freezing in winter and sweltering in summer. On small-time circuits (often called the Death Trail), available lodging was usually poor. Marriage was difficult unless husband and wife found work on the same circuit, and children were often left behind with relatives. Friendships with "civilians" (those not in show business) were rare, as vaudevillians were outside the mainstream of society and tended to rely on each other.

The comedienne's act was everything, her lifeblood. She was alone with her material and had to know how to lead up to the punch line and how to time the laughs. Even her entrance and exit were practiced over and over to perfection. She continually revised her material for different areas of the country, jealously guarding it as her own creation. Her routine had to please the theater manager at each stop, for he could simply cancel her act, leaving her stranded in a strange town with no income. Only a strong constitution and deep faith in herself enabled her to go on night after night.

Those who made names for themselves on the circuit were often tapped to work in films (sometimes segments of proposed films were first tried out on vaudeville audiences). The visual possibilities of film gave men and women a chance to express the comic spirit in a new way and spawned the first generation of film comedy greats. By the 1920s, vaudeville houses began adding movies and equipping the theaters for the new rage, the talkies. Some vaudevillians were able to make the transition

5

to radio or films, but many were left behind as vaudeville began its decline.

Certain comediennes were talented enough to consistently regale their audiences, no matter where they played. They became favorites of stage fans and early filmgoers, and are remembered for their unique contributions to comedy.

Lotta Crabtree

While still a child, Lotta Crabtree became an entertainment phenomenon of the California Gold Rush era. The miners who flocked to see the girl often pelted her with pouches of gold dust and tossed gold nuggets on stage when she performed. Her popularity grew as she matured, making her a beloved national figure of early American theater and the highest paid female performer in the country.

Lotta, christened Charlotte Mignon, was born November 7, 1847, in New York City to John Crabtree and Mary Ann (Livesey) Crabtree, both English immigrants. In 1851 John Crabtree left his bookstore and family to dig for gold in California. Although he found no gold, he sent for his family a year later, and they settled in the mining country in California's Grass Valley. Mrs. Crabtree ran a boarding house and persuaded one of her temporary boarders, actress Lola Montez, to teach young Lotta to sing and dance. She later arranged for her daughter to learn to play the banjo and do pantomime.

At the age of 8, Lotta made her debut entertaining saloon patrons in Rabbit Creek, California. Soon she and her mother were traveling by horseback to other mining camps, Lotta sometimes sleeping in the saddle. The curly redhead with enormous brown eyes easily established an immediate rapport with the entertainment-starved miners who came to see her, often improvising material just for them. Her paradoxical qualities of innocence and impudence fascinated and lifted the spirits of even the most downhearted.

Before every performance, however, Lotta suffered terribly, dreading the moment she'd have to walk out in front of a group of strangers. The crying, trembling child was held and sung to by her mother before facing the rough California audiences.

The Crabtrees moved to San Francisco in 1856 and Lotta divided her time between the city's entertainment halls and tours of the mining camps in Nevada and Oregon. Her earnings supported the entire family (which by then included two younger brothers). In 1858, the high-spirited performer made her stage debut as Gertrude in *Loan of a Lover*. The following year she was bestowed the title "Miss Lotta, the San Francisco Favorite."

Lotta and her mother left California in 1864 to tour the East and Midwest, and within two years, won the hearts of theatergoers with her burlesque of Jenny Lind in *Jenny Leatherlungs* at the Howard Athenaeum in Boston and appearances in both title roles in *Little Nell and the Marchioness* at Crosby's Opera House in Chicago. Her next success was at Wallack's in New York, playing six parts in *The Pet of the Petticoats*.

Lotta's outrageousness (she dared to smoke and show her legs on stage in the 1860s) was tempered by her kittenish mannerisms. According to the *New York Times*, Lotta was a "beautiful doll" who could generate continuous shrieks of laughter. From 1870 on, the tremendously popular entertainer toured with her own company, presenting plays such as *Little Bright Eyes* and *Mam'zelle Nitouche*.

Between engagements, Lotta traveled leisurely throughout Europe. She had many imitators, but none of them possessed that special eccentric quality which made her so loved. Because of her natural style of acting, she is credited with introducing a new school of technique to the early American theater. However, Lotta did not choose her life. She never overcame her terror of appearing in public. As a woman, she had to be comforted and pampered by Mrs. Crabtree before dancing out onto the stages in San Francisco, New York or London. Once the curtain went up, her fears melted and she became vivacious and carefree.

After a stage injury in 1891, she retired at the age of 43 to her country house on Lake Hopatcong in New Jersey where she painted, rode horses, and entertained. Lotta never married, and following her mother's death in 1905, became somewhat reclusive. She did return to San Francisco for "Lotta Crabtree Day" at the Panama-Pacific Exposition in 1915 and appeared at benefits for the soldiers and veterans during World War I.

Lotta lived at the Hotel Brewster in Boston during her last years. The hotel was one of many properties Mrs. Crabtree, an astute businesswoman, had purchased for her daughter. Lotta died there on September 25, 1924, at the age of 76, leaving nearly $4 million to needy actors, veterans, animal shelters and other charities.

A tall, ornate public fountain, donated by Lotta to the city of San Francisco on September 9, 1875, still stands in her memory. "Lotta's Fountain," built to provide water for horses and other animals, is located on a center island at the busy intersection of Geary and Market Streets, not far from Union Square. In 1974, it was refurbished, the water running once more, to remind San Franciscans of the impish Gold Rush performer who charmed her way into the hearts of everyone she met.

May Irwin

May Irwin (Madame Laughter) easily captured the love of her fans and was widely considered to be the funniest woman on the American stage during the late 1880s.

Born Georgia Campbell in Whitby, Ontario, in 1862, she first performed professionally in 1875 when her father's death left the family almost destitute. She and her sister Ada sang duets at the Adelphi Variety Theatre in Buffalo where manager Daniel Shelby renamed them May and Flo Irwin. Two years later, Tony Pastor caught their act on tour and booked them for his vaudeville center in New York City.

Blonde, robust May soon became known for her liveliness and flair for comedy. In 1883 Augustin Daly hired her for his stock company, breaking up the sisters' song-and-dance act. She played soubrettes in his productions and traveled abroad with the company in 1884 and 1886. The part of Susan in *A Night Off* brought her acclaim and led to a starring comedy role in the 1896 Broadway production of *The Widow Jones*.

A brief sequence from the play was filmed in close-up and titled *The Kiss*. The advent of moving pictures gave audiences the opportunity to be fully present while fires burned, horses galloped, or men fought. So the first time a kiss was filmed, it had an overwhelming impact on viewers. May made movie history when she embraced and kissed her costar John C. Rice. Though the film runs less than a minute, it was denounced by clergymen as immoral and caused the earliest stirrings of public interest in screen censorship. *The Kiss* is routinely shown today in film collections and in museums.

May also popularized a type of song called "coon-shouting," sung in Negro dialect to syncopated ragtime. She herself composed one song in that mode, titling it "Mamie, Come Kiss Your Honey Boy." Though her talents as an excellent raconteur were perfectly suited for vaudeville, May preferred the legitimate stage but always insisted that her vaudeville years had honed her technique. She was one of the least temperamental and most loved of notable women stars of the day. President Woodrow Wilson, a frequent vaudeville-goer, said May would make a good Secretary of Laughter.

"I'm honest with my audiences," May confided to a friend. "I never fool them . . . the public has learned that I will be there with every ounce of entertainment I can give. I respect my public."

Along with Sarah Bernhardt and Elsie Janis, May found animal acts so objectionable that she refused to play a bill that included one. She also reported exploitative animal trainers to the S.P.C.A.

May was married to businessman Frederick Keller from 1878 until his death in 1886. Two sons, Walter and Harry, resulted from that union. In 1907, she married her agent Kurt Eisenfeldt. She enjoyed being a homemaker, publishing her favorite recipes in *May Irwin's Home Cooking* in 1904. May not only took charge of her own career, but was also a sharp businesswoman. She amassed a fortune in property, realizing a million dollars when she sold the block between 54th and 55th streets on Lexington Avenue in New York City.

When invited to write articles or columns for publications of that era, May declined, stating that humor simply could not be turned on or off at will.

"Humor is spontaneous ... unanalyzable.... It is as mysterious as and less controllable than electricity," she claimed.

Whatever her reluctance to write about humor, she never failed to bring merriment to her audiences. When she was nearly 70, May agreed (on two hours' notice) to fill in for an ailing performer at the Palace. Claiming she was unprepared when she walked out on stage, she proceeded to tell jokes and then sang her old song "The Bully," from *The Widow Jones*. She packed them in for a solid week and accepted Eddie Darling's invitation to play on his upcoming old-timers' bill with Marie Dressler, Marie Cahill, Cissie Loftus, Fritzi Scheff and Blanche Ring.

"I'm the oldest of the lot," she volunteered.

May died in New York City on October 22, 1938.

Marie Dressler

"I was born with a terrific urge to please people, to make them happy," said perhaps the best remembered of early comediennes. Leila Koerber was born in 1869 in Cobourg, Ontario, Canada. A restaurant bearing her famous stage name has prospered for years in her hometown and continues to do a good business.

When she was 14, the girl used an aunt's name (her family objected to her stage aspirations), and joined a light opera company. Marie first became known for her comedic talent while working in legitimate theater. In 1892 she appeared in *The Robber of the Rhine* with Maurice Barrymore, and when the play closed, began singing in vaudeville. Joining Lillian Russell's company brought her recognition for her portrayal of Flo Honeydew in *The Lady Slavey* in 1896.

"Lady Slavey was my first big success," she recalled of her first taste of stardom. "It had taken exactly eleven years to make Broadway—eleven years of tank towns and hard work and little pay—sometimes no

pay at all. But it was worth it all to hang out of a window and watch my name in electric lights."

After the turn of the century, Marie returned to vaudeville and toured extensively. In 1907 she was a smash in London. Playing the part of Tillie Blobbs, the rooming-house drudge in *Tillie's Nightmare* brought Marie both fame and a signature song. From then on, "Heaven Will Protect the Working Girl" was associated with Marie Dressler.

Tillie's Nightmare led to Marie's recruitment for the movies by Mack Sennett in 1914. The entertainer went to Hollywood where she was immediately put to work in the classic silent film *Tillie's Punctured Romance* (an adaptation of the play). Her coworkers in that film were of the highest calibre: Charlie Chaplin (whom she greatly admired), Mabel Normand, Mack Swain, Chester Conklin, and the Keystone Kops. Elaborately staged, the film parodied the country girl–city slicker theme and was filled with earthy humor. Audiences loved it.

Marie worked in subsequent films with notable performers like Eddie Foy, and Weber and Fields. Years later, Joe Weber and Lew Fields were booked on the same bill at the Palace with a reunion of female old-timers. When the two men realized they were billed second after their old colleague Marie, they refused to go on.

During World War I, entertainers such as Marie and Charlie Chaplin worked to sell Liberty Bonds. One summer she was the guest of Mrs. Woodrow Wilson at the summer White House. She was also honored by American GIs in France when they named both a street and a cow after her.

"One company was always stealing her from another," she said of her namesake.

When the cow was killed during a siege of fighting, headlines of the "Marie Dressler" death caused considerable confusion among friends and fans back home.

"One bright day, I woke up to find headlines screaming, 'Marie Dressler' killed in line of duty," she said. "I had a hard time convincing people that the report of my death had been greatly exaggerated."

Unlike many silent film performers, Marie's popularity skyrocketed when sound pictures came along. Her first talkie was *The Callahans and the Murphys* (1927), in which she and Polly Moran played tippling neighbors. The two comediennes made three more films with the same story line.

Min and Bill, a 1930 talkie Marie made with Wallace Beery was one

Marie Dressler (left), Charlie Chaplin and Mabel Norman in *Tillie's Punctured Romance*.

of Metro's biggest financial successes. Her appearance in the film about two inhabitants of a dockside slum earned Marie the Academy Award for best actress of 1931/32. In 1933, they again teamed up for *Tugboat Annie* and her last film, *Dinner at Eight*, which included Jean Harlow and John Barrymore in the cast.

Wallace Beery once said, "Like my dear old friend Marie Dressler, my mug has been my fortune."

"I was born homely," she said of her lot to succeed in a profession where a pretty face was considered a definite advantage. Marie's life's work was to make others laugh and she took that responsibility seriously. One of her favorite lines had to do with work. "If ants are such busy workers," she would sometimes say, "how come they find time to go to all the picnics?"

Marie's fans did not desert her as she grew older. At the age of 63 she topped the Quigley Poll in both 1932 and 1933, the year before her death. Just two years later Shirley Temple began her reign as America's most popular box office star. She published two autobiographical books: *The Life Story of an Ugly Duckling* (1924) and *My Own Story* (1934).

In the latter, Marie wrote that she had enjoyed her celebrity status and the opportunity to meet so many wonderful people, among them seven different American presidents. She'd had "a full life to look back on. What more could any man or woman ask?"

Trixie Friganza

Many of the early female vaudeville headliners were big women: Marie Dressler, Emma Carus, May Irwin, Sophie Tucker, Stella Mayhue and Trixie Friganza. Trixie was the predecessor of women who get laughs by deriding their own shortcomings, whether it be lack of personality, sex appeal or physical attributes.

"When I started in show business I was thin enough to be blown through a keyhole," she'd say. "Now I can't even get through the door."

Her popularity with audiences was confirmed by critics, such as the one from *Variety* who declared her "a riotous hit," during her headlining reign at the Palace.

On November 29, 1870, Delia O'Callahan was born in Grenola, Kansas. At the age of 19 she appeared on stage doing chorus work in *The Pearls of Pekin*, adopting her mother's maiden name. Her first major role opposite Henry E. Dixey in *The Mascot* launched a show business career which within a few years led to her London appearance in *The Belle of*

Bohemia. From the mid-1890s until 1912, "Broadway's Favorite Champagne Girl" kept busy working in successful stage plays, among them *The Girl from Paris* (1901) and *The Orchid* (1908).

Next came vaudeville for which the plump entertainer was perfectly suited with her act, "My Little Bag o' Trix." The ample-figured performer cheerfully described herself as a "perfect forty-six," and constantly lamented her loveless existence in songs and jokes. One of the skits began with her already large body encased in layers of costumes which she peeled off as the act progressed. During the shimmy craze, she told other heavy women how to do the dance: "Walk fast and stop short."

Her personal life followed the same pattern of many of her peers. Marriages of women headliners rarely lasted because an enormous amount of time was consumed in maintaining their status. Male admirers were plentiful and more than willing to share the women's often extravagant lifestyles. Trixie never remarried after the failure of her marriage to Charles Goettler. Though the travel agency she had established for him was not profitable, the performer was knowledgeable about business dealings. Among her many properties was a South Carolina plantation.

The comedienne extended her talents to play character roles in films from the early 1920s until 1940. She appeared in a comic ballet number with Buster Keaton in his first sound picture *Easy Go* (also titled *Free and Easy*). Other screen credits include *Gentlemen Prefer Blondes* (1928), *Monte Carlo* (an early sound musical by Paramount in 1930 starring Jeannette MacDonald), and *A Star Is Born* (1937).

As age and an arthritic condition began to take their toll, the "Perpetual Flapper" curtailed her activities, though she was still entertaining GIs during the late forties. Trixie died at the age of 85 on February 27, 1955.

Irene Franklin

Surely Irene Franklin was an inspiration to the many women who became vaudeville performers after the turn of the century. Irene was born in St. Louis, Missouri, on June 13, 1876, and as an infant was carried on stage during a stock production of *Hearts of Oak*, a melodrama of that era. She went on to play child parts until her early teens when she toured Australia and England with her mother and sister.

Within a short time of returning home, both of Irene's parents died and the only work she could get was filling in at Tony Pastor's in New

York. Her act didn't catch on with audiences until pianist Burton Green convinced her that his special musical arrangements would enhance her singing.

"You're special," he told her.

Burton wrote down a melody Irene hummed for him, a tune she remembered her father playing on the piano. The attractive red-haired singer then wrote the lyrics and titled the song "Redhead." The new partners broke in their act playing small towns, then opened in New York. Irene's debut in American vaudeville launched a most successful career, with "Redhead" as her identification song.

Audiences loved her little-girl character dressed in a romper suit who lamented about the nasty comments she had to endure because her hair was red. Irene's characterization, expressive in both humor and pathos, was called "a work of art" by critics.

Burton and Irene fell in love and were married after Burton's wife, columnist Helen van Campen, agreed to a divorce. For the next two decades they were the most popular man-and-wife team with American audiences, as well as continually winning the praise of critics.

Irene wrote her own material and with her new husband composed more "kid songs" which like "Redhead" quickly caught on with her fans. One of her earliest bits was a tough streetcar conductor who gave passengers a hard time. She also performed satires on social issues such as feminism and prohibition. Her risqué song "What Have You Got on Your Hip? You Don't Seem to Bulge Where a Gentleman Ought To," referred to a man carrying a hip flask.

In 1908, the witty entertainer won a contest for the Most Popular Woman Vaudeville Artist, beating out well-known talents Eva Tanguay and Marie Dressler. Irene became part of the Big Four of women headliners in vaudeville who earned nearly $2,000 a week. (This was in contrast to a regular laborer's weekly wage of $15.) She shared the position with Nora Bayes, Eva Tanguay and Elsie Janis, who in 1930 became the first woman to produce a Hollywood talking picture, *Paramount on Parade*. The four women also received money from song publishers and the sale of phonograph records.

Lavish tips were expected of headliners like Irene who couldn't afford *not* to pay a gratuity to the musicians, spotlight men, transfer men or stagehands. A misplaced trunk, incomplete set or wrong musical cue could have severe effects on one's career. Irene seldom caused problems for her coworkers or those who hired her. Unlike some of the other highly paid entertainers of the day, she was not temperamental.

Irene had the ability to keenly observe a chorus girl or unhappy child and transform herself into that individual, complete with jargon and mannerisms. Her impersonations of an old farm woman at a railway station, a school teacher or a waitress were immediately identifiable. The singer's long, fiery hair was her most valuable prop and Irene used it to advantage during her act. In a few seconds she could skillfully arrange it into spitcurls, a matronly bun or youthful braids to enhance the portrayal she was about to do.

Through her years of immense popularity, Irene always credited Burton for his support and career guidance and underplayed her own talents.

"I sing badly, have only two notes," she'd say.

He in turn modestly declined to acknowledge that he was more than just a background musician and referred to being "just part of the scenery."

During the First World War, the couple went to France to entertain American servicemen from a truck which served as a stage. After Burton's death in 1922, Irene married a much younger pianist, Jerry Jarnagan, and returned to the stage, but her act was never as good. She appeared in theaters on the West Coast and in New York where she gave her final Broadway performance in *Sweet Adeline*, a hit musical of 1929. A few years later, Irene went to Hollywood to work in films which included *Change of Heart, Married Before Breakfast*, and *Garden of Allah*. Irene's career further declined with her husband's suicide in 1934. The last of her films was *Fixer Dugan* in 1939.

Though she had made a fortune during her career, Irene Franklin spent her last days in poverty, feeling that she had been forgotten. She died in 1941 at an Actors Fund Home at the age of 65. A few days earlier she had written a friend, "I don't think there are many who will remember me or who care."

Ruth Draper

Born in New York City on December 2, 1884, Ruth was the daughter of a well-known physician, Dr. William Henry Draper, and Ruth (Dana) Draper, daughter of Charles Dana, editor of the New York *Sun*. From her earliest years, Ruth was endowed with an uncanny ability to mimic people she observed. Her first audience was her family, and as she grew older, she exhibited her impersonations at parties and for charity events.

While in her twenties, Ruth continually worked to develop her character sketches, modeling them after that of English-born actress Beatrice Herford, whose monologues were becoming popular theater fare. Ruth's attention to nuances in both voice and gesture resulted in a cast of characters which fascinated other artists who saw her perform, among them Paderewski, Henry Adams, and Henry James, who even wrote a monologue for her. "You have woven your own very beautiful little Persian carpet," James told her. "Stand on it!"

Ruth began performing publicly to favorable reviews in New York City in April of 1916, and then, as World War I was coming to an end, entertained servicemen both at home and abroad. During her travels, she absorbed foreign dialects to expand her repertoire even more.

On January 29, 1920, Ruth finally made her formal professional debut presenting her monologues at London's Aeolian Hall. That launched a lifetime of traveling the world with her trunk of props to perform for large audiences (and many world leaders), always drawing critical acclaim. Besides her success in Europe, Asia and Africa, she was an immediate hit in the United States where she performed for President Harding in December, 1921, and enjoyed a nineteen-week-run at the Comedy Theatre in New York in 1928.

Ruth's act remained basically the same through the years, taking place on a bare stage with only a few props like a shawl or piece of clothing to change her appearance. She worked alone and varied her dialogue at every performance. Her repertoire included fifty-four characters in thirty-five sketches she had written herself. Ruth's individual characters would respond to invisible companions during her skits such as "Showing the Garden," "Three Generations in a Court of Domestic Relations," "An English House Party," or "The Italian Lesson" in which a wealthy matron converses with her four children, her tutor, her secretary, her cook, her manicurist, her husband, her lover, and various friends, all during an Italian lesson. Because of her expertise, audiences had no trouble imagining her invisible characters.

One monologue centered around a Southern belle attending a ball, another involved two Irish cleaning women, and "On a Porch in a Maine Coast Village" entailed recollections of two old women on a porch.

Dark Harbor, Maine, was home to Ruth when she was not touring. Though many awards were bestowed on her over a four-decade career, she was especially proud that in all that time, she had missed only one performance.

Following two performances in New York on December 30, 1956, Ruth died in her sleep at the age of 72. The shawls she had used to create her characters were draped over the coffin, as she had earlier requested.

Today her insightful characterizations are still enjoyed through the recordings of her work and are an inspiration to other performers in both drama and comedy. In 1960, *The Art of Ruth Draper* by Morton Dauwen Zabel was published. It contains the basic texts of many of Ruth's monologues along with a memoir of the talented monologist.

Ray Dooley

Ray was born Rachel Rice Dooley in Glasgow, Scotland, in 1891. She first performed as a young dancer in a Philadelphia minstrel show as part of a family act headed by her Irish father, Robert Rogers Dooley, a well-known circus clown. In 1906, at the age of 15, Ray eloped with entertainer Eddie Dowling.

The petite performer made her debut in vaudeville and in 1918 launched her comedy career quite by accident. Producer Raymond Hitchcock was making *Kitchy Koo* and one of the actors was too large to fit into the baby buggy used in a drugstore scene. Because of her size, Ray was elected to impersonate the baby.

Florenz Ziegfeld caught the act and hired her to play babies and brats in his *Follies* after World War I. Though she soon tired of portraying babies and pleaded with Ziegfeld for other parts, she did have luminaries for "parents." Fannie Brice, W.C. Fields, and Will Rogers were among those Ziegfeld cast for her act.

Ray and her husband worked as a team in the *Follies* for several years. Then Dowling became a producer. Ray starred in his production of *Sidewalks of New York* in 1927. The next year she joined W.C. Fields in *Earl Carroll's Vanities.* On December 27, 1934, Ray appeared in Dowling's revue *Thumbs Up* which ran for five months. Two musical hits emerged from that show, "Autumn in New York" and "Zing Went the Strings of My Heart."

After *Thumbs Up*, Ray retired to devote more time to her family which included a daughter and a son. Eddie Dowling went on to become an award-winning producer who presented three one-act plays in 1948. Ray returned briefly to the stage to play a straight dramatic role opposite her husband in *Home Life of a Buffalo.* The play dealt with a veteran vaudevillian who couldn't accept the fact or admit to his wife that vaudeville was through and his career finished.

After seventy years of marriage, Dowling died in 1976. Ray's death occurred at her home in East Hampton, Long Island, on January 28, 1984. She was 93 years old.

Charlotte Greenwood

Charlotte usually portrayed a gawky woman in hot pursuit of a man. Her schemes to find romance and a routine of high kicking and waving her arms windmill style delighted audiences during a long career which encompassed vaudeville, stage, screen, and radio.

On June 25, 1893, Frances Charlotte Greenwood was born to barber Frank Greenwood and his wife, Anna Belle (Higgins) Greenwood, in Philadelphia. When Charlotte was 1 year old, her parents separated. She attended public schools in Boston and Norfolk, Virginia, leaving school in the seventh grade when she moved to New York City. While still in her early teens, the tall, thin blonde with contralto voice got a job in the chorus of *The White Cat* at the New Amsterdam Theatre. After a few minor roles, she entered vaudeville, first in a sister act with Eunice Burnham, then in a high-kicking act with Sidney Grant, a short vaudevillian.

Charlotte gained recognition for her appearance in *The Passing Show of 1912* on Broadway. Two years later, she played the part of tall, lanky Letitia Proudfoot in the play *Pretty Mrs. Smith*. That portrayal led to a title role in a musical about the character titled *So Long Letty*, the first of a series of "Letty" shows, including *Linger Longer, Letty; Let 'er Go, Letty* and *Leaning on Letty* (which was taken on a world tour).

Essentially a physical comedienne, Charlotte used her limber body to get laughs. She'd flail her long arms and legs and walk about on all fours, her palms flat on the floor. "I'm the only woman in the world who can kick a giraffe in the face," she'd say.

On December 22, 1924, she married songwriter Martin Broones. They made their home in Beverly Hills with several dogs who were cherished companions of the performer. Charlotte loved white flowers of any kind and named Dickens and Shakespeare as her favorite authors. She preferred a simple diet and as an avid sportswoman, enjoyed swimming, golf and tennis year round. The only complaint she had about California living was that woodpeckers woke her up too early some mornings.

The performer ventured into radio in 1944, starring in the comedy-drama *The Charlotte Greenwood Show* for one season. She played a cub reporter on a small-town newspaper who was trying her best to get to Hollywood.

In real life, the comedienne had all the work she could handle in Hollywood, appearing in as many as six films a year. Her talent for broad comedy was evident in films such as *Parlor, Bedroom and Bath*, in which she romped across furniture chasing Buster Keaton. Her forty films include *Oh, You Beautiful Doll* (1949), *Oklahoma* (1955), and *The Sound of Laughter* (1963).

The tall, ungainly woman found her niche in show business and played it to the hilt. After a long and successful career, Charlotte died in Beverly Hills, California, on January 18, 1978.

Mabel Normand

Mabel was born in 1894 in Boston and had little formal education. Her father tried to make a living as a vaudeville piano player but finally gave it up. Mabel was 13 when she took a job with a women's magazine, working in the pattern department. The department head saw her potential as an artist's model and arranged for her to meet illustrator Carl Kleinschmidt, who hired her. She was soon established as a model, posing for such prominent artists as James Montgomery Flagg and Charles Dana Gibson.

In 1911 Mabel decided to try films and worked first in Vitagraph films and then at Biograph. She was a brilliant clown and mimic whose special gift was a complete naturalness before the camera. It was at Biograph that she met actor Mack Sennett and they immediately hit it off. Their amorous bickering was to last throughout Norma's life.

On August 28, 1912, Mabel and Mack arrived in Los Angeles to begin working on the first film for the newly formed Keystone Film Company. For 34-year-old Mack it was a dream come true. He owned one-third interest in a motion picture film company, and had free reign regarding the casting, directing, and final production of comedy films. He immediately hired comedians, bought equipment and began setting up an organization that would make fortunes for everyone involved.

In addition to Mabel, Mack hired Ford Sterling and Fred Mace, two friends whom he'd worked with at Biograph, to make up the original Keystone cast. Alice Davenport, Evelyn Quick, Victoria Forde, and Dot Farley became his supporting players. Other Keystone women comics included Emma Clifton, Phyllis Allen, Virginia Kirtely, Louise Fazenda, Polly Moran, Cecile Arnold, and Minta Durfee, who was wife of Roscoe Arbuckle.

Mack considered Mabel the best comic talent of the day, and planned to marry her. Petite and high-spirited, Mabel happily joined in the chaos at the Keystone Studio in Glendale, California. Whether surprising each other with jolts of electricity (the toilet seat in the men's restroom was wired) or buckets of water dumped on someone opening a door, the comics saw to it that madness reigned.

Mabel's roles ranged from the innocent dressed in rags to a Jezebel. Many felt that her ability to move audiences by her expressive facial nuances equaled Chaplin's.

On September 23, two split-reel comedies, *The Water Nymph* and *Cohen Collects a Debt*, premiered. Every week for the next five months, Keystone released two new comedies. Nonsensical titles like *Love's Sweet*

Piffle, Whispering Whiskers and *A Dozen Socks* reflected the humor of the films' creators. The rapidly paced Keystone comedies quickly became the rave of show business and the studio became known as the Fun Factory. Sennett's training in burlesque was an asset in knowing what would get laughs from the public.

Though slapstick comedy originated in the French films of Pathé and Méliés, Mack Sennett refined it with every camera trick and prop he could think of. He insisted that a gag take no more than twenty feet of film and carefully timed the gags to allow intervals for laughter. The intensity of the gags (incongruities and perilous situations were sure laughgetters) built until the film's climax.

Sennett was also an opportunist who made use of locations of other movie producers. He often sent one of the Keystone crews to film a comedy on an elaborate location being used for a more ambitious project. The full-reel comedy *The Battle of Who Run* was shot at Tom Ince's location for a Civil War picture. The enterprising filmmaker filmed the industry's Thanksgiving Ball and used it in a Keystone picture. The San Diego Exposition and the World's Fair in San Francisco also became backgrounds for two films.

Mabel became Charlie Chaplin's sparring partner when he joined the rough-and-tumble world of Keystone in 1913. Everyone but Norma doubted the talents of the English music hall comedian during his year with them. She had the distinction of directing Chaplin in six one-reel comedies shortly after he arrived. Thereafter, he felt confident to direct himself.

When Chaplin left Keystone, Roscoe "Fatty" Arbuckle joined the company. Arbuckle weighed 285 pounds but was a nimble man and a quick student of pantomime. Norma thought him terribly funny and suggested him for the leading role in *Passions, He Had Three*. Within weeks Norma and Fatty Arbuckle were gaining recognition as a top comedy team.

The limber, irrepressible performer (just five feet tall and weighing ninety pounds) insisted on doing all her own stunt work. She dove into rivers from high rocks, rode a bear, and was dragged through mud, thrown around by actors twice her size, and tied on railroad tracks. In *Mabel's Dramatic Career*, she is treated quite horribly by the villain, played by Ford Sterling. To film one ten-minute short called *A Dash Through the Clouds*, Mabel was filmed actually going up in an open-wing, box-kite airplane!

Audiences were thrilled as they watched Mabel wrestling with a toppling grandfather clock, being thrown from a horse, and hanging precariously from a roof. The adventurous actress spent considerable time recuperating in the hospital as a result of her fearlessness.

It was not unusual for leading ladies of the silent screen to request that soft music be played to put them in the proper mood. Before her physical-comedy stints, Mabel insisted on Jazz records played at their loudest!

In 1913 Mabel made movie history when she aimed the first custard pie at Fatty Arbuckle during the filming of *A Noise from the Deep*. Fatty got his revenge in subsequent pictures by firing pies at Mabel, seldom missing his target. Arbuckle became so expert at hurling pies, he could throw two at once in opposite directions. Some pies did a figure eight before hitting their mark. This special effect was achieved from a high stepladder out of the camera's range where a skilled fly-caster directed the pie's flight pattern.

At first, the pies sailing across the set were genuine custard, but a nearby baker devised a recipe for a flour, water, and whipped cream filling in a thick pastry shell which held up better while it was airborne. Two kinds of filling were used — lemon meringue for brunettes and blackberry for blondes.

The first melodrama produced by Keystone was *At Twelve O'Clock*, which set the format for several others. Mabel was bound and placed in front of a grandfather clock by the villain (played by Fred Mace). The clock was set to fire a bullet at twelve o'clock, but Sennett saved Mabel by moving the hands back with a pole stuck in through an open window.

In *Mabel's Awful Mistake* the comedienne played a country girl who is untied from the table in a sawmill just in the nick of time by her yokel boyfriend, played by Sennett. She was rescued from a railroad track by Sennett in *Barney Oldfield's Race for a Life*. After a wild chase which tested Oldfield's driving skills, the two men caught up with the train.

Mabel's fight scene with Dorothy West in *The Squaw's Love* was another first in the movie business. D.W. Griffith initiated the practice of using more than one camera to film a scene. He used three cameramen for the confrontation between the two women.

Mabel's off-screen pranks made the news and her lavish wardrobe was imitated by women admirers. While Mabel waited for Sennett to propose, she turned down many good offers to leave Keystone. But the filmmaker procrastinated. He hated the social whirl which centered around Mabel, and was happiest when working on his films. Finally they set a date for the wedding, but it never took place. Mabel came down with pneumonia and when she recovered, joined Arbuckle and a crew to make comedies in the East. They'd barely begun filming when Mabel was hit by a shoe thrown in a wedding shower of rice and shoes. A concussion put her in the hospital.

She wanted to leave Keystone and persuaded Sennett to assist her in getting a new contract. In 1916 the Mabel Normand Feature Film

Company was formed, with provisions for the star's own studio and choice of material, writer, and director. She had never fully recovered when she began working on *Mickey*, a six-reel feature about a tomboy raised by her miner father and an Indian woman, then sent to live with an aunt in the city. Accidents and financial problems plagued the eight-month project (*Mickey* had run over budget and Sennett used personal funds to complete it). The relationship between Mabel and Sennett became more strained and she left to work for Goldwyn Studios, where she made fifteen mediocre pictures. She returned to make four more films with Sennett between 1921 and 1923.

Mabel's personal life had become a shambles. Poor health and scandal over the murder of director William Desmond Taylor (Mabel had been with him shortly before his death) hastened the end of her career. She married actor Lew Cody and attempted a comeback in films with Hal Roach, but her popularity had decreased. A tubercular condition and years of reckless living led to an early death for the feisty comedy artist who died in 1930 at the age of 36.

The relationship of Mack Sennett and Mabel Normand was the inspiration for a Broadway play titled *Mack and Mabel*, starring Robert Preston and Bernadette Peters nearly a half-century later. On the CBS Studio City lot is a bronze plaque commemorating Mabel: "She brought laughter and beauty otherwise denied millions burdened with despair and drabness."

Belle Baker

Belle Baker (Bella Becker), born in New York City in 1895, was an engaging, emotional entertainer who excelled at portraying characters and singing. She introduced such Irving Berlin songs as "Michigan" and "Cohen Owes Me 97 Dollars," but became most familiar with fans for her rendition of "Eli Eli." She acquired the song "Put It On, Take It Off, Wrap It Up, Take It Home, Good Night, Call Again," when Fanny Brice arranged for her to meet song plugger Maurice Abrams. Belle not only liked the song, but married the seller who soon after became a music publisher.

Belle hated leaving her infant son Herbert behind while she toured with her act. In an attempt to soften her longing for him, she added a song about him to the routine. Herbert grew up to become a writer-producer for television and the movies.

In 1911, Belle debuted on Broadway in *Vera Violetta*, and went on to work in Florenz Ziegfeld's *Follies*. Vaudeville audiences never tired of hearing her sing "My Yiddische Mama" and "Little Man, You've Had a Busy Day." But because of a dispute over her refusal to work on Yom Kippur, she found herself no longer welcome on the circuit.

However, Belle continued to appear in revues and stage presentations. She also worked on the borscht circuit at places like Pop Nemerson's popular theater in the New York Catskills. In the thirties, Belle became a radio star appearing on the Ever-ready Blades' "Radio Gaieties" show. Hollywood also offered her work in *The Song of Love* (1929) and *Atlantic City* (1944).

The popular performer suffered a heart attack and died in Los Angeles on April 28, 1957. Some of her work has been preserved on recordings.

Carole Lombard

One of the most successful comediennes in the history of films, Carole Lombard appeared in forty-two talking pictures between 1928 and 1942. She became a legend in her own time, her beauty and wit a standard against which dozens of other comediennes have been measured in the decades since her tragic death.

Carole was born Jane Alice Peters on October 6, 1908, in Fort Wayne, Indiana, the youngest of three children of well-to-do Frederick Peters and Elizabeth Knight Peters. When she was 7, her parents divorced and she moved with her mother to Los Angeles where she attended Marian Nolks Dramatic School. Her film debut occurred in 1921 when Allan Dwan noticed the 12-year-old girl playing baseball in the street, and gave her a tomboy part in *The Perfect Crime* starring Monte Blue.

After her graduation from Los Angeles High School, Carole was placed under contract to Fox, but just as her minor film roles were bringing her attention, she was badly injured in an auto accident. Thrown through the windshield, she was also disfigured by a long cut between her mouth and one eye. Her film contract was cancelled and she spent a lonely year recuperating, the ugly scar leaving her depressed and convinced that her career was over.

"I snapped out of it," was all she would later say of overcoming her feelings of insecurity. Finally only two faint white lines were visible, but nevertheless she decided to learn all she could about lighting and camera angles once she returned to making films.

In 1927, the slender blonde joined Mack Sennett's group of bathing beauties. Sennett used her in several two-reel comedies, saying she was "a scamp and a madcap." Carole met comic Madeline Fields on the set and the two women immediately became friends. "Fieldsy" soon took over the business end of Carole's career as her secretary and manager.

Next transferring to Pathé, Carole made her first all-talking picture, *High Voltage* (1928), and then began freelancing with minor roles in films such as *Ned McCobb's Daughter* and *Fast and Loose*.

She was finally placed under a seven-year contract by Paramount and co-starred in *No Man of Her Own* (1932) with Clark Gable, the great comic masterpiece *Twentieth Century* (1934) with John Barrymore, and *Rumba* (1935) with George Raft. During the next two years, the comedienne worked in five films, all in the genre of a mid-thirties "screwball" comedy, with a crackling pace, hilarious dialogue and slapstick action. Two of these — *My Man Godfrey* (Carole plays a wacky heiress opposite William Powell) and *Nothing Sacred* (she and Fredric March play wiseacre lovebirds) — are considered to be among the best comedies ever produced.

The Lombard style developed during those films and the extremely feminine comedienne with a breathy voice became a favorite of moviegoers. Her characters possessed an earthiness combined with wide-eyed eagerness that served her well in her most memorable roles. In 1940, demands were made on Carole as a serious actress in *Vigil in the Night* and *They Knew What They Wanted*. She easily met the challenge with her sensitive portrayals in both films. Although carefree and explosive on the screen, she was most professional regarding her work.

For all the setbacks she experienced in her private life, Carole Lombard seemed to bounce back with a new enthusiasm each time, using humor to get through the rough spots. She was quite close to her mother, Bessie, calling her up on a whim at odd hours to tease her and chat about nonsense. A voracious reader, Carole got by on as little sleep as possible in order to fit in more living and learning.

"Most of all, I'm afraid of getting things too easily," she once said. "I like getting them the hard way. I might as well. That's the way I always get them."

Carole's marriage to William Powell in 1931 ended in divorce two years later, but they remained friends. She next fell in love with singer Russ Colombo, but shortly before their wedding, he was killed in a bizarre accident. A bullet fired from a supposedly empty old dueling pistol ricocheted and hit him. For some time, Carole kept the tragic news from Colombo's mother, who lay ill in the hospital with heart trouble. She even arranged for telegrams to be sent from Europe where Russ was supposed to be working.

In the mid-thirties, Carole and Clark Gable became the nation's most popular romantic couple. Even when *Photoplay* publicly revealed their affair in a relatively shocking article, there was no public censure. Once they were married in 1939, Carole severely curtailed her acting assignments, spending time at Gable's ranch in San Fernando Valley learning to be his hunting companion. She became an expert markswoman. She was known to use a mule skinner's vocabulary on occasion but her husband broke her of that habit.

"I will do the swearing in this family," he said.

One of Hollywood's highest paid stars, Carole was allowed to keep about one-third of what she earned. The rest was paid in income taxes. But she let everyone know that she considered the system fair and was happy to pay her share.

"I really think I got my money's worth," she said.

When war broke out, Carole was one of the first to volunteer to help sell war bonds. Her trips around the country generated millions of dollars for the war effort. In late 1941, she costarred with Jack Benny in *To Be or Not to Be*, yet another great film comedy, about a Shakespearean troupe in Poland fleeing the Nazis. In January, 1942, two weeks after completing work on the movie, Carole went on tour to sell defense bonds. Before her return flight home from Indianapolis, where she sold more than $2 million worth of war bonds, she turned to the crowd and said, "Before I say goodbye to you all — come on — join me in a big cheer — V for Victory!"

The crowd roared as she raised her hand to make the V symbol. That newsreel on January 16 was her last appearance before any camera. The plane she was traveling on crashed into Table Rock Mountain, thirty miles southwest of Las Vegas, Nevada, killing all eighteen passengers and three crew members. Carole's tragic death at the age of 34 shocked millions of her fans around the country. Jack Benny did not go on the air for his regular radio show that following Sunday night.

Clark Gable, who was inconsolable, received condolences from President Franklin Roosevelt and a citation from the government: "Your wife died in the service of her country. Her brilliant work for the Treasury this week in selling defense bonds in Indianapolis will be long remembered and honored by us all."

Some individuals who flew the American flag dropped it to half-mast in her honor. Among her friends were those who felt that Carole may have had a premonition of an early death.

"I never can see into the future at all," she once told friend and author Adela Rogers St. Johns. "I never can see myself growing old."

Chapter Two
Vaudeville Legends

Performers who made it into big-time vaudeville were assured of performing in the best theaters, and benefited from higher salaries and better working conditions than small-time vaudeville could offer. They were usually booked through the United Booking Office, created by the Keith organization which, with its successors, dominated vaudeville from 1900 on. This guaranteed many months of work on a circuit of major theaters around the country, where they were expected to perform only two shows a day. Instead of impromptu assistance during a performance, they could count on being backed up by a good orchestra and competent stage personnel.

Headliners on a bill could compete for the finer dressing rooms at theaters like San Francisco's Orpheum, Chicago's Majestic, or New York's Strand, Roxy, or Palace (the ultimate booking). Managers took care of business affairs, enabling the stars to channel all their energy into "killing them" night after night. Exposure in big-time vaudeville often resulted in offers of roles in legitimate theater revues or musical comedies. Such jobs meant getting off the circuit for awhile and settling down to work in one production for the duration of its run.

Of the nearly 20,000 vaudeville entertainers touring the country during vaudeville's heyday, around 750 made the big-time and only a handful of comediennes truly became vaudeville stars. They climbed to the top with the right material, a unique delivery, and an intense desire to hear the audience's laughter every time they walked on stage. Most importantly, it was each woman's individual spirit and ability to touch her fans in a special way that kept her on top, and later enabled her to also become successful in radio, the movies, and television, where she brought her humor to millions more.

Sophie Tucker

Her credo as a performer was to always look forward. "You can't grow stale or cling to a period," she claimed. "You must belong to your time."

Between the years 1884 and 1888 (Sophie's birthdate was never clearly established), a Russian tailor named Charles Kalish and his pregnant wife, Jenny Abuza Kalish, were on their way from Russia to the United States. Their daughter was born in Poland, and by the time they arrived in Connecticut she was 3 months old.

As a child, Sophie loved to sing. When not waiting on tables or working in the kitchen of her parents' restaurant near the Hartford railway station, she sang "Hello, My Baby" to customers enjoying their 25-cent dinners. The house specialty was Jenny's homemade gefilte fish.

Sophie soon was entering amateur contests and quickly became enamored of show business. A teenage marriage to Louis Tuck produced a son, Burt. After the union was annulled, the allure of show business caused Sophie to leave the boy behind with her mother while she went to New York.

A vaudeville performer passing through town had given her a letter of recommendation to Harry Von Tilzer, one of the most successful songwriters of that time. His compositions included "A Bird in a Gilded Cage," "Wait Till the Sun Shines, Nellie," and "I Want a Girl Just Like the Girl that Married Dear Old Dad."

Though Von Tilzer couldn't help the slim, fair-haired girl when she got to New York, she found a job much like the one at her father's restaurant, working in a cafe kitchen and singing requests of the customers. It was a start and she made good money while she considered other jobs with more of a future.

Her decision to enter small-time vaudeville meant giving up the big tips which she'd been sending home for her son's care, but she was determined to become a star. Sophie made her professional debut in vaudeville at the 116th Street Music Hall on December 9, 1906. Her first audition ended up with the booking agent insisting she go on in blackface, and she quickly became established as "The World-Renowned Coon Shouter" and "Sophie Tucker, Manipulator of Coon Melodies."

It was lonely on the road and after a year of traveling the circuit, Sophie got a job in burlesque and as a result was offered a part singing four songs in the 1909 Ziegfeld *Follies*.

The show's headliner, Nora Bayes, insisted that three of the songs be given to her, leaving Sophie with one. Sophie toured with the *Follies* until Nora's replacement, Eva Tanguay, wanted all four songs for herself, so Sophie returned to vaudeville at $40 a week. That episode launched a lifelong competition between Bayes and Tucker.

Sophie first sang what was to become her theme song, "Some of These Days," in 1911. Her forte in the early days was spicy songs like "There's Company in the Parlor, Girls, Come on Down." Critics were not kind to the entertainer in their scathing reviews, but Sophie eventually wore them down. They could not deny the mobs of ardent fans at every performance, so they had to concede her becoming a show business legend.

Audiences worshipped the bawdy singer who titillated them with her views on love and sex.

"Gentlemen don't love love," she'd tell them. "They just like to kick it around."

After her debut at the Palace in 1914, it was written in *Variety* that Miss Tucker possessed a "40-horse-power voice" and that she "just walked out and owned the place." The singer's voice nevertheless could be compassionate when rendering heartbreaking ballads. A few years later she took part in weekly concerts at the Winter Garden Theatre.

Sophie worked hard in her quest for fame. Fans were encouraged to visit her dressing room after the show. She kept the names and addresses of everyone she met on the road, so she could drop each a postcard before she played that town again, and send a Christmas card. Over the years her list of followers grew until she was mailing out 7,000 handwritten cards a year!

Sophie was a loud, sociable woman with a curiosity about everyone around her. She loved poker, betting on the horses, and playing cupid within her circle of friends, some of whom ended up marrying each other. Her son Burt was a favorite subject and everyone she knew had to hear of his handsome looks and scholastic feats. A framed photograph of him in military attire always stood on her dressing room table wherever she was playing.

As she built up a following and her salary increased, she shared her good fortune with the stagehands and orchestra leaders who worked with her by giving them generous tips. She also invested a great deal of money in exclusive material for her acts and for new gowns and jewelry in which to perform, though many felt that her garish costumes were in the worst of taste.

Her London Cabaret debut in 1922 was followed by cabaret work in England, Australia, and South Africa. After one such tour of English music halls, Sophie asked to be billed as "Madame" at the Palace, but fellow entertainers gave her such a razzing that she quickly went back to being just plain Sophie.

Vaudevillians sometimes called the Keith theater chain "the Sunday

School circuit" because of its strict censoring of performers' material. One Keith theater manager told the flamboyant entertainer that she couldn't sing "Who Paid the Rent for Mrs. Rip Van Winkle While Rip Van Winkle Was Away?" Sophie quit the show.

Of the "hot numbers" she sang, Sophie explained that they were not immoral. "They have to do with sex," she said, "but not with vice."

Sophie's second husband was younger comedian Frank Westphal, whose act consisted of pushing his piano on stage, removing his coat, hat and rubber overshoes, doing his low-key musical act, then putting his coat, hat and rubbers back on and pushing the piano off stage. After their marriage, Sophie included him in her act for awhile until he decided he'd be happier running a garage. Sophie set him up in the car business but couldn't resist generating a little publicity by putting up a sign reading "Sophie Tucker's Garage." Frank bowed out of the marriage shortly after that faux pas by his wife.

Sophie's third and last marriage, to manager Al Lackey, ended after four years. "I'm living alone and I like it," she sang, following the divorce. She later claimed her love life "set me back a million."

Sophie made headlines when she returned to the Palace in 1932 to perform on a bill with the team of Smith and Dale and dancer Bill Robinson (seats then cost from twenty cents to one dollar). Ed Sullivan wrote for the *New York Graphic* that, "She just about tears the roof off the place."

One night while Sophie was onstage a fire broke out. She continued singing as spectators were ushered out of the theater to safety. Backstage, Bill Robinson suffered from smoke inhalation but later continued the show with wet dancing shoes. "The grand and glorious days of the Palace ended with that fire," Sophie proclaimed.

Elected president of the American Federation of Actors in 1935, Sophie Tucker became the first woman to serve in that position. She had her own radio show and worked in films during the 1930s. Of the feature films she appeared in, many have weathered the years and are still being shown on television. They include *Broadway Melody of 1938* (1937) starring Judy Garland and Robert Taylor, *Thoroughbreds Don't Cry* (1937) with Mickey Rooney and Judy Garland, and *Follow the Boys* (1944) starring George Raft as a USO hoofer and featuring a routine by W.C. Fields.

Late in 1938 the performer opened in the musical comedy *Leave It to Me*, which was a success both on Broadway and on tour. In 1941 she played herself in the New York production of *High Kickers*. Sophie was popular with American servicemen in both world wars, and once received considerable publicity for canceling a nightclub date to visit the wounded in a New York hospital.

The entertainer's autobiography, *Some of These Days*, a culmination of her show business journal over the years, was published in 1945. Her honest and earthy recollections earned good reviews, the *Library Journal* calling it "frank and racy." She generously donated her time and the proceeds from the sale of deluxe editions of her book to various religious and theatrical charities, homes for the aged and youth camps.

That same year *Variety* reported that Sophie was headlining at $3,500 a week in Boston, delighting her faithful fans by slipping her rowdy rendition of "Tax on Love" past the Boston censors. She was at her best when appearing in nightclubs. Hecklers didn't faze the exuberant Sophie, who could subdue the wildest audiences with her salty language.

As the years added girth to her figure, Sophie continued to wear glamourous costumes, but changed the lyrics of many of her songs from "red-hot mama" to "big fat mama" and introduced new songs like "I May Be Getting Older Every Day (But Getting Younger Every Night)," "Life Begins at Forty," and "I'm the 3-D Momma with the Big Wide Screen."

The veteran entertainer frequently appeared on television and was a popular guest on the *Ed Sullivan Show* during the fifties and sixties. She interspersed her songs with philosophical meanderings.

When she was 69, Sophie delivered a homily which found posterity in *Bartlett's Quotations*. "From birth to age 18, a girl needs good parents. From 18 to 35, she needs good looks. From 35 to 55, she needs a good personality. From 55 on, she needs good cash."

She gave a command performance at the London Palladium in late 1962. The following year a musical titled *Sophie*, which was based on the early years of her life, was presented at the Winter Garden in New York.

Though Sophie was a hard taskmaster to those who worked for her (Ted Shapiro played piano for her for forty-two years and always addressed her as "Miss Tucker"), she was a sympathetic woman.

Eddie Cantor once said of her soft-heartedness, "Sophie would cry at a card trick." Many of her acquaintances who were down on their luck could depend on "good old Soph" for a personal loan.

"Anything for a friend," she'd say.

The entertainer's many farewell performances in later years became the source of jokes, as she could never really retire. She was still singing "I'm the Last of the Red Hot Mamas" a few weeks before her death. That song said it all.

In 1966 Sophie Tucker died at the age of 82, leaving behind months of advance bookings at nightclubs across the country. More than 3,000 of her loyal fans came to pay respects to their beloved Sophie.

Fanny Brice

For forty years Fanny Brice was a star in the theater, vaudeville, movies and radio. She called everyone "kid" and used earthy language, keeping her vulnerability well hidden behind a joking, mugging exterior. A flair for comedy dialogue and devastating mimicry, along with a flawless handling of song lyrics, placed Fanny in a class by herself. When she died in 1951, *Variety* mourned the loss of "one of the greatest singing comediennes in the history of the American theater."

Fannie Borach, the red-haired, blue-eyed daughter of a saloon keeper, was born in 1891 on New York's crowded Lower East Side, where her attendance in the public schools was sporadic. "I ran away from every school I ever went to, or if I didn't, I was thrown out," she once said.

She absorbed the various European accents she heard in the tenements, accents she would later use in dialect songs. As a girl, her renditions of ballads of unrequited love evoked pathos at the amateur contests she entered. At 13, she worked her way into show business by winning amateur nights (and five-dollar prizes) at all three of Frank Keeney's theaters. Another souce of income was a movie house job that entailed singing, playing piano and working in the projection room.

"Listen, kid!" she was to say years later, "I've done everything in the theater except marry the property man."

When she was 15, Fanny talked her way into a chorus line job in the George M. Cohan–Sam Harris review *Talk of the Town*, but didn't last long. George Cohan noticed that she couldn't dance and fired her, yelling, "Go back to the kitchen." Though humiliated, the gawky, thin-legged girl found a job in the cast of *A Royal Slave*, playing an alligator! Next she began singing songs written by the young Irving Berlin. He suggested she sing one of the songs, "Sadie Salome," with a Yiddish accent, and she had a big hit.

She appeared in *The Transatlantic Burlesque* and *College Girl* in which Florenz Ziegfeld saw her perform, and though his policy was to hire only the most beautiful young women for his productions, he made an exception. He immediately offered Fanny $75 a week to appear in his *Follies of 1910*, which starred Bert Williams and Lillian Lorraine, and her career was established. Fanny's original contract, which was written on stiff paper, had to be replaced because it became literally worn to pieces from the proud young woman's constant handling and showing it to friends.

"The individual hit of the show," *Variety* proclaimed, writing about the 1910 production. Starring *Follies* roles were to follow in 1911, 1916,

1917, 1920, 1921 and 1923, with her salary escalating to $3,000 a week. Of her good fortune she said, "I've been poor and I've been rich. Rich is better."

Fanny's first marriage was to Frank White, a barber she met while touring in 1911, and lasted only a short time before being annulled. Fanny was soon starring on the stage in musical comedies *The Honeymoon Express*, *Nobody Home*, and *Why Worry?*

She was a natural for vaudeville, quickly becoming a headliner and playing the Palace for the first time in February, 1914. For the next two decades, she delighted audiences with her hilarious impersonations of salesgirls, Jewish mothers, and fan dancers. Burlesque dancing numbers, especially her classic "Dying Swan Ballet," were favorites with Palace crowds for years.

Fanny had been compensated for her plain looks by enormous talent and comedic style and could get laughs by merely grinning or making the slightest gesture. Brooks Atkinson of *The New York Times* proclaimed her "the burlesque comic of the rarest vintage."

Of her talent to captivate an audience, Fanny said, "You get your first laugh — boom! you're going. You lose yourself, you become whatever it is they're laughing at, but it isn't you."

Over the years her vaudeville routine grew from twelve to forty minutes long! Writer Blanche Merrill supplied much of Fanny's special material. The busy comic's repertoire included monologues with a heavy Jewish slant like the one ending with Mrs. Cohan reprimanding her kids at the beach, saying "Why didn't you do it when you were in the water?"

Fanny was convinced that ". . . the audience has to like you . . . and you must set up your audience for the laugh you are working for."

Her fans loved her lampoons of sultry Theda Bara and Camille (W.C. Fields played the maid). She sang humorous songs as well as tragic ones like "The Song of the Sewing Machine," about the plight of women in the sweatshops, "Second-Hand Rose," and "My Man" (introduced in 1921). She became internationally famous with "My Man," a song that referred to her second husband, gambler Nicky Arnstein. Fanny stood by him while he served a two-year sentence (1924–1926) in Leavenworth for his involvement in the disappearance of $5 million worth of securities. A daughter, Frances, and a son, William, resulted from that marriage.

Fanny wore a cave woman dress and snake headdress in an "Adam and Eve" sketch with Bobby Clark in the *Music Box Revue of 1924*. Also on the program was her lamenting immigrant's song, "Don't Send Me Back to Petrograd." In 1925 she starred in *Fanny*, a stage comedy written for her by David Belasco, then returned to the musicals *Fioretta* and *Sweet and Low*.

Fanny's film debut in 1928 was in *My Man*, in which she sang "I'd

Fanny Brice

Rather Be Blue Over You," "I'm an Indian," and "Second-Hand Rose,"
as well as the title song. *My Man* was called a "singing silent film" because
not all theaters were yet equipped to show it as a talking picture.

That first picture was followed by the all-sound musical *Be Yourself*,
in which she again wins, loses, then wins back her man. Her Jewish
dialect song "Cooking Breakfast for the One I Love" debuted in that film.

Next Fanny played herself in *The Great Ziegfeld*, a 1936 Oscar-
winning three-hour extravanganza starring William Powell and Myrna
Loy, *Everybody Sing*, in which Fanny did her "Baby Snooks" routine
with Judy Garland, and *Ziegfeld Follies* (1946).

Hollywood never figured out how to tailor Fanny's extraordinary talents to the screen, so most of her roles were from her previous vaudeville sketches and the *Follies*. A remark usually credited to movie mogul Sam Goldwyn actually originated with Fanny when she said, "A verbal agreement is not worth the paper it's written on."

In 1930 Fanny and showman Billy Rose were married by Mayor Jimmy Walker of New York City. During their courtship, Rose had written "More Than You Know" and "How Lucky Can You Get?" especially for Fanny. She recorded both songs and headlined her husband's production of *Crazy Quilt* soon after their marriage.

Her career as a radio singer with George Olsen's orchestra in 1932 lasted only until the radio series ended. After Ziegfeld's death, she starred in the Shubert *Ziegfeld Follies* in 1934 and again in 1936, the latter marking her last Broadway stage appearance. Fanny's marriage to Rose ended in 1938.

"I've played in London before the King and in Oil City before miners with lanterns in their caps," the comedienne later reminisced of her extensive stage performances.

The following year Twentieth Century–Fox released *The Rose of Washington Square*, a thinly veiled story of Fanny and Nicky Arnstein. A backstage plot about a *Follies* girl who loves a bum, it starred Al Jolson, Alice Faye and Tyrone Power. Both Fanny and Nicky later received an out-of-court settlement from the film studio because neither one had given permission to the movie makers to portray their relationship on the screen.

Though she was one of the major headliners in vaudeville, Fanny became known primarily for her bratty character of "Baby Snooks," whose pranks included cutting the fur off her mother's mink coat, pasting it all over her little brother Robespierre and selling him as a monkey to a neighbor boy for fifty cents. "Thirty years of show business, and I had a hit as a 4-year-old baby," she said.

The routine originated when Fanny spoke baby-talk for her friends at a party. She later used it in her "Babykins" skits in vaudeville and finally became "Baby Snooks," whose "Why-y-y, Daddy?" became familiar with millions of listeners of one of the top radio shows between 1938 and 1949. Hanley Stafford played the part of "Daddy," at his wit's end in dealing with Snooks for ruining his fishing equipment or lying about a broken window (she told him a lion had jumped through it):

Daddy: Even if a lion did jump through the window, why did the pieces of glass fall on the outside?
Snooks: Well, the lion jumped in backwards.

Snooks wore out three "mothers," who were played by Laline Brownell, Lois Corbett, and Arlene Harris. She was also a frequent guest on the *Fleischmann–Rudy Vallee Show* and other popular radio programs, playing the character of the annoying little girl. Fanny said of the Snooks character, "I don't have to work into it. It's part of me."

Fanny also starred in *The Fanny Brice Show*, a comedy which was first broadcast in 1944. She played a teenager named Irma, and Hanley Stafford again did the honors as her father. Danny Thomas played their postman.

The comedienne's characterizations were continually reshaped over a long period of time until they fully developed. The last character she created was a Pennsylvania Dutch girl which she had spent considerable time on, but her public never got to see her.

Through the years, Fanny retained a soft spot for fellow performers, especially vaudevillians who, after the demise of vaudeville, couldn't find work in other areas of show business. She preferred not to make it public that she generously supported many of them. Other outside interests included oil painting, collecting children's paintings, cooking, and interior decorating, a talent she put to use in decorating the homes of her friends the Eddie Cantors and Ira Gershwins.

In later years, Fanny suffered from a heart condition and had made plans to retire, but a massive cerebral hemorrhage ended her life at the age of 59 on May 29, 1951, just two weeks before her NBC contract ran out. Instead of the regular show which had been scheduled for the evening of her death, a short eulogy was delivered by Hanley Stafford during a musical tribute to her memory.

Mae West

Mae West was an iconoclast who kept censors busy for decades, continually causing controversy in vaudeville, the theater, radio, and film during a sixty-year career. She was a female pioneer who wrote, directed and produced her own skits, plays, and movie scripts in which she portrayed a shameless gold digger who kidded about sex and loved to thumb her nose at the establishment. She could get the most suggestive ideas across without uttering one lewd word. When asked, "Haven't you ever met a man who could make you happy?" she answered, "Sure. Lots of times."

Mae was born in 1893 in Brooklyn, New York, to John and Matilda West. John was called "Battling Jack" and tried his luck at boxing before

Mae West

becoming a detective. Matilda spoiled the girl and told John, "Let her go; she's different." While still a toddler, Mae attended vaudeville matinees with her mother, who had always hoped to be an actress herself. Mae began singing and dancing on Brooklyn stages at 7 (she debuted at the Royal Theatre), then played child parts in stock companies and musical shows.

In 1911 Mae wed handsome song-and-dance man Frank Wallace, but soon decided she didn't like the married life, so she encouraged him to join a show just beginning a forty-week tour. Though the union wasn't officially dissolved until more than thirty years later, they never got together again, and Mae pretended she'd never been married. "I'd have to give up my hobby," she'd say when asked about matrimony.

In 1912 she received her first review in *Variety*. "The eccentric type," the critic noted, following her debut in the musical review *Vera Violetta*, starring Al Jolson. After performing in *A Winsome Widow*, Mae teamed up with her sister Beverly in a vaudeville act in which Mae dressed up as a man, and for the first time used material she'd written herself.

When her sister quit, Mae was back doing a single again, accompanied by pianist Harry Richman. She danced the shimmy wearing provocative costumes and began breaking house records. In 1918 her dancing was a hit in the Broadway musical *Sometime*, which costarred Ed Wynn, but after two years in musical comedy, Mae returned to vaudeville. She was a draw wherever she played, and the Christmas issue of the *New York Dramatic Mirror* featured her on the cover.

"It wasn't what I did, but how I did it," she wrote in her autobiography years later. "It wasn't what I said, but how I said it."

Mae spent much of the 1920s studying the subject of sexuality by reading Freud, Jung, and Adler, and writing and appearing in her own plays, which usually received negative reviews. The first of these Broadway productions was *Sex*, a play about a group of prostitutes in a Montreal bordello.

In spite of the critics, who found it inept and crude, the play enjoyed a successful run until it was raided by the New York police. Amid great publicity Mae was fined $500 and sentenced to ten days on Welfare Island. Though she had to don prison clothes, she insisted on wearing her own silk underwear under them.

Another of her plays, *The Drag*, which featured homosexuality, was considered too "vulgar" and closed after two weeks. *The Wicked Age* was despised by critics but loved by theatergoers.

Diamond Lil (1928), accepted by the public and critics alike, proved the most successful of the lot, running for 323 performances. Her invitation to the Salvation Army captain to "come up and see me sometime," became famous. It was Diamond Lil, "the bad girl with the good heart," that established the type of character Mae West would play again and again, the blonde femme fatale never at a loss for words, as in one scene when her escort says he's a politician. "I don't like work, either," she replies.

The hourglass figure, lavish gowns draped with diamonds, hand-on-the-hip pose and suggestive drawl became trademarks. Though not especially beautiful by show business standards, Mae exuded sexual confidence with her sauntering strut and sultry glances.

"I'm my own original creation," she would say. At times she'd even lapse into speaking of "Mae West" in the third person. Charlie Chaplin and the Marx Brothers were favorite performers of hers because they too created their own characters.

After two more plays, *The Constant Sinner* and *Pleasure Man*, and a final return to vaudeville with an act at the Academy, Mae departed for Paramount Studios in Hollywood. There she wrote spicy scripts and appeared in a string of films, the first one *Night After Night* with George Raft (her off-screen lover) in 1932. It was in that film that she introduced to the screen her famous line, "Goodness had nothing to do with it."

Costar Raft said of her, "In this picture, Mae West stole everything but the cameras." Her comment about him: "When they make a man better than George Raft, I'll make him too."

During a guest shot on Edgar Bergen's Sunday evening radio show *The Chase and Sanborn Hour* in 1937, Mae and Don Ameche played Adam and Eve in a Garden of Eden sketch written by Arch Oboler. Mae's steamy dialogue with the serpent and her repartee with dummy Charlie McCarthy caused such a national furor that she was consequently banned from radio. Heated congressional debate threatened punitive action against NBC for failing to conduct their programming in the public interest. Though network executives had approved the script prior to the broadcast, they and the sponsor, Chase & Sanborn Coffee, publicly apologized to listeners the following week.

In 1940 Mae teamed up with W.C. Fields in the unforgettable *My Little Chickadee*, in which they wrote their own dialogue. By the end of each filming day Fields was inebriated, even though no one could catch him sneaking a drink. Finally, Mae discovered that his dressing room water cooler was filled with gin!

Cary Grant was her leading man in both *I'm No Angel*, a circus picture in which Mae played a lion tamer, and *She Done Him Wrong*, an adaptation of *Diamond Lil* considered by many to be her best movie of the lot.

The humorist also sang in the films, and hired top musicians such as Duke Ellington and their orchestras to accompany her. Mae both shocked and delighted audiences with one-liners like "Between two evils, I always pick the one I never tried before," and "I used to be Snow White but I drifted."

Her movies of the thirties were extremely profitable and kept Paramount (then on the verge of bankruptcy) solvent during the Depression. In 1935 Mae's earnings were close to half a million dollars, more than anyone else's in Hollywood. The box office queen wisely invested her earnings in California real estate.

The Kansas Restaurant Association publicly paid her tribute for making feminine curves fashionable again. American women finally had an excuse to end the dieting brought on by their attempts to look like

Marlene Dietrich and Jean Harlow. Britain's Royal Air Force contributed to Mae's immortality by naming an inflatable life jacket after
her, and a lush, cream-colored rose became known to gardeners as the
Mae West Rose.

The last Mae West film of that era was *The Heat's On* (1943), which
along with most of her other films, is still shown today on television and
in art cinemas.

In 1944 her production of *Catherine Was Great*, based on the life of
Catherine the Great of Russia, ran on Broadway for six months before going on tour. Three years later she starred in a comedy *Come On Up* and
in 1949 in a revival of *Diamond Lil*, which toured around the country.

Mae was always close to her mother (she considered her mother's
death the worst event of her life), and her sister Beverly, but concluded
that spending time with other women was a waste of time, so she limited
her friendships to men only. She had her own behavior code: No drinking, no smoking, no married men. "I never needed to take away another
woman's man," she said.

During the fifties, an entourage of muscular young men were
featured in Mae's nightclub acts. One of them, Paul Novak, became her
devoted companion and remained with her until her death. She regularly
appeared on television and radio shows, and recorded three albums. Her
autobiography, *Goodness Had Nothing to Do with It*, in which she
boasted of marathon sex with her many lovers, was published in 1959.
Mae claimed that the few times she felt herself falling in love, she ended
the relationship. She feared the loss of her identity.

Mae's 1970 film comeback in a cameo role in *Myra Breckinridge*
earned her the title of "world's oldest sex symbol."

"I'm proud to be 82, because I know I don't look it," she declared,
preparing to appear in yet another movie, *Sextette*, with Tony Curtis.
Age did take its toll in other ways, however. During her later performances, she was wired with an electronic prompter which also picked up
highway patrol signals. Along with her lines, Mae sometimes repeated
snatches of traffic reports.

During her life, the woman whom George Jean Nathan called the
"Statue of Libido" broke down barriers with sociological satire that
changed the entertainment world. "I was the first person to bring sex out
into the open," Mae told writer Lewis Lapham in 1964. "Before I came
along, nobody could even print the word on billboards."

Though she always dressed extravagantly for her public and admitted that she spent over three hours on her makeup and hair before she
considered herself presentable, Mae did not attend Hollywood parties.
Going to prizefights with her manager Jim Timothy was a favorite
diversion.

She lived quietly in the apartment she'd acquired in 1932 when she had first moved to Hollywood, and gave infrequent interviews from her golden shell bed. In spite of the many men she had known, the renowned performer insisted that her only important love affair had been with her audience, and that it had endured for a lifetime. On November 22, 1980, Mae West died at the age of 87.

Bea Lillie

Considered one of the best comic wits in the world, Bea Lillie filled theaters with laughter on both sides of the Atlantic for nearly forty years. Barely five feet, three inches tall, the slender, blue-eyed entertainer wore her short-cropped hair tucked under a hat, giving her a girlish look. The toast of two continents, she could convulse an audience with a simple facial expression or gesture.

"I don't depend entirely on dialogue . . . nor on stage business performed during the dialogue," she once explained. "It's what I do *after* I say my lines that counts. I never calculate a gesture . . . in advance. If I were consciously aware of what I was doing, I couldn't function at all. . . ."

Beatrice Gladys Lillie was born in Toronto, Canada, on May 29, 1898, the second child of Irish-born John Lillie and her Spanish-English mother, Lucie Shaw Lillie.

"Four Lillies were enough for any bouquet," remarked Bea of her family. Both parents had emigrated to Canada. Her mother, Lucie, was a singer who ran a "vocal studio" in their home, and encouraged Bea to become a soprano and her older sister Muriel to be a concert pianist. John Lillie left the house from time to time, perhaps to escape the continual piano scales and vocal exercises of his musical family.

Lucie enrolled young Bea at the Rich Concert and Entertainment Bureau to learn "dramatic gestures, elocution and mime." There Harry W. Rich painstakingly taught Bea gestures to denote the lyrics she sang. She learned to subtly suggest happiness, sorrow, birds flying, or farewell to summer by delicate motions of the arms and fingers. As soon as Mr. Rich felt her proficient, he billed her in his catalog as a "Character Costume Vocalist and Impersonator." Years later, when she was an international comedienne summoning laughter with a certain movement of her head or hand, Bea admitted that the grueling labor had paid off for her.

The girl hated school and fretted about her prominent nose during her childhood. On Sundays, Lucie directed the choir, Muriel played the organ, and Bea sang, until she was kicked out of the choir for making faces during the sermon. At home, Bea and Muriel often ended up with sore bottoms for playing tricks on guests at their mother's weekly musical soirees. Once Bea, who loved to enter contests, sneaked into a Toronto burlesque house and tried to win a piano by singing. She was in trouble when her mother found her consolation prize, a box of chocolates.

Professionally, Lucie, Muriel and Bea were known as The Lillie Trio — High Class Entertainers. Their promotion announcements noted that "they can be engaged as a whole, double, or single." The three Lillies were hired for local gatherings and toured theaters in the area, once ending up stranded in northern Ontario after their manager took off with all their money.

When she was 14, Bea was sent to St. Agnes' College in Bellevue, where she fought boredom with devilment. When chosen to lead the girls on their morning walk, she detoured from the usual route and led the procession inside a bank so she could get a closer look at a handsome young teller. Someone at the bank notified the teachers, who were waiting to reprimand her when she returned. A few weeks later, she was again disciplined for sneaking away from a dance with the same handsome young man. Bea desperately wished to become a serious ballad singer, so as soon as the law permitted, she left school for good.

In the meantime, her mother and Muriel had gone to England, so in late 1914, Bea went to join them, singing in a ship's concert on the way over (John Lillie joined them a few years later). No jobs were forthcoming for their "Beatrice and Muriel" sister act, so Muriel played a piano in a movie house and Bea found work in London stage shows, filling the roles of men who were going off to war. "I became sort of a paid, professional transvestite," she later said of the top hat and tails costume she wore.

Several months later, Bea was hired as a seriosinger for *Not Likely*, a new André Charlot "intimate" revue, which emphasized a witty cast rather than elaborate costuming and sets. With a three-year contract at fifteen pounds a week, 16-year-old Bea debuted, singing "I Want a Toy Soldier Man," and didn't cause a stir. For the next few war years, the young singer appeared in all of Charlot's revues in straight roles but gradually realized that her real potential in reaching audiences lay in comedy. She was, in her own words, a "natural-born fool."

After Bea was nearly fired one night by a stage manager for her antics in the chorus line, Charlot realized she'd been miscast and put her in *5064 Gerrard*, which opened almost simultaneously with the German Zeppelin raids on England. Dressed in farmer's overalls and carrying a milk pail, Bea was a hit singing Irving Berlin's song "Take Me Back to

Michigan." From then on, Beatrice Lillie's comedic touches were a part of every Charlot revue, and the critics soon took notice. Wartime shows were packed by men in uniform who appreciated Bea's "take me back" songs about Alabama, Maine, Florida, and other home states. Before long, Gertrude Lawrence was hired as an understudy for Bea, and that association initiated a lifelong friendship.

In 1920, Bea was married to the Honorable Robert Peel, who was a descendant of Robert Peel, Prime Minister to Queen Victoria and the man largely responsible for originating London's police force, the "Bobbies," or "Peelers." A year later, they became parents of a son, Bobbie.

Bea soon returned to the London stage in Charlot's revues until Charlot entered into a partnership with American producer Arch Selwyn, and took a revue consisting of the best sketches from over the years to New York in 1923. Headlining the show were Bea, Jack Buchanan and Gertrude Lawrence. Despite the warnings that "Americans will never fall for this English stuff," *André Charlot's Revue of 1924* opened at Times Square Theatre on January 10, 1924, and was extended from six weeks to nine months with sold-out performances, giving the Ziegfeld extravaganzas competition. A highlight of the show was Bea's rowdy satire on Britain's naval strength, "March with Me," in which she roamed the stage dressed as Brittania, Queen of the Waves. In "Tea-Shop Tattle," she played Gwladys, an arrogant waitress. The show was hailed by the critics and Beatrice Lillie was a star in America.

For the next fourteen years, Bea sailed back and forth between London and New York, appearing in dozens of shows and cabarets. Her mother brought Bobbie to visit her as often as possible and the telephone bills were astronomical. Bea ventured briefly into typical musical comedy, but admitted that her impish talents and inspired moments of madness were better suited to revues, where she relied on the audience to coach her. "I am best in a sketch in which I can invent my own business and do whatever comes into my head," she said.

In 1925, Bea's father-in-law died and her husband became Sir Robert, fifth baronet. The comedienne became Lady Peel but had no desire for a life of "social nonsense" the position entailed. Her husband tried different lines of work to keep the debt-ridden Peel estate solvent: movie writing in Hollywood, sheep farming in Australia, leading an orchestra in England. Bea continued with her career.

Her American counterpart, Fanny Brice, came into her life on opening night of André Charlot's *Revue of 1926* in London. "I was a trifle uneasy about Fanny," she later recalled in her autobiography, *Every Other Inch a Lady.* "We had barely met . . . and I was doing a burlesque of her, while Gertie mimicked Sophie Tucker, 'the last of the red-hot mamas.'"

Needless to say, Fanny loved the show, and later when Bea and Gertrude rented a house in New York, Fanny was a frequent visitor among their other theatrical friends.

Up until that time, Bea's long, dark hair had been worn braided and coiled into buns over her ears, but on a yachting trip one weekend, she impetuously cut off her braids and went swimming. For a while, she wore the braided plaits of severed hair every time she appeared in public. Then one night at a party, one of the plaits fell off and her secret was out. The hair was auctioned off for charity and the Lillie crop and ever-present hat became her trademark.

In the late twenties, Bea appeared in the Rodgers and Hart musical farce *She's My Baby* with Clifton Webb and Irene Dunne, then Noel Coward's *This Year of Grace*. Bea and Noel initiated a friendship which would endure in spite of occasional screaming arguments over the years. They performed together not only in the play, but at charity events and nightclubs, where they were always requested to sing their duet from the show *Lilac Time*.

Bea made her vaudeville debut doing a sketch Noel had written for her, "After Dinner Music." It involved an aging prima donna in a red wig and moth-eaten gown who sings for her guests. Bea hyped it somewhat for vaudeville, catching a tablecloth and spilling china on the floor, tripping over chairs, and shattering a light bulb with a high note. Though she said, "I'd never been so nervous in my life," she was a hit.

There were many attempts to analyze Bea Lillie's talent over the years. Some felt the contrast between her apparent good breeding and flippant irreverence to be the secret for producing hilarity. Critic Harrison Down once noted, "It is like entering a drawing room and beholding a duchess performing like a crazy downstairs maid."

Bea's transatlantic commuting continued as she worked in London in Charlot's sleek and sophisticated productions. Requests to entertain at the Royal Palace alternated with invitations to star-studded parties hosted by William Randolph Hearst and Marion Davies at San Simeon.

Bea introduced the song "Mad Dogs and Englishmen" to Chicago audiences in *The Third Little Show* in 1931. The following year she portrayed Sweetie the Nurse in Shaw's *Too Good to Be True*, and a madcap coed in *Walk a Little Faster*.

Her first movie, *Exit Smiling*, completed in weeks, was puzzling to Bea, who often worked months to get a single gesture just right. She appeared in *Dr. Rhythm* with Bing Crosby, and *Walk a Little Faster*, but soon gave up on films. "The inspiration of live-audience reaction stimulates my creative juices and establishes a subconscious bond between us," she said, also mentioning that men as a rule seemed to resist laughing at women performing comedy.

Sir Robert Peel, the husband she had seldom seen since the early days of their marriage, died in 1934 of peritonitis at the age of 36. His 13-year-old son Bobbie became Sir Robert Peel, sixth baronet, and Bea was left with the family debts.

In *At Home Abroad* with Ethel Waters and Reginald Gardiner (1935), Bea, as Mrs. Blodgen Blagg, tried to purchase "two dozen double damask dinner napkins" and Reginald Gardiner did his original imitation of wallpaper. Bea and Reginald teamed up again in 1936 to star in *The Show Is On* with Bert Lahr. "I believe she could make people laugh in a dark room ... by the inflection of her voice," Reginald said of his friend.

And Bea, who was adept at burlesqueing Ruth Draper, proved his point by appearing on radio shows—she was regularly heard on *The Fred Allen Show*, *The Rudy Vallee Show*, *The Big Show*, *Information Please*, and *Manhattan Merry-Go-Round* during the thirties. The performer's life was a whirl of work and parties. For one period, she doubled at the new Rainbow Room and appeared in *The Show Is On* at the Winter Garden Theatre. Once in a while, she left New York to visit Fanny Brice in California, where Fanny would try her best to sneak garlic into Bea's food. (Bea's food tastes were simple. She didn't care for sweets, preferring plain dishes such as "boiled chicken in jelly, Irish stew, corned beef and cabbage, and beer ... after the show, I have a pitcher of lemon juice and water.")

"To stay with Fanny was usually good for your soul," Bea recalled of their long talks about their children, a mutual interest. Years later she would regret not having been chosen to play Fanny Brice in a movie.

Bea opened *Happy Returns* by riding a white horse on stage, then just prior to World War II she returned to England where she stayed for the duration of the war. Bobbie joined the Royal Navy and his mother entertained Allied troops in England, Europe and the Middle East. When her son was reported missing in 1943, Bea continued working, but stopped every young sailor she saw to inquire about Bobbie. She later was notified that he'd been killed on Easter morning, 1942, in a Japanese raid on Colombo Harbor in Ceylon.

In 1944, Bea returned to the United States to appear in Billy Rose's *Seven Lively Arts*—wearing a mermaid costume—and received a five-minute ovation from her ecstatic fans. Her role won her *Billboard's* Donaldson Award for the best feminine lead in a musical show.

Ethel Barrymore initially suggested that Bea sing "There Are Fairies at the Bottom of Our Garden," saying it was just her style. Bea resisted until her accompanist Sam Walsh tricked her into singing it by playing the introduction one night. From that night on, the song was forever ruined for other singers attempting to sing it straight.

It was in *Inside U.S.A.* that Bea sang about the wonders of the industrial city in "Come, O Come to Pittsburgh." That was also the show in which Bea Lillie first whirled a long string of pearls around her neck, emitting a delighted "Whee-e-e." The pearls circled her body in a downward spiral until they landed on the floor. After that she perfected rotating her head to get the desired results every single time with a flexible string of pearls six feet long, and delighted in twirling them at the slightest provocation.

"I find the exercise invigorating, though there's always a certain risk, when getting started, of loosening your front teeth," she explained. "It's touch and go whether you choke to death."

In the early fifties, Bea settled into an East End Avenue apartment in New York overlooking the East River with two kittens, which she said liked her furniture better than catnip. After first touring, *An Evening with Beatrice Lillie* opened on Broadway to rave reviews. Walter Winchell called the show a "Lilliepalooza." Friend Helen Hayes called it "Bea's triumph." In the cast along with Bea were old friend Reginald Gardiner, Xenia Bank, Florence Bray, and John Phillip, for a long time associated with her as a co-performer, director and producer. Bea next replaced Rosalind Russell in *Auntie Mame*, and made the rounds as a guest on television shows hosted by Carson, Griffin, and Cavett.

After the *Follies of 1957*, she portrayed Madame Arcati in *High Spirits*, based on Noel Coward's *Blithe Spirit*. A couple of "Lillie touches" added to the costume were long-eared bunny slippers and bicycle clips. Actress-comedienne Phyllis Newman later recalled opening night of *High Spirits*: "I think Beatrice Lillie is the funniest woman I've ever seen.... When I saw this vision come onto the stage with bicycle clips holding her dress together and an insane hat and little bunny slippers I screamed.... She kills me."

When not at the theater, Bea walked and window shopped for exercise. After decades of partygoing, her fondness for big gatherings faded, and fans no longer ran across news photographs of her (often in an oversized fur coat, and *always* a hat). Calling herself "Beatrice van Gone," she devoted more time to her oil painting, which she had taken up during World War II. Her canvases, sometimes sold at charity auctions, most often revealed flowers, landscapes, and Pekingese dogs, her favorite pets over the years. (She swore one named Mr. Lee could say "I love you," "I want the ball," and "Up yours.") In later life, the ageless, supremely funny entertainer settled down to write her autobiography, paint, and enjoy her many friends.

Bea will always be remembered as an exacting mistress of absurdities. "Unless things are funny," she once said, "they are apt not to exist for me at all." Whether doing a clog dance in galoshes, vocalizing while perched in a wobbly silver moon above the stage, or simply twitching her eyebrows, Bea Lillie possessed a sparkling comic genius. Just the mention of her name brings a smile, then, "Bea Lillie! I'll never forget the time she . . ."

Chapter Three
Funny Women of Radio

Radio took root in the 1920s and rapidly expanded into all phases of American life. For the first several years, a headset was required, making it impossible for more than one person to hear an incoming broadcast at the same time. In 1927, the first coast-to-coast program was broadcast, making radio history. The Rose Bowl football game, originating in Pasadena, California, was broadcast over the NBC network. As the use of radio increased, advertisers began to sponsor portions of each program. The revolutionary medium's sweeping influence was so feared by newspaper publishers that they refused to print radio logs or mention the word "radio" in their newspapers.

With the onset of the Depression, movie houses, regional stock theaters, and nightclubs closed but radio flourished, continuing the process of cultural homogenization which had been initiated by films. The dome-shaped mahogany console became the most imposing piece of furniture in many living rooms, and families depended upon "the box" to provide hours of laughter, sorrow, chills and adventure. The shows filling the airwaves were innocent by today's standards, incorporating the optimistic messages that crime does not pay, and that goodness is rewarded.

Increasing numbers of listeners tuned in to hear the daily news, music, drama, science fiction, mystery, westerns, variety and game shows (quiz show prizes started at $5!), amateur hours, children's shows, women's shows, and of course, comedy. Helping to carry the country through the depressed thirties and war-torn forties, radio comedy provided much-needed humor, nourishing a trait so evident in the American character — the ability to laugh in the face of terrible hardship.

In all, more than 1,500 nationally broadcast network and syndicated programs were transmitted during the golden years of radio. Without sophisticated polls, radio programmers had to rely on fan mail to gauge the popularity of a program and its cast. Comedy shows, presented during quarter-hour, half-hour, and one-hour segments of the day, were measured by the same criterion of success as other shows — the facility to capture the imagination of radio listeners and transport them through the magic of pure sound emanating from soundproof studios with microphones.

Radio offered imaginative comedy with no restrictions — listeners could "see" anything radio could create. Unhindered by the physical substance of sets, costumes, or makeup, they perceived characters and settings in as many different ways as there were listeners. Each individual could enjoy a program according to his or her own mental and intellectual abilities.

Many talented comediennes worked in radio, often in husband-and-wife teams. Listeners welcomed these radio families (with their assorted neighbors and friends) into their homes, routinely gathering around the radio for their favorite shows. Those funny women who captured the imagination of millions of fans during those golden years will always be remembered with wistful nostalgia.

Gracie Allen

George: Did you ever hear that silence is golden?
Gracie: No, what station are they on?
George: It's an adage, you know what an adage is.
Gracie: Oh sure, that's where you keep your old trunks.

The unique talent of Gracie Allen to be unconsciously funny made Burns and Allen the greatest husband-and-wife comedy team of all time. They became so popular with American audiences through their stage, radio, movie and television appearances, that even though they retired their act in 1958, fans can still recite Gracie's lines.

Grace Ethel Cecile Rosalie Allen was born in San Francisco on July 26, 1906. Her father, Edward Allen, whom Gracie considered "the best clog and minstrel man in San Francisco," worked in West Coast vaudeville. She had a brother George who was not interested in show business and three sisters, Bessie, Pearl and Hazel, who as the Allen Sisters, won many Irish dancing contests around the San Francisco area with their complicated clogging routines.

As soon as Gracie graduated from The Star of the Sea Academy, a Catholic school for girls, her mother accompanied her to local social events and fairs where she sang Irish songs, danced and gave a dramatic recitation about an Irish waif.

All four sisters were then hired by Larry Reilly, a headlining actor

Gracie Allen

on the West Coast vaudeville circuit. The Allen girls danced jigs and played Irish colleen parts in their appearances with Larry Reilly and Company. When Reilly was offered a good booking in the East, only Gracie went with him. Bessie, Hazel and Pearl, preferring not to leave their boyfriends, opened a dancing school.

Gracie left Reilly during that ten-week tour in the East because her feelings were hurt when he dropped the "& Co." from a theater billboard.

In 1922 the petite brunette with a mellow off-stage voice met George Burns (Nathan Birnbaum), who had been in show business since childhood. He'd been a partner in various vaudeville endeavors including a dog act, a roller skating act, a Russian Mazurka dancing routine and an act with a seal. At the time he was teamed with Billy Lorraine. A friend told Gracie that the act of Burns and Lorraine was splitting up, so she should ask Lorraine if he'd take her as a partner, because "Burns is terrible."

By mistake, Gracie instead approached George Burns and asked him for a job, calling him Mr. Lorraine. George hired her the next day and told her to quit calling him Lorraine. He wrote a new act which they took to Newark to break in with Gracie playing straight to his jokes.

George later told Gloria Steinem during an interview for *Ms.* magazine, ". . . the audience sort of giggled at Gracie . . . and nobody laughed at my jokes."

He reversed their roles and the team of Burns and Allen was on its way. Gracie's ability to deliver the most incredible lines with absolute sincerity made her unique.

The following year *Variety* reported that though both Burns and Allen had good deliveries and winsome personalities, they needed better material. Nevertheless, they managed to work steadily and during their second year together were booked on the Orpheum Circuit on the West Coast.

By then George had fallen in love with Gracie and proposed to her, but she planned on marrying Irish songwriter-dancer Benny Ryan. George bought some time by arranging for them to get a raise. Gracie explained the raise to Benny and told him the wedding would have to be postponed a little longer.

During their tour Gracie had to be hospitalized for an emergency appendectomy. Gracie asked George to notify Benny, but George didn't do it — as a result Benny didn't send flowers, but George surrounded her hospital bed with baskets filled with them.

The problem of their material was solved when they bought a sketch called "Lamb Chops" from writer Al Boasberg in 1926. They were breaking in the new act in small-time theaters in Ohio and had two days off before opening at the Keith Theatre in Cleveland. Gracie had reconsidered George's proposal and married him in Cleveland.

"Lamb Chops" went over so big, the couple were signed by the Keith circuit for an unprecedented five-year contract and their salary almost doubled. *Variety* again reviewed their act and agreed "Lamb Chops" was "funny stuff." George later recalled that because all the girls fellows dated in those days always wanted a nice dinner, their routine went as follows:

"Do you like to love?"
"No."

"Do you like to kiss?"
"No."
"What do you like?"
"Lamb chops."
"A little girl like you, can you eat two big lamb chops alone?"
"No, but with potatoes I could."

After the sketch Gracie and George would dance off together into the wings.

George always walked out on stage before each show to see which way the air was blowing in order to keep his cigar smoke downwind of Gracie's face while they were working. Once they were being considered for the Eva Puck and Sammy White parts in the London production of the hit musical *Show Boat*. Knowing that the producer was in the audience at the Palace made George so nervous he forgot his pre-show check and blew smoke into Gracie's face during their entire act. The producer declined the offer if George was included in the deal.

While on the road, a dry cleaner once ruined one of Gracie's dresses and would not make restitution. That night on stage Gracie abruptly stopped in the middle of her scatterbrained prattling about her family to warn the audience about the cleaners, then picked up with George where she had left off. She got paid for the dress.

Though the couple hired writers, George often wrote Gracie's jokes. His part in the routine was to ask the questions, then to listen to her answers with growing incredulity, all the while puffing on his cigar.

"Really?" he'd comment. "Is that so?" "You don't say," as Gracie would explain that she always kept the emergency brake on in case of emergency, or that she cleverly had shortened the electric cords on the lamps to save electricity.

In 1929 Burns and Allen went to England as "The Famous American Comedy Couple" to play the Holborn Empire and the London Palladium. The English public and critics alike loved them.

She once said of herself, "The onstage Gracie may look poised . . . but the real Gracie is shy, a little self-conscious, and before every performance of my life, panicky."

Their radio debut took place in London in 1930 when they made a series of radio broadcasts for the BBC. Back home the following year, Eddie Cantor invited Gracie to appear on his network radio program, *The Chase and Sanborn Hour*. Eddie used George's lines and Gracie was a hit.

Cantor: Do you remember the Gettysburg Address?
Gracie: I think they live in Buffalo now.
Cantor: In Buffalo?
Gracie: Maybe they moved.

The appearance successfully launched a radio career for Gracie and George. Guest spots on a show called *Guy Lombardo and His Royal Canadians* followed, and their popularity grew. Though there were several other husband-and-wife teams using similar material (like Jesse Block and Eve Sully), none ever became as successful as Burns and Allen. When Lombardo left the show in 1932, they inherited his air time and *The George Burns and Gracie Allen Show* began its nineteen-year run. Tootsie was played by Alvia Allman and Muriel by Sara Berner.

"Oh, George, I'll bet you tell that to all the girls," became a familiar line to radio listeners.

The comedy team had a backup routine to use for emergencies like the broadcast where their script pages fell and scattered in all directions, the day the studio lights went out, or the time George didn't have his reading glasses.

George would say, "Gracie, let's talk about your brother." She'd reply, "Which brother do you want to talk about, the one who's in love or the one who sleeps on the floor?" and they were good for ten minutes. Their clever survival plan worked fine but one time completely baffled their host Rudy Vallee, who frantically shuffled through the pages of the script.

The couple used successful gimmicks from time to time to keep audiences interested. In the early 1930s Gracie searched for an imaginary lost brother who had hurt his leg falling off an ironing board while pressing his pants. She kept popping up on other radio shows looking for him until NBC put an end to the gag. Her real brother George, a San Francisco accountant, kept a low profile until the commotion blew over.

Shortly after their radio debut, the team entered another medium. When Fred Allen became ill and couldn't make a movie short, Burns and Allen were asked to fill in, a stroke of luck that began a string of shorts produced in New York studios.

In 1932 they were called to Hollywood to make *The Big Broadcast* for Paramount. They signed a two-year contract to make feature pictures and moved into a twelve-room Beverly Hills home with an Italian-tiled swimming pool. It was there that Gracie and George raised their two adopted children — Sandra Jean, born in 1934 and Ronald John, born in 1935.

Their new career as movie stars was disappointing because though the plots were intriguing, all they were called on to do was perform segments of their stage routines. Gracie's ability to sing and dance did enhance their appearance in some of the films like *Damsel in Distress* with Fred Astaire.

They made over a dozen films, among them *International House*, a comedy about an inventor, a movie that stands up well after fifty years. It was during the making of that movie that they became friends with their costar, the irascible W.C. Fields, who didn't like being topped by Gracie's funny lines. They teamed up with him again in *Six of a Kind*, a movie about a cross-country motor trip featuring Fields' pool-shooting routine.

The Big Broadcast of 1937 was a satire on the radio industry and besides Gracie and George, starred Martha Raye, Jack Benny, and Benny Goodman and his orchestra. The comedienne appeared without George in *The Gracie Allen Murder Case*.

Away from the microphone, Gracie cherished her time at home and in her garden. For a hobby she painted and in 1938 gave an exhibition of her surrealistic-style creations in a Manhattan gallery. Two of the canvases were named *Man Builds Better Mousetrap and Buys Mohair Toupe*, and *Eyes Adrift as Sardines Wrench at Your Heartstrings*.

She wrote a widely syndicated newspaper column for awhile and as a guest in 1939 on the radio program *Information Please*, did quite well in the company of experts. Gracie also gave a credible performance opposite Jimmy Cagney in a serious Irish playlet for a Screen Guild show.

As another gimmick in 1940, she entered the Presidential race on the Surprise Party ticket, and appeared unannounced on several network shows to air her political theories. When asked which party she was most closely affiliated with, the candidate replied, "Well, I may take a drink now and then, but I never get affiliated."

During World War II, Gracie and George performed on special radio shows for wartime appeals and military recruitments. On their own program, they made spot announcements urging Americans to stay on the job and informed them about critical meat, gas, and rubber shortages. Gracie's humorous observations made the messages more appealing.

Speaking of gasoline rationing, she said, "I had the impression that gasoline came out of wells in the ground . . . and I've often thought how convenient it was for the filling stations that those wells were always found under the busiest street corners."

In 1950, after nineteen years on the radio, *The George Burns and Gracie Allen Show* made a smooth transition to television in a half-hour sitcom for CBS. Added to the show were son Ronnie, announcer Harry Von Zell, and Bea Benaderet and Larry Keating as their neighbors Blanche and Harry Morgan.

The first fifty shows were televised live, so in order for the episode to come out to the minute the actors had to slow down or speed up on cue. And there was no way to correct a slip in dialogue. The new format was especially demanding of Gracie, who had to memorize the entire script because her lines usually made no sense in relation to preceding lines. Every spare moment was spent memorizing lines.

"Gracie was everything," George always said of his wife's contribution to their act through the years.

Viewers felt protective toward her and loved her dizzy misunderstandings. In one show she explained her method of putting two roasts in the oven. "When the little roast burns, the big one is done."

After a commercial for Carnation Milk, Gracie often wondered aloud how the sponsors got milk from carnations. The team's vaudeville routines were used at the end of each show before George told Gracie to say goodnight.

After Gracie retired in 1958, she survived several mild heart attacks. On August 27, 1964, she died at the age of 58.

Gertrude Berg

One of the most successful writers and performers of comedy material in all facets of show business was Gertrude Berg, who was born in a Jewish section of Harlem on October 3, 1899. She was the only child of Jacob and Diana Edelstein, and from the time she heard her first radio show as a child, she was determined to become a writer.

After her graduation from Wadleigh High School, Gertrude took extension courses in playwriting at Columbia University, where she met engineering student Lewis Berg, whom she later married. They became parents of a daughter and a son. The budding playwright's first radio script about two salesgirls named Effie and Laurie made it onto the air but was cancelled after the first show because of the author's liberal views on marriage. Then Gertrude wrote a script about what she knew best — Jewish family life — and she began her career as creator and voice of the beloved Jewish mother, Molly Goldberg.

After hearing the young woman enthusiastically read her script, radio executives offered Gertrude a contract for $75 a week. Out of that she had to pay the cast. From its premiere in late 1929 until the show went off the air permanently in 1949, she wrote every script in longhand for *The Rise of the Goldbergs*, a total of 4,500 broadcasts.

Her characters, and often her actors as well, were drawn from life. She hired store clerks and elevator operators to portray themselves on the show when the script required outside characters. Famous alumni of the show include Joseph Cotten, Marjorie Main, Everett Sloane, Jan Peerce, Ann Bancroft and John Garfield.

Eventually the series aired five times a week, becoming second only to *Amos 'n' Andy* in longevity and popularity. Along with *Amos 'n' Andy*, the Goldberg program blazed the path for future radio shows with recurring characters in familiar settings — shows the listeners could quickly settle into. Set in the Jewish ghetto of the Lower East Side of New York, the Goldbergs invited listeners to eavesdrop while matriarch Molly calmly helped them cope with urban living. The adventures of Molly, her husband, Jake, their children Rosalie and Sammy, and Uncle David became a radio staple. Gertrude became so closely identified with her character that even her friends called her "Molly."

"Yoo Hoo, Mrs. Bloom," was a national cliché. Molly fluttered, shrugged and brought drama to even minor events.

"If it's nobody, I'll call back," she instructed family members. "Enter, whoever," was another of her many hallmark lines.

When Sammy came home late and admitted he'd been playing marbles and forgotten the time, she chastised him. "Playing marbles, ha? A marble shooter you'll gonna be? A beautiful business for a Jewish boy!"

Crediting her sense of Jewishness to her grandparents, Gertrude once said, "We scarcely spoke Yiddish at home. You'll notice there's no dialect, just intonation and word order."

In 1949, *The Goldbergs* easily made the transition to television, drawing thirteen million viewers. The show (with Philip Loeb playing husband Jake) ran for several years and resulted in an Emmy Award for Gertrude.

"I'm miserable when I'm not working," she explained of her willingness to always take on yet another project. Speaking of her early years in radio, she once recalled the simpler ways of radio broadcasting when she and the cast would still be rewriting the script at air time, and if street noises were needed, she'd place a microphone on the windowsill overhanging Madison Avenue. "It was fun because we did it ourselves," she said.

During a hiatus in the radio show in the late 1940s, Gertrude wrote her autobiography and a Broadway show, both titled *Me and Molly*. The show ran for 156 performances before closing. She later starred in the 1950 movie *Molly*, for which she also wrote the screenplay. The film concerns Molly's former suitor, played by Philip Loeb, who pays the Goldberg family a visit.

Returning to radio three years later, Gertrude wrote and starred in *House of Glass*, playing Sophie the cook, at a Catskill Mountain resort hotel. In 1959 Gertrude played a plump Jewish widow involved with an elderly Japanese man (played by Sir Cedric Hardwicke) in the Broadway play *A Majority of One*. Her memorable portrayal of Mrs. Jacoby, who had lost a son in World War II, played against Sir Cedric's widower who had lost a daughter in Hiroshima, earned her a Tony Award.

The prolific actress and writer (who even wrote a Molly Goldberg cookbook) suffered a heart attack and died at the age of 66 on September 14, 1966. She was scheduled to star in *The Play Girls* on Broadway the following January. The production was based on one of her ideas.

Marian Jordan

Marian Jordan played good-natured Molly on *Fibber McGee and Molly*, a major situation comedy radio program which originated from Chicago in the 1930s. The Jordans had earlier worked on radio in *The Smith Family* and the sitcom *The Smackouts*, set in a grocery store always "smack out of everything."

Her "Tain't funny, McGee!" in response to Fibber's corny humor became a national catch phrase. The popular show depicted life in small-town America and emphasized the quirks of odd characters who came in contact with the McGees. Fibber, a habitual bungler and braggart, was played by Marian's husband, Jim Jordan. Radio audiences in those days wanted fallible characters with whom they could easily identify. When Fibber periodically opened the McGees' overstuffed closet, the contents noisily tumbled out for several seconds — CRASH! THUD! CLAPPETY–CLUNK! ... WHAM! BANG! CLATTER! ... Jangle ... Plink!

"Got to clean that hall closet one of these days," Fibber would muse after the avalanche. "Fibber McGee's closet" became a cliché in most households and is still referred to today by those who remember it.

Marian Driscoll, daughter of a coal miner, was born in 1898 and raised in Peoria, Illinois, a typical Midwestern farming town. For years vaudeville entertainers joked about "laying eggs" in Peoria, a town with a reputedly poor appreciation of showfolks. Marian, a piano teacher, met Jim at a choir rehearsal at St. John's Church and married him in 1918. They later used their remembrances of hometown Peoria in presenting their radio home of 79 Wistful Vista to listeners.

Marian was responsible for bringing the show closer to reality after the first few years on the air, insisting happenings on the show should reflect what might really be happening back home in Peoria. Fibber's whopper-telling image was softened during the remaining years of the show.

A gifted voice imitator, Marian was integral to the popular program. In addition to Molly, who spoke with an Irish brogue, Marian played the parts of Mrs. Wearybottom, youngster Sis, Old Lady Wheedledeck, Lady Vere-de-Vere and Teeny, the nasal-voiced little neighbor girl. Fibber couldn't escape Teeny's tiresome questions ("Whatcha doin', huh, mister, whatcha doin'?"), and went to great lengths to avoid her.

Fibber McGee and Molly was an institution which enjoyed one of radio's longest sponsorships—fifteen years by the Johnson Wax Company. The stars were paid $3,500 a week and because of their popularity, RKO Radio Pictures signed the couple to work in films. They were also heard regularly on the popular *Breakfast Club* show. As is the case today, the success of one show led to others similar in format. The low cost of producing a program of that type was also an advantage. Later on, listeners could tune in to *The Great Gildersleeve* (who began as a neighbor of the McGees), *The Aldrich Family*, and *The Adventures of Ozzie and Harriet*, which took place at "1849 Rogers Lane."

All through the Depression and World War II, nearly one-third of all households with radios tuned in every Tuesday evening for a half-hour of spirit-lifting fun with the McGees. Fibber was the lovable fool so popular with radio fans during the years of high unemployment and feelings of personal inadequacies. Wishful thinking about his superhuman feats as a skyscraper construction worker, wild-game hunter, or football hero provided escape. And Molly was always there when his ego crashed back to earth, such as the time he ran for a touchdown for the neighbor kids and was knocked unconscious by a pint-size tackler.

Following the attack on Pearl Harbor in 1941, the Jordans incorporated messages into their programs, reminding listeners to buy defense bonds and stamps. The themes of their shows often referred to government rationing programs and the black market. In one episode, Fibber decided to buy some beef on the black market, the meat turned out to be spoiled, and the lesson learned was passed on to listeners. In late 1943, the McGees rented a spare room to Alice Darling, a giddy, man-crazy war plant worker, who was played by Shirley Mitchell. When the Allied forces invaded France on D–Day, the Jordans' comments, interspersed with news bulletins, replaced their regularly scheduled show.

The series continued until 1952 when the Jordans switched to doing a fifteen-minute weekly program. Marian's career ended in the late 1950s when she was stricken with cancer. She died in 1961. The entertainer was so popular that the show's ratings dropped one season while she was off because of illness. Throughout all her years in radio, Marian maintained a loyal following of fans who never touched their radio dials until they heard her kindly voice say "Goodnight, all."

Bernadine Flynn

Bernadine Flynn played Sade in *Vic and Sade*, the immensely popular daytime serial in the 1930s and early forties. The show was patterned after creator Paul Rhymer's formative years in Bloomington, Illinois, and became a classic of American humor. Named best in its category in 1940, the show often entertained as many as seven million listeners. Instead of relying on jokes, Rhymer supplied his characters with amusing small talk about everyday life in "the little house half-way up in the next block" in "Crooper, Illinois, forty miles from Peoria."

Bernadine was born in Madison, Wisconsin (circa 1907), and later attended the University of Wisconsin as a drama student. After college she moved to New York and found work on Broadway, including a part in Eugene O'Neill's *Strange Interlude* (1928). When she heard that Chicago offered opportunities in radio drama, she went there and landed parts on the *Rin–Tin–Tin* adventure program and the Great Northern Drama series.

In 1932 the crisp-voiced brunette became Sade Gook, a mercurial small-town housewife who usually had the last word in family disputes. Her life revolved around worrying about her husband, Vic, and son Rush, her Thimble Club meetings, Main Street washrag sales, and gossiping with her friend Ruthie Stembottom.

Vic (played by Art Van Harvey) had a distinct Indiana Hoosier accent and called Sade "Kiddo." He played a local accountant who counted the days between business trips to Chicago. For at-home diversion he often joined Mr. Gumpox and his horse Howard (who suffered from dizzy spells) while they made the rounds with their garbage wagon.

The Gooks chatted about the latest escapades of acquaintances with peculiar names like Reverend Kidneyslide, Y.Y. Flirch, Rishigan Fishigan from Sishigan, Michigan, and twins Robert and Slobbert Hink. Fans of the program wrote to NBC for recipes to many of the eccentric dishes Sade whipped up in her kitchen, such as "stingeberry jam" and "beef punckle ice cream."

The last regular *Vic and Sade* show was broadcast in late 1944 and titled "Goodbye." Bernadine Flynn, who had so expertly portrayed the Midwestern homemaker, died in 1977.

Jane Ace

Jane Ace got into radio by accident. While waiting in a radio studio for her husband, Goodman Ace, to finish his fifteen-minute show *Ace Goes to the Movies*, she was motioned to the microphone to help him fill in for the following broadcast which failed to come through. Her witty repartee enabled the couple to ad-lib for fifteen minutes. Their impromptu performance generated fan mail and landed them a contract for their own local show.

Jane Sherwood was born in 1905, the daughter of a Kansas City clothing salesman. The blond teenager attended the same high school and dancing school as Goodman Ace, and in 1928, against her father's advice, they were married. Her bridegroom was convinced that the medium of radio would prosper.

After the couple's Kansas City contract ran out, they were offered a show with CBS in Chicago in the fall of 1931. That led to a contract doing *Easy Aces* four times a week for CBS in New York. Besides performing, Goodman also wrote and directed the fifteen-minute show which was later switched to the time slot against *Amos 'n' Andy* three times a week. In most parts of the country, it was heard on Monday, Friday and Saturday evenings. The Aces also made over a dozen short subjects for RKO films during the mid-thirties.

Jane's glib comedy style was mainly responsible for the show's success. The theme song *Manhattan Serenade* led listeners into each episode of life with the Aces. As the dippy, upper-class Manhattan housewife, Jane busied herself with problems at the country club, unmarried girl friends, her maid (played by Helene Dumas), her friend Betty (played by Ethel Blume) and their boarder Marge (played by Mary Hunter, who also supplied the laughter for each show).

"Damon and Runyon, that's us," Jane proclaimed of her long friendship with Betty.

Jane became known for her malapropian sayings which she claimed she heard all around her. Her Jane Aceisms on the show included "time wounds all heels," "up at the crank of dawn," "familiarity breeds attempt," a "thumbnose description" and "we're insufferable friends."

After fifteen years, the show ended after a dispute with a sponsor and Goodman accepted a contract to write the Danny Kaye show. While cleaning out their Ritz Tower apartment, the Aces found 1,300 transcriptions of their old broadcasts. Many were edited and sold to over a hundred local stations, which resulted in *Easy Aces* reaching more listeners and earning the couple more money than the original airing. In 1947 *Easy*

Aces became a thirty-minute show called *Mr. Ace and Jane*, which included music and a live studio audience. A brother for Jane was added to the show — Paul, who hadn't worked in twelve years because he was waiting for the dollar to settle down. The longer version was not as successful as its predecessor and went off the air in 1949.

Goodman became a comedy writer for some of television's leading performers, including Milton Berle and Sid Caesar. Jane became interested in astrology and the Christian Science religion. She later returned to radio with her own show, *Jane Ace, Disc Jockey*, on NBC. During the thirty-minute program, she spun records, filling the intervals between tunes with her nonsense. Within a few years, Jane retired from show business. She died in 1974.

Portland Hoffa

Portland Hoffa was another wife who joined her husband at the microphone. Born in Portland, Oregon (circa 1903), the daughter of optometrist Frederick Hoffa, she was named after the city. Before meeting Fred Allen, the dancer worked as a chorus girl in *George White's Scandals*. While dancing in *The Passing Show of 1922*, a musical comedy revue playing the Winter Garden, the slim, vivacious showgirl met Fred. They married in May, 1927, and Portland became the "dumb dame" and dancer in his act. In 1930 they appeared in another successful revue, *Three's a Crowd*.

When the Great Depression threw a shadow over their future as stage performers, Fred decided to audition for radio. His nasal twang went over and he was hired for *The Linit Bath Club Revue*, a thirty-minute program on Sunday nights. Portland played various "dizzy dames" on the show, and listeners found her high-pitched voice hilarious. (Her husband claimed that she sounded to him "like a small E-flat Frankenstein monster.")

Fred's satirical scripts about society and politics quickly led to offers of other shows. In 1935 the couple settled into *Town Hall Tonight*, which was extremely popular with small-town audiences, for five years. Portland always opened one segment of the show by calling in her shrill voice, "Mr. A-a-allen . . . Mr. A-a-allen." Then she'd tell him the latest news about her relatives. When Fred asked why she was rushing off to buy tweezers, she explained: "Papa sat down on a rose bush yesterday and some of the thorns are missing."

Following *Town Hall Tonight*, they worked in a similar series titled

Allen's Alley, a radio classic which debuted in 1942 and ended on June 26, 1949. Their partnership provided much laughter and the mention of Portland Hoffa still brings a smile of recognition from those who loyally tuned in the Allen shows during those years.

Minerva Pious

Also on *Town Hall Tonight* was a talented comedienne named Minerva Pious. As a child, Minerva had come to America from Odessa, Russia, where she was born in 1909. She became a pianist and while accompanying a singer who was auditioning for the Allen show, met the comedian. The singer persuaded her to do a few of her dialect characters for Fred, who immediately hired her. That was the beginning of a career which encompassed not only radio, but films and Broadway.

Minerva played Jewish housewife Pansy Nussbaum, one of the four major characters on *Allen's Alley*. Mrs. Nussbaum, who spoke in a Jewish–Bronx accent, became known for her humorous, misconstructed phrases: "You were expecting maybe the Fink Spots . . . or Talooraloora Bankhead?" She was especially fond of "chopped liver cacciatore" and "herring du jour."

Minerva's talents as a dialectician got her parts on many other radio shows, including *Duffy's Tavern* (Shirley Booth played Miss Duffy), the *Philip Morris Playhouse*, the *Kate Smith Hour*, and on Sammy Kaye's show, where she played Gypsy Rose Rabinowitz.

Mary Livingstone

Mary Livingstone was a permanent member of her husband, Jack Benny's, radio show cast. She kidded Jack about his stinginess and like Gracie Allen, talked about the foibles of members of her family.

Sadye Marks was born in 1908 in British Columbia, the daughter of local vaudevillians. She and her teenaged chums once heckled Jack Benny during one of his performances. Years later, he saw her working in a May Company department store, and they began dating when he was between tours. After their marriage in 1927, she joined his vaudeville act as foil and singer. Her radio debut was on the Canada Dry program in August of 1932. On short notice one night, she assumed the bit role of corny poet Mary Livingstone, a fan of Jack Benny's who was visiting him at the studio. That led to other appearances by the flippant girl who amused listeners with her witty putdowns which punctured Jack's pomposity. Over the years Mary was a significant factor in the popularity of the *Jack Benny Show*. Her skepticism, along with Rochester's candid observations about his boss's frugality, greatly strengthened Jack's radio personality. In 1949 she legally changed her name, claiming, "Even my husband calls me Mary." Widowed in 1974, Mary lived in Los Angeles until she died of heart disease on July 11, 1983.

Hattie McDaniel

Hattie McDaniel, a well-known radio comedy star and the first black person to win an Academy Award, at one time had to take in washings in order to continue her career.

Born in Wichita, Kansas, on June 10, 1898, Hattie was the thirteenth child of Baptist minister Henry McDaniel and Susan Holbert McDaniel. The family later moved to Denver where the girl's musical talents were nurtured by her mother, a church vocalist. Young Hattie and her brother Otis wrote their own songs and performed in small-town tent shows. At 17, she sang on the radio with Professor George Morrison's Negro Orchestra in Denver, reputedly the first black female to sing for radio. The following year, she won a gold medal from the Women's Christian Temperance Union for reciting *Convict Joe*. She was soon touring on Shrine and Elks circuits in the south, and by 1924, was headlining on the Pantages vaudeville circuit where she was called "the colored Sophie Tucker."

Hattie found it rough-going those first years, hiring herself out as household help between bookings. She hit bottom when she found herself with no job and no money in Milwaukee. She finally got hired as a ladies' room maid at Sam Pick's Suburban Inn. One night the manager asked the help to volunteer their talents to fill out the stage show and Hattie sang "St. Louis Blues." That ended her maid's job. She starred in the floor show for the next two years until she landed a legitimate stage role in the touring company of the operetta *Showboat*.

In 1931 she decided to try her luck in films, but ended up on the *Optimistic Doughnut Hour* on radio station KNX in Los Angeles. There she was featured as Hi–Hat Hattie for almost a year before getting her first movie part in *The Golden West*.

Making the rounds in Hollywood resulted in a few more parts for her but to keep eating regularly she took in washings. Gradually more roles came her way and she was able to support herself without a second job. A few of the many movies she appeared in were *Blonde Venus* (1932), *Babbit* (1934), *The Little Colonel* (1935), *Music Is Magic* (1935), and the notable *Show Boat* (1936) in which she played Mammy and sang "I Still Suits Me" with Paul Robeson.

Unfortunately, black women in those days were usually relegated to playing maids or other stereotypical characters. Hattie established a near-monopoly during the thirties and forties in playing genial black servants, but always with her own touch of humor, intelligence and irony. For this she received both criticism and praise. She herself didn't see the casting pattern to be a problem, and took all the work that came her way.

"I portray the type of Negro woman who has worked honestly and proudly to give our nation the Marian Andersons, Roland Hayeses and Ralph Bunches," she said.

Hattie coveted the part of Mammy in *Gone with the Wind* so much that when she was tested she said she "opened my heart and let the tears flow out." She not only got the part, but was immediately put under contract by David Selznick and called upon to begin making screen tests with Hollywood's leading ladies who were competing for the role of Scarlett O'Hara. One of the three required scenes for the finalists involved Scarlett getting into her corset with Mammy's assistance. The role of Mammy brought Hattie an Oscar for best supporting actress in 1939. She donated the statuette to Howard University and continued making movies until 1949.

In the meantime, Hattie had renewed her acquaintance with radio. She not only had been cast as Mammy on *The Maxwell House Showboat*, but in 1947 took over as the star of *The Beulah Show*, which revolved around the life of a Negro domestic. "Somebody bawl fo' Beulah?" became familiar to listeners tuning in each week to hear about Beulah's problems with her employers the Hendersons, girlfriend Oriole, and shiftless boyfriend Bill.

The part that earned Hattie $1,500 a week had been played by white men since the character's inception in 1940. She portrayed Beulah (and appeared on *Amos 'n' Andy* and Eddie Cantor's show as a guest) until she fell ill in 1951 and was replaced by Louise Beavers, and later Lillian Randolph, both black performers. Oriole, Beulah's girlfriend, was played by Ruby Dandridge, then Amanda Randolph, and finally Butterfly McQueen.

Widowed once, Hattie had married and divorced three more times. She died on October 25, 1952, at the Motion Picture Country House in San Fernando Valley, California. The round-faced entertainer with an infectious low chuckle opened the gates for other black performers. In her family alone, her brother Sam and a nephew were inspired to become film actors. Hattie McDaniel worked for nearly every major film studio and can still be enjoyed in reruns of many of the seventy movies she made.

Joan Davis

In 1908 Madonna Josephine Davis was born in St. Paul, Minnesota, the daughter of a train dispatcher. Though neither her father nor mother had ever shown an inclination for performing, young Jo was a natural ham. Her parents allowed her to sing wherever she found an audience and by the time she was old enough to start school, she had three years' experience as a performer. Along the way, comedy was added to her song-and-dance act and Joan was signed to tour on the Pantages theater circuit.

"I read *Variety* before the first-grade primer," she would later recall.

With her mother and a tutor, she took to the road performing as "The Toy Comedienne." From time to time they would return to St. Paul where the girl could catch up on her formal schooling. During her high school years, she stayed off the circuit and graduated from the Mechanics Arts High School as valedictorian and star of the debating team.

The seasoned performer then honed her comedy talents by studying Charlie Chaplin. She also gradually developed her own broad style with slapstick, hard pratfalls, and outrageous facial distortions. By her twentieth birthday, she had played every vaudeville circuit in the country, as well as summer camps, benefit shows and amusement parks.

Five months after Joan became a show business partner of young actor Si Wills, she married him. They barnstormed for a while, then played the Palace in New York, billed as Wills and Davis. "Two a day in vaudeville was beautiful," she later reminisced.

When the decline of vaudeville became evident, the couple decided to try their luck in Hollywood, moving there with their 1-year-old daughter Beverly in 1934. Shortly after their arrival Joan was hired by Mack Sennett for a hillbilly part in *Way Up Thar*.

That debut led to more than twenty other films including *Wake Up and Live* (a 1937 film about the Walter Winchell–Ben Bernie feud), *Thin Ice* (a musical released that same year with Sonja Henie and Tyrone Power), and *Hold That Co-ed* (a 1938 critically acclaimed musical comedy with John Barrymore). Shown now on television, these films bring back Hollywood's world of the thirties with smart factory girls in upswept hairdos, big-hearted chorines, and snappy switchboard operators who helped handsome detectives solve murders.

The early forties proved successful for Joan as a guest comedienne on radio shows. She was Gracie Allen's replacement on the Burns and Allen show when Gracie was ill. When Rudy Vallee left his program in 1943 to serve with the Coast Guard, Joan inherited his show. *The Joan Davis Show* on NBC centered around the misadventures of the characters who inhabited the Swanville Tea Shop. Verna Felton and Shirley Mitchell were also in the cast. Joan was also a regular on the variety show *The Village Store*. Before long she was voted top comedienne in a newspaper poll and won the *Motion Picture Daily's* Fame Poll. After her marriage broke up in 1944, she divided her time between homes in Bel Air and Palm Springs.

"What a breeze," she said of her radio years. "It was stealing money."

In 1945 Joan signed a four-year radio contract with the United Drug Company for four million dollars. An astute businesswoman, she created her own production company for future films and the hit NBC television series *I Married Joan*, which premiered in 1952. The comedienne (who memorized all her lines because she felt restricted using a TelePrompTer) portrayed the inept wife of a domestic-relations court judge (played by Jim Backus). Beverly Wills, her sound-alike daughter who had inherited her mother's rusty voice, played Joan's sister on the sitcom. The star's "comic zest and vitality" were praised by *Variety*.

"I've never worked so hard in my life," she said of playing Joan Stevens on the show. "I'm glad I took care of myself as a little girl."

Joan's duties as president of Joan Davis Productions, where she was addressed as JD, in addition to starring in the weekly show, took their toll. There was little time for her favorite pastimes of fishing, playing golf, or going through her extensive joke file. "I don't go to sleep," she said of her demanding schedule. "I fall down unconscious."

Worn out, she quit playing the role in 1955 and the program went into reruns, tying with *Queen for a Day* as the highest-rated daytime show. In 1959 Joan Davis retired completely from show business leaving her daughter a legacy of "a cracked voice and a lot of negatives" of her movies and *I Married Joan* television series, which is still being rerun. The comedienne, whom Fanny Brice once said should play her in the movies, died of a heart attack on May 24, 1961, at the age of 53.

Eve Arden

The hit television show *Our Miss Brooks* became so much a part of Eve Arden's life that she named her daughter Connie after the main character — not surprising for someone who adopted her stage name from a character in a book and a cosmetic jar. That happened during the 1930s when Eunice Quedens (born in Mill Valley, California, on April 30, 1912) was trying to make it big in show business. Eunice Quedens' career actually had begun when she was sixteen.

"I was dumped by my mother and my aunt at the Henry Duffy office in San Francisco and told to get a job acting," she said.

She worked with the Duffy Company for over a year before joining the Bandbox Repertory Theatre, a group of young actors who toured the "citrus circuit" through southern California. After a year and a half of traveling with an old Ford and a trailerload of props, she was hired to appear in the revue *Lo and Behold* at the Pasadena Community Playhouse. Tyrone Power and Kay Thompson were also in the show's cast.

Lee Shubert noticed her and hired her for the part of Fanny Brice's mother in a *Ziegfeld Follies* skit in 1934. She next worked in *Parade*, a Theater Guild production in which her satirical singing of " Send for the Militia" won the praise of Brooks Atkinson of the *New York Times*. Then she was back to the *Follies*, this time as a featured player and understudy for Fanny Brice.

Movie roles followed (the first as a gun moll in *Oh, Doctor* in 1937) with Eve usually playing the wisecracking sidekick to the leading actress, as she did with Joan Crawford in *Mildred Pierce* in 1945. In *Stage Door* (1937) she wore a live cat around her neck as a fur piece!

In addition to appearing in over thirty movies, Eve found time to work on Broadway in *Very Warm for May* (1939), *Two for the Show* (1940), and *Let's Face It* (1941), in which she played opposite Danny Kaye.

Her movie role as a Russian sniper in *The Doughgirls* (1944) brought her fame as a leading film comedienne. Radio wanted her, so Eve was soon working on broadcasts with Danny Kaye, Ken Murray, Jack Carson and Jack Haley.

In 1947, Eve became the proprietress of the Sealtest Village Store, the setting for the weekly music and comedy offered by the radio show *The Village Store*. When offered the lead part in a radio show called *Our Miss Brooks* in 1948, Eve immediately accepted because she found the character of the cynical English teacher "thoroughly likeable." Critics wrote that the program was one ". . . which has the makings of a Hooper hit," and ". . . there just isn't anyone in the business who can handle feline dialogue as well as Miss Arden."

After the show's premiere, there was criticism by some in the teaching profession for presenting teachers in an undignified way. Eve defended the show by saying that she saw Miss Brooks as an involved teacher at Madison High who went out of her way to help her students.

"We tried to wipe out the notion that all teachers were fuddy-duddies," she insisted. "It just isn't so. Teachers are like Miss Brooks . . . warm, romantic, realistic, attractive . . . she's typical."

Eve had based the character on two of her own teachers — Lizzie Kaiser and Ruth Waterman. Ruth had taught her in the third grade. "She had dimples, big brown eyes, and was always smiling," Eve recalled. "I try to give Miss Brooks that same smiling quality."

After being criticized for dressing beyond a teacher's salary, the actress then bought the clothes she wore for each show, keeping in mind what a teacher could afford.

Many teachers around the country agreed with her attempts to present them in a better light. They wrote letters thanking her for making them more human by dispelling the staid, unmarried stereotype. "We're not all social left-overs," one wrote. Educators' associations honored her with citations and speaking invitations.

Amid her stacks of fan mail one day, Eve found an unusual request from a woman she'd never met, but she agreed to it. A short time later, she was maid of honor at the Chicago teacher's wedding!

Eve was married to Hollywood literary agent Edward Bergen from 1939 to 1947. She met actor Brooks West in 1950 during a summer stock tour of *Over the Rainbow*. She married him the following year and they eventually became the parents of two boys and two girls. West worked as a regular in the CBS television comedy series *My Friend Irma* during the early 1950s.

In 1952 a poll conducted by *Radio–Television Daily* named Eve Arden as Woman of the Year in Radio. While she was known to radio listeners only as buoyant Miss Brooks, in real life she chose to undergo psychoanalysis. "My real reason for getting my psyche explored," she explained afterwards, "was to avoid making major mistakes in raising our children."

Connie Brooks' reign as the nation's favorite teacher was extended and the show was moved to television for a four-year run. Eve took to the new medium with gusto, and developed the knack of directly addressing her viewers and throwing caustic one-liners their way.

The adventurous schoolmarm, though she knew better, often got involved in her charges' crazy schemes — like breaking into the principal's office: "It sounds risky, far-fetched, and impractical . . . we'll get started right after school."

Besides having to contend with a tyrannical principal and various addle-brained students such as Walter Denton (played by Richard Crenna), Connie Brooks' romantic hopes were continually thwarted. Stolid biology teacher Philip Boynton was more interested in his frog McDougal than in her.

On the radio show Jeff Chandler played Mr. Boynton, but it was felt he didn't look the part for television so he was replaced by Robert Rockwell. When the show was reformatted in 1955 (the setting was changed to Mrs. Nestor's Private School), the object of Miss Brooks' affections became gym teacher Gene Talbot, played by Gene Barry. Gale Gordon portrayed Principal Osgood Conklin in both versions of the show.

"I do love Miss Brooks," Eve said when the series ended in 1956 and went into reruns, "but enough of a good thing can be too much."

That same year Gale Gordon and Richard Crenna joined Eve in the making of *Our Miss Brooks* for the movie screen. At the end of the movie, Connie Brooks' dream finally came true when she became Mrs. Boynton. Several years of reruns brought Eve new fans from all over the country.

"People are going to have to go to Siberia to escape me," she laughed. Everywhere she went she was recognized by her fans. "They come up . . . and say something nice about Miss Brooks," she said.

Her return to television on *The Eve Arden Show* lasted but a short time due to poor audience response. From 1967 to 1969 she costarred with Kaye Ballard in the successful series *The Mothers-in-Law* on NBC. The pair played next-door neighbors whose son and daughter had married. Herbert Rudley played Eve's husband for the two seasons it was on.

She continued to work in the theater, appearing in the road versions of *Auntie Mame* in 1958 and *Hello Dolly* in 1967. Brooks West often toured with his wife, appearing in *Auntie Mame, Little Me, Under Papa's Picture* and other roadshows. They also worked together in the spellbinding film *Anatomy of a Murder* in 1959. West died in 1984 at the age of 67.

The actress-comedienne worked in more than fifty films over the years, the later ones including *The Strongest Man in the World* (1975) with Kurt Russell and Phil Silvers, and *Grease* (1978) with John Travolta and Olivia Newton–John. In *Grease*, Eve had come full circle. She was once again back in high school, this time playing the principal!

Minnie Pearl

The "Queen of Country Comedy" has pleased many fans with her cornpone humor for over fifty years. Her stage attire always remains the same — a cotton dress, black Mary Jane shoes, and flower-decked hat with the dangling $1.98 price tag still intact. After greeting the audience with a toothy grin and an ear-splitting "Howdee-e-e," she tells them all about the goings-on down home in Grinder's Switch.

Sarah Ophelia Colley was born in 1912 in Centerville, Tennessee, the pampered daughter of prosperous lumberman Tom Colley and his wife, Fanny, a pianist.

"I guess I always wanted to be funny, she says, "and my parents and four older sisters encouraged me."

Sarah attended Ward-Belmont College, a fashionable girls' finishing school in Nashville. Adept at playing the piano by ear, she often entertained at parties but soon discovered that "while I was playing the piano, the cutie-pies were out smooching in the rumble seats with all the good-looking guys."

After college, Sarah traveled throughout the South giving dramatic readings and picking up colloquial expressions of the different areas she visited. When a theater career did not materialize, she took a job with the Wayne P. Sewell Producing Company of Atlanta, Georgia. For the next six years, she lived out of a suitcase, traveling to rural communities where she roomed in private residences and produced shows with local talent.

"I got to know the people very well," she said. "Warm-hearted, down-to-earth country girls, I loved them for their honesty and the humorous way they looked at life. From them, Minnie Pearl grew.... Her name is really a tribute to the many Minnies and Pearls I came to know as a back-hills producer."

In 1937, Sarah's father died, and she was called home to care for her mother. She took a job with the WPA running a recreation room for children at $50 a month. She remembers that period as the lowest ebb of her life: "There I was at 28, a failure. No husband. No career. Minnie and I seemed destined to be small-town unknowns."

Then she was asked to fill in at a bankers' convention in Centerville. Using the local humor she had absorbed, country gal "Cousin" Minnie Pearl performed singing and comedy routines about country life and her determination to "ketch a feller." Bob Turner of Nashville was so taken with the character, he arranged for an audition with the Grand Ole Opry. She passed and was scheduled for a trial on the show.

Her first performance in November of 1940 brought her ten dollars, stacks of fan letters, and a new career. Minnie joined the Opry, thus initiating an era of solo comics with that country showcase. For the next thirty years, she worked alongside the greats in country music. She toured the United States playing theaters, nightclubs, fairs, rodeos and concert halls, always ending up back in Nashville every Saturday night for the radio broadcast from Ryman Auditorium (later replaced by the $15 million Grand Ole Opry House).

"I love those Grand Ole Opry folks and the people of Nashville like a family," she says today.

Minnie was also in the cast of a musical variety radio show called *River Boat Revels* in the early forties, and through the years has been a familiar guest on many television variety shows, including the *Mike Douglas Show*, the *Dinah Shore Show*, and the *Tennessee Ernie Ford Show*. Recordings of her humor include the single hit *Giddyup Go-Answer, Monologue* and *How to Catch a Man*.

"She's apple pie and clothes dried in the sun," Sarah says of her character. "The price tag on my hat seems to be symbolic of all human frailty."

During World War II, the entertainer visited hospitals and traveled to Europe to lighten the lives of servicemen. Sarah caught her own "feller" when she met ex-commercial airline pilot Henry Cannon while touring Army installations. When they married in 1947, he became her business manager and whisked her to her engagements around the country in a silver Cannon Beechcraft.

"I'm the luckiest gal in show business," she's often said. "I married my transportation."

The Cannons live in a sprawling, two-story, white-brick home (with swimming pool and tennis courts) next door to the Tennessee governor's mansion in Nashville. Tennis and swimming keep Sarah so trim that Minnie's dresses are cut from the same pattern as that first yellow dress in 1940. Her own designer clothes share closet space with Minnie Pearl's modest frocks. She says that the character is like an alter ego, an extension of herself.

If she weren't a comedienne, Sarah would like to be a television producer or director. Her worst experiences over the years were when "folks didn't laugh." An old pro at sizing up her audience, she never has a set routine, but chooses material from her memory storehouse to fit each group. She finds that senior citizens groups especially are tickled at Minnie Pearl's racy country humor.

Many honors have come her way, but she was especially pleased in 1965 when she became the Nashville Woman of the Year and in 1968 when she was elected to the Country Music Hall of Fame. Hats worn by

Minnie Pearl are displayed in the Hall of Fame, the Roy Acuff Museum, the Tennessee Museum, and the Minnie Pearl Museum, which opened in December, 1984.

Located just across the street from the Country Music Hall of Fame in Nashville, the Minnie Pearl Museum is a yellow gingerbread house just like the one Sarah imagines her character would choose for a cozy home. The museum's theme is "It's Always Christmas at Grinder's Switch." Visitors can view the photos and handmade dioramas about young Sarah's transformation into Minnie Pearl, and watch videos of the performer's frequent television appearances. Upside down on the ceiling hangs a replica (fifteen feet in diameter) of her famous hat. The gift shop offers memorabilia, handmade dolls and preserves, and copies of *Minnie Pearl: An Autobiography.*

For forty-four years, Minnie Pearl wore the same pair of shoes, having them refurbished from time to time. Now they have appropriately been retired to the museum. Minnie Pearl visits there regularly, to chat with fans and sign autographs.

"She is uneducated but timeless, ageless in the knowledge of the hills," Sarah says of Minnie Pearl's appeal. "She pokes fun at life, herself, at others, but without barbs."

Pleased with the way her life turned out, Sarah says, "The Lord granted me this break which I don't deserve. One of the bright spots of my life is that people tell me they have laughed and felt a little better . . . that's all I ask of life, of my career . . . that people find happiness in Minnie Pearl."

Ann Sothern

Harriette Lake was born one cold January day in 1912 in Valley City, North Dakota, where her mother, a concert singer, was on tour. She and her two younger sisters were given early musical training. By the time she was in high school, Harriette was chosen to represent the state of Minnesota in a competition among young American composers. She continued her musical studies at the University of Washington in Seattle, then moved to Hollywood where Mrs. Lake was a vocal coach at Warner Bros. Harriette worked briefly first with Christie Comedies, then at MGM.

In 1930 Florenz Ziegfeld heard the young woman sing and hired her for the chorus of the Broadway musical *Smiles.* That led to singing roles in *America's Sweetheart* and *Everybody's Welcome* on Broadway the following year. In 1933, she played the feminine lead in both the road company and New York production of *Of Thee I Sing*.

When the show closed, Harriette accepted the invitation from Columbia Pictures to return to Hollywood. The studio changed the color of her hair from red to platinum and gave her a new name — Ann Sothern. She began playing ingenue roles, but soon tired of them, preferring instead to sing with the band of Roger Pryor, a musician she married in 1936. Finally MGM put her under contract. Portraying a character named Maisie Revere, Ann Sothern was a sensation in the film *Maisie*. "One of the brightest and liveliest comediennes in the business," a critic wrote.

Ann's first marriage ended in divorce, and she married actor Robert Sterling in 1943. A daughter, Patricia Ann, was their only child. That union also was later dissolved.

There were nine *Maisie* films in all, and though the critics often faulted the story material for being flimsy, the silky voiced star won their praise. Ann made other pictures but everyone still referred to her as "Maisie." The character became so well known that she received mail addressed to "Maisie, U.S.A." Ann was captivated by the limelight and lifestyle a movie career afforded, such as a chauffeur-driven limousine. She didn't like to drive a car, but did ride a motorcycle back and forth to the MGM studios during the war years.

In 1945, Ann brought her impudent character to radio. The role was unusual for those times. Most women on radio were portrayed either as man-hungry or scatterbrained, sometimes both. But Maisie was independent, sophisticated and perfectly capable of outwitting her boss. Listeners tuned in for the latest of Maisie's misadventures as a Good Samaritan secretary who worked for a wealthy lawyer named Mr. Dorsey. The revised radio version of *Maisie* in 1949 centered around a sharp-tongued shop girl continually in hot water for talking back to rich customers. That syndicated series entertained a devoted following of fans until 1952.

During the late forties, Ann became critically ill with hepatitis and barely survived. For more than two years she couldn't work, except to tape-record the *Maisie* radio shows. After her recovery, she returned briefly to Broadway and starred in several television plays. Critics and fans alike were happy to see the saucy performer again.

In 1953, Ann made an easy transition to television where she again played a zany but shrewd secretary named Susie on the TV show *Private Secretary*. Having gained weight during her illness, the performer wore slimming black outfits on camera and was seldom shown from the waist down. Former movie heavy Don Porter portrayed Susie's boss, Peter Sands, a no-nonsense theatrical agent. Ann Tyrell appeared as the receptionist and Jesse White played a shifty rival talent agent. Susie McNamara's scheming behind her boss's back continually got her into trouble (she once poked holes in his new briefcase to make a home for a stray cat), but she emerged cocky as ever at the end of every program. The show was chosen to be shown to American armed forces overseas.

By the time the final segment of *Private Secretary* was televised in 1957, Ann Sothern was a woman with considerable wealth and clout. She owned ranch land in Idaho and presided as president of several corporations. But she was not ready to give up television, and introduced her own program, *The Ann Sothern Show*, in which she played an assistant hotel manager named Katy O'Connor. After the first season, there was a shuffling of characters and Don Porter was hired to replace the hotel manager, played originally by Ernest Truex. Hence viewers were able to enjoy the pair's old *Private Secretary* relationship, only in a different format, until the show ended in 1961.

In 1965, Ann embarked on her most unusual role — playing a talking automobile. In *My Mother the Car*, lawyer Dave Crabtree (Jerry Van Dyke) bought a 1928 Porter in a used-car lot after it told him it was the reincarnation of his mother. Misunderstandings abounded because Dave was the only one who could hear Ann's voice. After the show went off the air a year later, Ann continued to do guest spots on other series (*The Lucy Show* and *Love American Style*) and in 1980, worked in the movie *The Little Dragons*.

Marie Wilson

Marie Wilson was born Kathleen Elizabeth White on August 19, 1916, in Anaheim, California. After the death of her father, the family moved to Hollywood, where Marie managed to get a movie contract. While still in her teens, she became the sole support of her family. The attractive young starlet made her movie debut in *Babes in Toyland* (1934). After appearing in *The Great Ziegfeld* in 1936, she began working regularly, sometimes doing four films a year. Those included *Boy Meets Girl* (with Pat O'Brien and James Cagney) and *Satan Met a Lady*, a tongue-in-cheek version of *The Maltese Falcon*.

Marie was also in demand for nightclub and stage show appearances, but was usually cast in archetypical dumb blonde roles that emphasized her well-endowed figure. Those who knew her, however, found her both intelligent and witty, qualities which were never allowed to surface in her character portrayals.

In June, 1942, Ken Murray hired her to do a satirical strip-tease act in his "Blackouts" show in Los Angeles. During her five years under his employment, she ran up a record of 2,332 consecutive performances and her salary had increased from $250 a week to $1,000.

Marie's career really took off when she got her own radio show, *My Friend Irma*, on CBS in 1947. Writer-producer Cy Howard, the creator of the role, had to persuade the hesitant young woman that it was right for her. Marie eventually agreed to play the part of Irma Peterson, a gorgeous but vacuous blonde secretary. Her more level-headed roommate Jane was played by Cathy Lewis and Gloria Gordon was Mrs. O'Reilly, owner of their boarding house.

The weekly half-hour shows focused on the romantic escapades of Irma and Al, a jobless, down-on-his-luck schemer, and Jane and her millionaire boss whom she hoped to marry. The show immediately attracted a substantial following of listeners. It quickly climbed up in the Hooper ratings and by 1948, moved into sixth place. And popularity polls showed Marie ranked among the top five for radio performers in the country.

In 1949, Marie appeared in the movie version of *My Friend Irma*, in which her con-man boyfriend lends her apartment to two soda jerks. This was the screen debut of Dean Martin and Jerry Lewis. The following year, she made *My Friend Irma Goes West*, again with Martin and Lewis.

"Irma" next moved to television. The debut of the show was broadcast from CBS's new Hollywood studios in 1952 and ran for two seasons. Irma's on-screen shenanigans took place mostly in her New York apartment, and usually concerned Al, Jane, and Jane's suitor, a wealthy financial expert played by Brooks West (Eve Arden's husband).

After her television series ended (and went into several years of reruns), Marie returned to the nightclub circuit and the making of comedy films. Groucho Marx and William Bendix shared billing with her in *A Girl in Every Port* (1952) and Robert Cummings was her costar in *Marry Me Again* (1953). She departed from her familiar roles when she portrayed the ill-fated French queen Marie Antoinette in an all-star movie epic titled *The Story of Mankind* (1957). Marie's last movie was *Mr. Hobbs Takes a Vacation* in 1962. She continued working, doing the voice-over for a television series, *Where's Huddles*, two years before her death. She died in Hollywood in November, 1972, at the age of 56, following surgery for cancer.

Marie was married twice, first to Allen Nixon, then producer-writer Robert Fallon. She and Fallon had an adopted son, Gregson. The comedienne, who fashioned a radio and television career out of playing a scatterbrained blonde whose antics caused trouble for others, is remembered for her friendliness and compassion. She was known for being kind-hearted and charitable to anyone in need—strangers and friends alike.

Judy Canova

Wearing pigtails and a straw hat and toting a battered suitcase, Judy was a steady presence in show business for nearly fifty years. She usually played the country bumpkin, her hokey get-ups reflecting on her upbringing in the hills of Georgia.

Juliette Canova was born in Starke, Florida, in 1916, and while still in her teens, accompanied her brother Zeke and sister Annie to New York City where they performed a hillbilly act in nightclubs. Judy's contribution to the routine was yodeling and playing her "gittar."

Broadway work followed with parts in *Ziegfeld Follies of 1936*, *Calling All Stars* and *Yokel Boy*. She later toured in *No, No, Nanette*. Hollywood beckoned and the young performer went West to appear in more than a dozen films during the thirties and forties. Judy, along with Donald O'Connor, Peggy Ryan, and other young players, set the tone of the period. In one spook picture, Judy's pigtails stood on end with fright.

Among Judy's films still being viewed on television are *Sis Hopkins*, a 1941 comedy with Susan Hayward in which Judy stars as a country girl in a snooty girls' school; *Sleepytime Gal*, a 1942 comedy musical with Jerry Lester; *Chatterbox*, a 1943 movie about a dude ranch costarring Joe E. Brown; and her last film, *The Adventures of Huckleberry Finn*, made in 1960 with Tony Randall and Eddie Hodges.

After singing regularly on the Edgar Bergen–Charlie McCarthy radio show and making guest appearances on others from the late thirties on, Judy became the host of her own *Judy Canova Show*. It premiered on NBC in 1945 and ran for twelve years. Judy portrayed a country girl from Cactus Junction living in Hollywood with her aunt, who was played by Ruth Perrott, then Verna Felton. Her jokes reflected her southern rural background.

"When I found out we are what we eat, I stopped eatin' pig cracklin's and sow belly," she proclaimed.

One of her gags was a favorite with radio listeners. Someone would say, "One of my ancestors was a Knight of the Royal Order of the Bath— or don't you know the Order of the Bath?"

Judy would reply, "Why, shore—on Saturday night it was Paw first and then all the kids in the order of their ages."

The hayseed comic was recorded on RCA Records and when

television came along, she succeeded in that medium as well. Her television credits include *Police Woman*, *The Alfred Hitchcock Show*, *Love American Style*, *The Johnny Carson Show* and *Love Boat*, on which she made her last appearance in 1980.

The twangy-voiced entertainer who made a career of playing "hicks" died on August 5, 1983. She was 66 years old.

Chapter Four

Early Stand-Up Comics

Until the late 1960s, it was extremely difficult for a woman to persuade a theater or nightclub owner that she could make people laugh without a man by her side to feed her the lines. And if she did talk her way into a job, she still had to convince his patrons. Only a dauntless individual would walk into the spotlight of a smoky cabaret and rely only on the words she uttered to win over a tough nightclub audience.

The rooms she played were a whir of activity, with people table-hopping or going back and forth to the restrooms. A few feet from where the comic stood were tables of noisy customers who were preoccupied with summoning a waiter, impressing their dates, or arguing with companions. Drunken hecklers were an occupational hazard that took special handling. They talked over her punch lines or yelled, "Go home where you belong." It was hard for a fledgling comic to remember the next joke, let alone concentrate on her timing and delivery, while confronted with a barrage of remarks questioning her femininity.

Besides the obstacles she faced in finding steady work, the stand-up comic sometimes received little or no support from her family and friends. They didn't understand her pursuit of such an "unladylike" and potentially dangerous occupation that entailed keeping such late hours.

Some women, through stamina and an unwavering belief in themselves, eventually made it. Despite the frustrating nights when they "bombed" and went home soaked with flop sweat, they thrived on the challenge to become a show business phenomenon and kept returning to the microphone. They pioneered the way for future women stand-up comics by proving that funny was funny, despite the sex of the messenger.

Moms Mabley

Jackie "Moms" Mabley appeared to be a cantankerous old woman for over fifty years. Tottering on stage in her runover shoes, frumpy dress with slip showing, and knit cap ("but I'm *cle-e-ean*"), her onstage mannerisms and homilies were perfectly in character with a wary observer of the world. In her gravelly voice she regaled audiences (whom she addressed as children) and saw no contradiction in the combination of her religious beliefs and her racy material.

"I really just talk about life," she said, "and I never did anything you haven't heard on the streets. . . . My slogan is: by all means do what you want to do, but know what you're doin'."

Through the years Moms was always carrying a torch for some well-known entertainer like Cab Calloway who "treats me so bad, chillun." One of her favorite subjects was "ugly old men," one of whom "worked in a doctor's office, standing by the door making people sick." Another well-known line was, "An old man can't do nothin' for me except to bring me a message from a young man."

After a half-century in show business, Moms finally gained national recognition when racial barriers came down during the 1960s. Her toothless grin ("I never could work with them in") and croaking voice became familiar to millions of American television viewers.

She claimed that every comedian had stolen from her except Jack Benny and Redd Foxx. "But it makes no difference," she philosophized. "God always gives me some more."

Loretta Mary Aiken was born one of twelve children of the town grocer in Brevard, North Carolina, in 1897. She was of mixed black, Cherokee and Irish ancestry. Great-grandmother Harriet Smith, a former slave, was her spiritual mentor who told her to put God first in everything. "She was the most beautiful woman I ever knew," Moms said.

After entertaining at church fund-raisers as a child, she ran away at the age of 16 to sing, dance and tell jokes in vaudeville. "I was pretty and didn't want to become a prostitute," she explained of her decision to enter show business.

Her work was restricted to the black vaudeville circuit, TOBA (Theatre Owners Booking Association). The performers claimed the initials stood for "Tough On Black Asses." Bessie Smith, Pigmeat Markham, Tim "Kingfish" Moore, Peg Leg Bates and Louis Armstrong were among the many great black performers playing the circuit in those days. Along the way she also met another entertainer, Jack Mabley, and decided to use his name for her stage work.

"He took a lot off me," she said of her early boyfriend. "The least I could do was take his name."

The young performer was befriended by partners in the act Butter-beans and Suzie and taken to New York by them in 1927. (Ed and Suzie Edwards were famous for double-entendre jokes and one of the first black acts to do topical humor.) Moms played the black circuits all through the South and became a hit at popular black clubs like Connie's Inn in Harlem, Atlantic City, and Chicago, but for years remained unknown to white audiences.

She appeared in rooms with Duke Ellington, Count Basie and other big bands of that era and eventually was in demand for fifteen-week stints at the Apollo Theatre in Harlem, where she presented a new song-dance-comedy routine every week! For years she headlined at the Howard Theatre in Washington, D.C., and the Royal in Baltimore. Moms sometimes told her northern audiences about the delicacies her southern relatives sent her at hog-killing time — "neckbones with a whole lot of meat" to eat with cracklin' bread and "gre-e-eens, you understand what I me-e-ean."

"My baby brother Eddie Parton and I write the material," she noted. "In thirty-five minutes on stage, I can keep laughter in a certain range, building higher and higher 'til when I tell the last joke, they're all laughing like mad."

Comedian Godfrey Cambridge once stated that the humor of contemporary black comedians such as Moms Mabley, Bill Cosby, Nipsey Russell, and Dick Gregory could be "traced back to the satire of slave humor."

Film work consisted of bit parts in *Mom's Boarding House* and the more familiar *The Emperor Jones*, the 1933 adaptation of Eugene O'Neill's play. It was the first film (and the last for a long time) to star a black man. Paul Robeson, the star, was criticized for daring to depict the character as a proud, tough southern black.

Moms' first television appearance was in *A Time for Laughter*, an all-black comedy special produced by Harry Belafonte in 1967. Guest spots followed on shows hosted by Mike Douglas, Flip Wilson, Bill Cosby and the Smothers Brothers. When she received an invitation to appear on the popular *Ed Sullivan Show*, she declined because her act would be limited to four minutes. "Honey, it takes Moms four minutes just to get on the stage," she explained.

In her private life Moms resided in a luxurious home, and wore stylish clothes and furs. She also owned a chauffeur-driven Rolls Royce bearing a monogrammed license plate.

Her first endeavor as a recording artist earned her a gold record titled *Moms Mabley — The Funniest Woman in the World* (Chess Records).

Moms Mabley at the U.N. and *Moms Mabley at the Geneva Convention* were also big sellers, as well as her stag party hit *Now Hear This* (Mercury). Along with Jonathan Winters, Lenny Bruce, Phyllis Diller, Homer & Jethro, Shelley Berman and the Smothers Brothers, Moms was considered a top comedy recording star of the 1960s.

Of the difficulties of being a black female performer, she once spoke of "some horrible things done to me. I've played every state in the union, except Mississippi. They ain't ready."

In spite of the hardships she endured, Moms was a moderate in civil rights who chastised urban rioters during the 1960s. She spoke out against the violence which followed Martin Luther King's death.

"They ain't civil rights people, they're looting people using the least excuse for their own selfish use."

Moms' career was in full swing in the early 1970s with dates at top white showplaces such as the Kennedy Cultural Center in Washington, D.C., and the Copacabana in New York. Metropolitan audiences came to hear her comments on controversial issues and fictional conversations with world leaders including President Lyndon Johnson ("What you want, boy?"). She spoke out against abortion and blamed national problems on a government which didn't follow the Ten Commandments.

Speaking of Redd Foxx and herself, she said, ". . . now we've made it. . . . It's too bad it took so long. Now that we've got some money, we have to use it all for doctor bills."

At the age of 76, the rubber-faced comedienne starred in a comedy called *Amazing Grace* portraying Grace Teasdale Grimes, an honest woman who cleans up a corrupt city government. Friend Slappy White, Butterfly McQueen and Stepin Fetchit were her costars.

"I wanted to do something to make my children (one daughter and one son) and great-grandchildren proud of me, like all mothers do," she said of her acting role.

The film was an overdue success for Moms, who said, "I try not to be bitter. I would have liked to have gotten my chance earlier, but that's the way things were in those days."

The popular entertainer suffered a severe heart attack while working on the picture, but returned after three weeks to complete the filming wearing a pacemaker. Though her arthritis was getting worse and her weight much lower than normal, she was planning to make club appearances, working from a wheel chair if necessary. Disregarding her doctor's orders, she continued to smoke.

Of old age, she warned, "You wake up one morning and you got it."

Moms died on May 23, 1975, in White Plains, New York. At her funeral comedian Dick Gregory lamented, "Had she been white, she'd have been known fifty years ago."

For the short time the spunky comic was allowed to share her insightful humor with American audiences regardless of race, she succeeded in every aspect of show business she entered, and recordings of her work are still sold in record stores across the country. Her distinctive talent for humor, which she considered a "gift from God," came from within.

"I just tell folks the truth. If they don't want the truth, then don't come to Moms. Anybody that comes to me, I'll help 'em. I don't say anything I don't mean."

Jean Carroll

Jean Carroll (born circa 1915) was an innovative stand-up comic who wrote her own material for vaudeville. Her routines about everyday incidents set her work apart from other comedy acts. Bits about her husband, daughter, mother and father brought resentment from some who went to see her, but she didn't see what the fuss was about and continued to joke about the members of her family.

"I used to do that routine about my daughter being a hippy with the dirty sneakers and dirty blue jeans, but why a beard? And you know people would actually come to me and say, 'Does your daughter really have a beard?' I'd say, 'No, I made her shave it, but I let her keep the mustache.'"

Jean's career began in the 1920s when she was in her early teens and living in the Bronx. After being spotted in an amateur show in New York City by a talent scout for MCA, her mother allowed her to quit school to go on the road in a dance act. A backstage tutor was available to teach school-age youngsters like Jean who were in show business. When she and the other girl, Pearl Saxon, were deserted by their male dancing partners who took off with the troupe's music and wardrobe, they borrowed money for clothes and became a duo.

Her comedy work began when Marty May offered her a job after hearing her clown around in the green room of a theater where they were waiting to go on. The two of them did an improvisational type of humor, unusual for those days because most acts were timed down to the minute. If seventeen minutes were called for on a particular bill, the performer knew just which parts of his routine could be combined to equal that length of time.

Jean met dancer Buddy Howe in 1934 when he worked on the same bill with her and May. They fell in love, so she wrote an act for the two of them, taught him to read lines, and the partnership of Carroll and

Howe was born. Elegantly attired Jean provided the humor and Buddy performed acrobatic dances and acted as straight man.

"If she changed the words, I was gone," he once said, referring to his wife's habit of ad-libbing.

The attractive couple had no trouble getting good bookings, eventually doing two a day at the Palace. In 1936, they married and left for England for a four-week engagement at the London Palladium and ended up staying in that country for three years.

After returning home, Jean kept the act updated with routines about her shopping experiences and the family. When telling the audience that her mother had lived with them since she had lost her father, she said, "He's not dead, he's hiding." An interest in people, a good ear for dialect, and the knack of embellishing enabled her to write humor that would appeal especially to local audiences along the circuit, whether rural or metropolitan. She and Buddy were rewarded by the total dedication of their fans, many of whom could recite the material from their previous appearance.

"You felt you were bringing something into people's lives," Jean said of the warm reception they received everywhere they appeared.

Carroll and Howe spent two years with the USO before Buddy was called into the Army. By the time he was discharged, Jean was appearing in Chicago as a very successful single act, so he decided to become a talent agent. In May of 1948, shortly after Israel had been declared an independent state, the comedienne appeared for the United Jewish Appeal at Madison Square Garden. She was introduced as a "very funny lady" to the crowd, by then teary-eyed from the moving music and speeches. The tough spot didn't faze Jean. She brought down the house when she stepped up to the microphone and said, "I've always been proud of the Jews, but never so proud as tonight because tonight I wish I had my old nose back."

Jean continued to perform alone until she retired during the fifties to become a doting grandmother.

Sally Marr

In October of 1948, Sally (claiming to be just a Brooklyn housewife) introduced her son, Lenny Bruce, to the Arthur Godfrey audience, proclaiming that her only son was destined for stardom. After seeing Lenny impersonate Jimmy Cagney, Humphrey Bogart, and Edward G. Robinson, all speaking in German, the audience agreed!

In reality, Sally (Sadie Kitchenberg) was stagestruck while still a child. In 1919 she entered a beauty contest judged by Valentino. The twelve-year-old did a "hootch dance" while the band played "Hindoostan." When a man came around later to sign her up, her father would not allow her to take the job.

She went on performing just the same—her early entrance into vaudeville, numerous first prizes in Charleston contests, and work as a crazy-leg dancer keeping her in the limelight. From then on, Sally saw every acquaintance as an audience to be won over. In social settings, she'd charm others with jokes and teasing patter. An early marriage to Mickey Schneider turned out to be a mistake and she shunned the responsibilities of motherhood shortly after her son, Leonard Alfred Schneider, was born, in much the same manner as her own absentee mother had done. Lenny was left in the care of his father while Sally continued to enter dance contests.

Once in a while she'd see Lenny, whom she called her little "malted-milk face," and take him to a burlesque show. When Mickey planned to remarry, Sally agreed to take Lenny for awhile, but the day-to-day chores of raising a child were more than she could handle. Two weeks later, she called Mickey to come get him. He and his new wife took Lenny home with them and raised him.

A string of dreary jobs followed for Sally. She worked as a maid for Tony and Rita DeMarco of the popular dance team, ran dancing classes for youngsters in Riverhead, and worked for an elderly Jewish publisher who took her dancing at the Roosevelt Grill. She and another woman made up the Marsalle dancing duo. When business was bad, she found work as a taxi dancer in Times Square. Among the stage names she used through the years were Boots Malloy, Sally Marsalle, and finally Sally Marr.

Her career picked up when the war came along and there was a sudden demand for entertainers. In 1942 she began working professionally when Mickey went into the Army and young Lenny joined the Navy. Her first jobs were as an emcee in bars in Flatbush. She told risqué jokes and threw in some dance steps when the attention of the audience lagged. Her bits about a Jewish mother and about the goings-on in a dance school went over big. Gradually she worked her way to comic status, and started to buy other comedy writers' material to augment her own.

Better club dates in Manhattan eventually led to a job at Club 78 at 78th Street and Broadway where she did jokes, sang a little and danced. Sally was a wisecracking trouper who energetically worked a room to get laughs.

To Lenny, she was a pal who could break him up. She passed along to him her ambivalent attitudes about show business, especially her disapproval of the exorbitant salaries paid to top entertainers. After her own career ran down, she transferred her attentions to Lenny.

Sally was living on Livingston Street in Brooklyn when Lenny and stripper Honey Harlow decided to get married. For a while they all lived together in the fifth floor, walk-up, one-bedroom apartment in which Lenny painted everything black and gold, including the bathtub! Sally later moved to the West Coast where she found work in burlesque and the movies. In 1952 she appeared briefly in *Star!*, Fox's film about an aging actress's decline. Bette Davis played the star trying to make a comeback and Natalie Wood was her daughter.

Lenny got custody of his daughter Kitty after his divorce from Honey. When a series of nursemaids didn't work out, Sally took her granddaughter to raise so her son could pursue his career unhampered. Whenever Lenny called to check on Kitty, Sally expected a detailed report on how his club act was doing. A marriage to a man twenty years her junior lasted but a short time, and Sally continued playing supporting roles in films. Some of her later work included parts in *Every Little Nook & Cranny*, starring Lynn Redgrave and Victor Mature for MGM in 1972, and *Fast Foxtrot in Burbank* the following year. Now 78 years old, the retired entertainer still resides in Hollywood.

Phyllis Diller

Phyllis celebrated her thirtieth anniversary in show business on March 7, 1985, and says she isn't about to slow down. A veteran of hundreds of television guest appearances, her own specials and series, thirteen movies, Broadway roles and theater in the round, she's made recordings and commercials, written several books, and draws capacity crowds at major clubs around the world. She is planning her eighth tour of Australia and appears frequently in Canada, England, and Monte Carlo.

The popular comedienne's performing attire is as outrageous as ever—fright wigs, spangled dresses, gold ankle boots. "I found that the greatest way in the world to say 'Hello' to an audience is to relate to something funny you're wearing," she explains.

Her machine-gun delivery punctuated with that trademark cackle still fractures fans who are eager to hear the latest about her legendary cheap husband, "Fang": "Once he took us out for doughnuts and coffee. The kids loved it—they'd never given blood before"; her fat mother-in-law, Moby Dick: "I don't know what her measurements are. We haven't had her surveyed yet"; sister-in-law Captain Bligh; and her own sleep-around sister: "It took a driving instructor two days to teach her how to sit up in a car."

Phyllis still puts herself down as well and can get laughs with jokes she's used for a decade or more, like the one about her visit to the beauty parlor: "I was there five hours — and that was just for the estimate."

Phyllis was born in 1917 in Lima, Ohio, the only child of older parents. Her father, Perry Driver, was an insurance salesman. Encouraged by her mother, Frances, young Phyllis developed her talents as a pianist and vocalist. A favorite childhood memory is "standing in a barn when I was 6 and singing opera tunes to a flock of sheep."

Phyllis says she started to think funny as a child and even though she's been known since high school as the life of the party, admits that she is really shy. After some time at a Chicago music conservatory, she realized ". . . I wasn't Melissa Mozart," so she began training as a music teacher at Bluffton College in Ohio. It was during her senior year there that she met Sherwood Diller.

They were married in 1939, moved to San Francisco, and within the next ten years became parents of Peter, Perry, Sally, Suzanne, and Stephanie.

"I had nine dolls which I adored . . . so I thought 'I'll have nine children' . . . but I bogged down at five . . . they were *terribly* expensive. I had no idea!"

Phyllis loved to read and wanted to become a writer, but none of the books she started ever got written. "I remember the little kids were all around the floor, the little rug rats . . . and I was writing on the top of a small upright piano so they couldn't get at my papers," she later said in a *Writer's Digest* article.

The family needed more income, so Phyllis looked for work. After answering an ad for a copy boy at the *San Francisco Chronicle* and being turned down, she landed an assignment with the *San Leandro News Observer* in the late fifties. She had to visit all the shops that advertised with the paper and write articles about them. That led to writing her own household-hints-and-humor column for the paper and later, a job writing ads for radio station KSFO in San Francisco. It was then she learned the art of sharp, condensed writing, so valuable to a comedy writer. She now edits her words so tightly she can deliver twelve punch lines per minute: "For radio you have 120 words a minute . . . I treated it like a telegram."

In an interview for *Movie Digest* in 1972, Phyllis admitted that early married life was not easy.

"My husband was in-between jobs frequently and I had to go to work to help support the family. I was . . . unsure of myself. I would crack jokes at the laundromat and act happy-go-lucky. I wasn't."

Phyllis Diller

One day while she was out looking for a job, she stopped in a strange church and heard a minister speak of positive thinking. That prompted the reading of numerous self-help books, one of them Claude Bristol's *The Magic of Believing*, which attests to a person doing almost anything he or she is determined to do. "I read that book over and over for two solid years," Phyllis said, "and I began to believe . . . and my belief in myself changed the entire course of my life."

Bristol's book also taught the harried working housewife how to concentrate on what she really wanted instead of trying to do too many things at once. By focusing all her attention and energy on one goal, she succeeded. Through the years, Phyllis has given away many copies of that book to friends and still speaks of how *The Magic of Believing* cured her of her fearfulness.

While Phyllis was growing more certain about her goals, Sherwood kept telling her that her one-liners were being wasted on the laundromat crowd and at the grocery checkout line. He urged his wife to expand her audience.

One day Phyllis called the Red Cross and said, "I have an act; where do you want it?" She was sent to the veteran's hospital at the Presidio.

"I pushed a piano into a room that had four guys in it. I played, sang and told jokes while they yelled, 'Leave us alone; we're already in pain.' I kept thinking, 'Is this show business?' But I was committed."

Not at all familiar with nightclubs, she visited a few with a friend before auditioning at the Purple Onion in San Francisco, the launching pad for many entertainers during the fifties. Others starting then in North Beach were Mort Sahl, The Kingston Trio, Johnny Mathis, and Rod McKuen. After her audition, the 37-year-old housewife was told she'd be called back for an appearance. During an interview with Sandy Payton on WIOD Radio in Miami (February, 1984), Phyllis recalled that appearance at the Purple Onion where she did her first original bit on stuffing a turkey: "I was petrified. I shook. I was a blur on stage . . . I sweat . . . It runs down your back, it runs into your shoes."

But the audience laughed, her trial engagement was subsequently held over for eighty-nine weeks, and she was on her way. For the next four years, she had no agent, writer, publicist, or manager, "just me and my material." She slithered around the piano with her long cigarette holder, lampooning current celebrities, and perfecting her routines about housekeeping and life with Fang.

While working at a club in New York, Phyllis's pianist felt she belonged on the *Jack Paar Show*, so he doggedly called the show again and again until one day she was summoned for an audition. She walked into an office and auditioned cold in front of three men. They put her on the Paar show *that night!*

"Time stood still," she recalls of that experience. "At the end of the bit, there was that electric moment when I *knew*."

Many laughmakers besides Phyllis became established from exposure on the *Jack Paar Show*. Hermione Gingold, Dody Goodman, Jonathan Winters, Dick Gregory and Nipsey Russell are just a few who were given a chance there.

Phyllis's forte has always been a rapid string of simple jokes—"a setup and a payoff and the quicker the better . . . I want volume business. . . . My goal is that everybody in the audience understands the joke at the same moment."

Often asked why she uses her looks and shortcomings to get laughs, she explains that comedy is based on error, so that if there isn't something wrong, there's no comedy.

"I *was* ugly. I had a badly broken nose, very crooked teeth, and the wrong hairdo. That gave me a head start on being funny."

Her jokes about her miserable cooking, grease fires in her sink, and other household tragedies quickly caught on. She claimed to have a tan from the light in her Princess phone. Her husband, Fang ("He has one tooth two inches long, what would *you* call him?"), and the rest of her fictitious family became familiar to television viewers.

The Dillers divorced in 1965 and Phyllis married actor Warde Donovan (they are now also divorced). Some felt her first divorce would have an effect on her career and she'd have to revise her material but Phyllis kept Fang in the act.

"Fang is purely a figment and bears no resemblance to either of my former husbands," she insists.

The comedienne starred in her own show, *The Phyllis Diller Show*, on ABC during the 1966–67 season, and in *Beautiful Phyllis Diller Show* on NBC the following year. By the end of the 1960s, Phyllis joined the ranks as a top comedy record maker, along with Jonathan Winters, Moms Mabley, Homer & Jethro, Lenny Bruce, the Smothers Brothers, Bill Cosby, Pigmeat Markham, Shelley Berman and Allan Sherman.

In 1971 Phyllis emerged from a brief absence with a face lift, straightened teeth, and a new nose. She had again ignored the advice of "crepe hangers" who told her cosmetic surgery would wreck her career, and didn't change her routines at all. Pleased with both the physical and psychological effects, she talked freely about it, perhaps doing more than any woman in America to take the stigma out of the plastic surgeon's scalpel.

"I wanted to bring it out of the closet," she says.

Once firmly established as a top comedy star, Phyllis decided to return to her music: "I think I did it for my mother who programmed me to be a pianist." Starting in 1971, she appeared as guest pianist (her piano virtuoso name was Dame Illya Dillya) playing mostly Beethoven and Bach with symphony orchestras from Honolulu to Fort Lauderdale. After performing with nearly 100 different ensembles over a ten-year period, she gave her farewell concert in 1981.

While she loved the excitement and fulfillment of playing, she admits that practicing became drudgery, so she had to reestablish her priorities. "I'd rather make people laugh," she says.

Phyllis feels that the rhythm and timing of music are extremely beneficial to a comedian and points out that many comedians are also musicians: Sid Caesar was a concert saxophone player, Johnny Carson and Charlie Callas play drums, Phil Silvers played a clarinet, Jack Benny had his violin.

"If I weren't in the humor business, I'd like to be in fashion or writing," Phyllis says, now that she's proved herself musically.

As an author, she has already become quite prolific. Her most successful books include *Phyllis Diller's Housekeeping Hints* (Doubleday, 1966), *Phyllis Diller's Marriage Manual* (1967), *The Complete Mother by Phyllis Diller* and *The Joys of Aging and How to Avoid Them* (1981). One Diller hint for homemakers is to replace the labels on store-bought pickles with personalized ones noting month and year, then draping the jar with a cobweb so it looks as if it just emerged from the fruit cellar. In the latter book, she warns that no matter how cleverly you disguise your age, your driver's license can give you away if "Your license is not issued from a state but says, 'Territory,' as in 'Territory of Montana.'"

She freely gives advice on how to appear younger: "Airbrush disco colors on your orthopedic shoes," or "Have braces put on your false teeth." She says times have changed since the fifties, so "Instead of dating one guy, invite a SWAT team up to your apartment."

While researching a book, Phyllis records gags on index cards, which are then arranged in chapter order. After she has enough material, these comic "bricks" are cemented with "mortar" words to form the text of the book.

When all the beauty and exercise books by famous screen and television stars were topping the best seller lists, Phyllis also had tips to share.

"Just because my anatomy has been rearranged several times by natural disasters, childbirth and some cooking accidents doesn't mean I can't give advice as well as Jane, Linda and other beautiful stars," she said. "Next to gold and jewelry, health is the most important thing you can have."

Her special beauty secret is the facelift which she recommends "if you're tripping over your neck." She has reservations about some of the new wonder drugs since she asked her doctor if a new medicine would relax her. "No," he answered, "you'll just dig being tense." The comedienne also warns women about taking iron supplements in excess: "I've got so much iron in my blood that I attach my earrings with a magnet."

Phyllis writes seventy percent of her own material and buys the rest which she restructures, then tries out on stage. "A comic is responsible for his or her own material," she says. "You stand alone and just do it — you either make it or you die alone."

Phyllis respects only "true comic material" and worries about the trend of performers who "rely only on filthy words to get laughs." Her advice to newcomers is that they are not going to be "discovered," but must work and work the clubs and someone who can help them will come along. Nor should they let others dissuade them. Some people advised Phyllis to give up her "stupid" laugh: ". . . if I could tell you how many commercials I've been hired to do just to get my laugh," she says. "Life is a do-it-yourself kit, so do it yourself. Work. Practice."

Phyllis tries not to miss Johnny Carson's monologue and tells of one memorable appearance on his show.

"It was the biggest laugh I ever got," she says. "I was playing saxophone with Johnny on drums, Los Angeles [Mayor] Sam Yorty on banjo and Jimmy Stewart on accordion. They all started and a little later I came in with one terrible, high, screechy note. Johnny said, 'Hold it,' then proceeded to dress me down at length. I sat in silence. Just as we all were about to begin again, I said, 'What was it about it you didn't like?' It was a perfect set-up with his bawling out, then split-second timing with my line." Everyone cracked up.

Phyllis considers Bob Hope her "guru, buddy and patron saint," and has costarred with him in movies and on stage. When she accompanied him on a Christmas jaunt to Vietnam, Hope remarked that the war would have been over in three days if Phyllis had cooked for the enemy.

Over the years, Phyllis has been the recipient of humanitarian awards, patriotic citations and honorary degrees. More recently she received the AMC Cancer Institute Humanitarian Award and was inducted into the Ohio Women's Hall of Fame. She lives in Los Angeles and presently donates her time and talents to the Parkinson's Foundation and the Better Speech and Hearing Foundation of which she is National Chairperson. She often donates items to be auctioned off at fund-raisers around the country from little theater groups to charities such as Reye's Syndrome Foundation.

"There's a lot of sadness in the world," she says.

Phyllis often hears from fans who say she made a difference in their lives. One man told her that she was responsible for making his mother's last years more bearable. After watching Phyllis do her turkey-stuffing routine on television, the woman began to see the humor in everyday situations.

Television viewers were invited into Phyllis's twenty-two-room, English-style Los Angeles home during an *Entertainment Tonight* show in March of 1984. The tour began on a charming brick walkway bordered by white pillars and flowering plants leading to the entrance of the seventy-two-year-old structure, which she bought sight unseen. Phyllis said the elegantly furnished house is a total reflection of her, and not what the public might expect. She is also a devoted mother and a good cook.

"That woman is madness," she said of her stage personality, "but I'm a totally organized, normal person."

Naming many of the rooms began when Bob Hope gave her his portrait in 1966. She placed the gold-framed painting on a large easel in the corner of one room which she then christened the Bob Hope Salon. An oak-paneled alcove with stained-glass windows is the Gothic Alcove, a mirrored phone booth is John Wilkes Booth, and the guest powder room is Edith Head. The comedienne's study is filled with photos of show business friends, including her favorite performer, Tim Conway. Her office, originally the Bach Room, still houses a concert piano and German bass. At one time Phyllis *collected* pianos and pump organs!

"When we have people who can play jazz, the room comes to life," she told viewers.

The master bedroom remains unnamed and is filled with "things I dearly love" — artwork by her daughter, old hand mirrors tied with ribbons, antique evening purses, and her treasure — a black and gold harpsichord.

"You have to be basically an elegant person to succeed in comedy," she concluded. "If you don't have taste, your comedy will never make it. That's one of the true secrets of comedy."

Another well-kept secret created quite a stir when Phyllis crashed a stag lunch at the Friar's Club on October 20, 1983. "I had seen *Victor/ Victoria* and *Tootsie*," she said afterward. "I thought, 'That looks like fun.'"

Accompanied by her attorney, she attended the roast (for Sid Caesar) wearing a boy's suit and man's fedora over slicked-back hair. She was introduced to her unsuspecting fellow comics as "Phillip Downey." Her disguise worked perfectly. She sat through the whole roast with 2,000 men without being recognized. "People I'd known for thirty years looked right at me ... it was fun."

Her disguise didn't work so well in late 1984 when her famous cackle gave her away while she was traveling incognito, dressed as a nun. In her Sister Louise persona — wearing a habit, rimless glasses, and no makeup, Phyllis had been enjoying her privacy whenever she traveled. But on that Los Angeles-to-New York flight, she blew her cover.

Phyllis feels that women still have an extremely difficult time of being comediennes, but that funny women like Pudgy, Elayne Boosler, and Maureen Murphy are emerging.

"Men do not want women to be funny ... men want women to be fluffy little airheads," she says. "Men don't want women to be aggressive, but to become a real comic, you *have* to be aggressive ... to be aggressive and yet stay feminine, that's the trick."

Phyllis Diller was once flat broke and totally without confidence.

Now she needs three secretaries to handle her travel arrangements and mountains of correspondence. By learning to believe in herself and working with a fierce determination, she has succeeded as a comedienne, musician, actress, recording star, and author.

The veteran entertainer says she keeps up her energy by eating properly and genuinely loving what she does. She describes her life as "glorious — I'm enjoying the fruits of my labor." She also likes to reminisce about earlier times.

"My favorite memories are being with my mother and laughing a lot, and being with the children when they were little, especially taking them to the beach."

Totie Fields

Sophie Feldman was born in 1931 and her own mispronunciation of her name remained with her for life. While still a toddler, Totie's family moved from Hartford to Boston, where during high school, she sang in small clubs before heading for New York.

After three disappointing years of trying to get established, Totie got a booking at the Copacabana in 1963. Critics hailed her "slambang" performance and she was on her way with a spot on the *Ed Sullivan Show*. By that time, Totie had completely dropped the singing to expand the humorous patter between songs into a full routine. Her television debut led to more than two dozen appearances on Sullivan's popular Sunday evening television program.

Just four feet, eleven inches tall and weighing 170 pounds, Totie admitted an addiction to bagels and cream cheese and used her vital statistics to get laughs.

"I come right out and say I'm fat," she explained of her method of preempting hecklers. "I think I'm precious at this weight."

She loved to share her bizarre diets with the audience and often told amusing anecdotes about her husband, George, and her sister Rose. When she talked, her beautifully manicured hands fluttered around the friendly face so familiar to millions of talk-show viewers. As her popularity grew, the good-natured comic with the raucous voice was booked into nightclubs across the nation.

"I must do clubs," she said. "That's where I get the feeling for this business."

During the 1960s Totie's salary reached $200,000. She drove a Lincoln Continental and though overweight, spent a large part of her salary (she once estimated the amount at $100,000) on beautiful clothes, including bulky fur coats.

"I break all the rules and wear everything," she once said of her passion for clothes. "Ruffles, ostrich feathers, fox coats. You look fat in fox anyway," she reasoned, "so if you start fat, you only look a little fatter."

During the early 1970s the rotund performer was better paid than other leading female comics and was called "the number one stand-up comedienne on the saloon circuit," by *Playgirl* magazine in 1975.

Tragedy struck the following year. Totie underwent cosmetic surgery and complications resulted. About a month later, her left leg was amputated because of a blood clot. The spirited performer refused to give up — she immediately started working on a new act while she was still in the hospital.

"I don't want anyone feeling sorry for me," she said of her refusal to accept others' pity.

Totie's determination to resume her career won her the respect and affection of millions of Americans. After her ordeal, she returned to the stage (using an artificial limb) before a celebrity-packed house in Las Vegas. The performance was recorded and later presented to television viewers as "Totie Returns."

She entertained around the country, playing long engagements at the Sahara Hotel in Las Vegas, where audiences applauded her idea to market her own line of clothes for big women, with size labels of 3, 5, and 7.

"Mentally it will make us feel better," she joked.

Following the loss of her leg, Totie had continued health problems in spite of her positive attitude. She not only had to fight diabetes, but had to undergo more surgery and suffered two heart attacks. In every interview, the entertainer always spoke of her feelings of deep gratitude to her husband, George, for his support through her ordeal. The couple had two daughters, Debbie and Jody.

In January of 1978 Totie was named Entertainer of the Year by her colleagues. Seven months later she died of a heart attack in her Las Vegas home. The resilient performer was just 48 at the time of her death.

Chapter Five

Funny Women of Television

Shortly after World War II, the technology of television began to evolve. Television stations built to transmit signals were constructed in the late forties and antennas sprouted on roofs in communities all around the country. Everyone was intrigued by a box that not only talked, but transmitted a picture, fuzzy though it was. This revolutionary medium, besides providing a new avenue of entertainment and employment opportunities for many Americans, soon became a dominant force in our lives, profoundly influencing our thinking and lifestyles.

The first people having access to a television set (initially a small screen surrounded by a huge wooden cabinet) were afforded "free" entertainment and information to an extent unprecedented in history. Within a few years, Americans became more of a national society, reducing to a great extent the forces of regionalism. Information was presented on a global scale, making it possible for millions to witness world events such as a coronation, inauguration, or funeral of a world leader.

In the beginning, television tapped ex-burlesque performers and local talent for musical and variety shows. The infant medium soon drew stars from radio, often imitated radio show formats, and of course adopted the concept of using advertising dollars to sponsor programs.

Comedy shows were among the first aired and became a staple of the industry, though presented in different formats through the years. Television made it possible for entertainers to become nationally known overnight. The medium's mass audience is of such incredible size that viewers of a single episode of a series of average popularity could fill the largest Broadway theater to capacity for twenty years of performances.

Of the many talented comediennes who prevailed through television's mercurial love affair with American viewers, certain gifted funny women achieved superstardom and will always be warmly remembered. Through the syndicated reruns of their shows, they continue to bring laughter to fans all over the world.

97

Imogene Coca

At the mention of the "Golden Age of Television," one show in particular comes to mind—*Your Show of Shows*, starring the unlikely team
of raucous Sid Caesar and wistful Imogene Coca. For four seasons, the
show was a TV trailblazer which dominated Saturday night prime-time
viewing, resulting in 160 ninety-minute shows, televised *live*. And unlike
many other top shows of that era, *Your Show of Shows* withstood the test
of time, as witnessed when a compilation of sketches was shown more
than twenty years later. Caesar and Coca are still as funny as ever.

Imogene Fernandez y Coca, born in 1908, was the only child of
Joseph Coca and Sadie Brady Coca. Her father, the leader of a
Philadelphia orchestra, loved to gamble, sometimes using his band's
payroll to stay in the game. Sadie Brady had run away from home to
work in Howard Thurston's magic act. Imogene studied music and dance
from age 5 on, and was regularly shoved on stage to play moppet roles.

When she was through grammar school, her parents allowed her to
choose between high school and a full-time career. She chose the latter,
becoming a regular variety show performer whose specialty was ballet
and tap-dancing. At 15, she left for New York where she made her
legitimate debut playing a chorus girl in *When You Smile* on Broadway
in 1925. After the musical's short run, she found work in nightclubs, and
then became Leonard Sillman's dancing partner in a vaudeville act playing the Palace. After a few more minor stage roles, Imogene returned to
vaudeville and toured under the names of Jill Cameron, Donna Hart, and
Helen Gardner.

When Leonard Sillman decided to produce the revue *New Faces* in
1934, Imogene got her break, and was hired at a weekly salary of forty
dollars. (One of the other new faces in the revue belonged to Henry
Fonda.) During rehearsal one day, the petite (five foot three inches) girl
borrowed a camel's hair overcoat from one of the men and proceeded to
parody a stripper. She strutted provocatively, her alluring smile promising erotic adventure. First pulling up a sleeve to reveal her arm, next raising the hem of the coat to show her ankles, she then happily peered down
the front of her coat. While prancing around, she removed the belt and
played with it for a while. Finally she yanked open the coat, but she was
facing the *rear* of the stage at the big moment. Sillman liked the bit and
put it in the show.

The review gained Imogene recognition from critics and for the next
several years she worked regularly, alternating between Sillman's Broadway revues and touring stock companies. While appearing in the 1935

Sillman production *Fools Rush In*, she met actor-musician Bob Burton. They married that same year and continued working together. A few years later, *Straw Hat Revue*, in which they were both appearing at the Tamiment Summer Playhouse at Bushkill, Pennsylvania, was brought to Broadway by director Max Liebman. Imogene's satirical portrayals in several of the sketches brought down the house.

When World War II broke out and her husband joined the armed forces, Imogene, disappointed that her hard work wasn't bringing in a regular income, moved to her mother's home in Philadelphia. Before she had settled into retirement, she was coaxed back to New York to audition for *Oklahoma*, and though she was turned down for the part, she resumed working in nightclubs, this time coming to the attention of the critics who praised her "light lunatic touch." She was offered a long engagement at Cafe Society Downtown, followed by stints at the Blue Angel, and clubs in Chicago. Two popular numbers were her "Cavalcade of Oldtime Movie Stars" and her satire of Phil Spitalny's all-girl orchestra.

In 1948, Max Liebman, who remembered Imogene from the weekly revues he had staged at Tamiment, asked the road-weary entertainer to become part of his initial television project, the *Admiral Broadway Revue*. Despite the skepticism of his associates, he felt he could make her a star.

Sid Caesar would head the cast and the writing would be done by two young Canadians, Lucille Kallen and Mel Tolkin, also Tamiment alumni (Mel Brooks later joined them). The show debuted on NBC on January 28, 1949. Imogene repeated some of her successful routines from earlier revues and talented comedienne and singer Mary McCarty, who was co-featured, performed several of her previous nightclub skits. She did her Happy Hypochondriac and Miss Bubbles Winecellar of Giddy Heights, Indiana, who loved her job as a wine taster.

Imogene and Sid Caesar hit it off from the moment they met. "I felt a certain chemistry between us," he said later of their meeting. "Right away, I called her 'Immie' and that's all I ever called her."

At an early rehearsal, Liebman was looking for sketches and Imogene suggested a routine she and her husband had done earlier in the theater: "It was one of those going-to-the-movies pantomime things. . . . It went over so well that when Sid and I went with Max into *Your Show of Shows*, we continued doing pantomime numbers, and before we knew what was happening, we had become a team."

The following year *Your Show of Shows* premiered on February 25, 1950. The wildly inventive company remained essentially the same with Carl Reiner and Howard Morris. Imogene's husband became her advisor and arranged much of the music used in her sketches. At the end of hectic days at the studio, they relaxed at home with their French poodle Apricot.

Liebman was producing the equivalent of a revue every week! More than thirty years later, Sid Caesar recalled those "90-minute live takes" and the pressure of memorizing an entirely new show every week forty weeks a year.

"Sunday was our day off," he said. "I'd stand under the shower and shake."

Saturday night television viewers became addicted to the variety show with the soaring ratings. Those responsible were showered with awards. Imogene's mobile face and pixieish mannerisms delighted audiences. The pantomimes she performed with Sid often had to do with a married couple on an outing. Through their facial gestures and body language, they could turn a driving lesson, picnic, or simple act of hailing a taxi into a complicated, frustrating situation, guaranteed to get laughs. Not as quiet—but just as funny—were their lovemaking sequences in different languages.

Takeoffs on silent films were performed by the company with Carl Reiner and Howie Morris usually featured in the moralistic melodramas. The players also became adept at lampooning musical films with inane plots and predictable endings, and poked fun at the more serious ones such as "A Place at the Bottom of the Lake," in which "Mildred" keeps talking about how happy their married life will be through all of "Montgomery's" attempts to strangle her. (He finally gives up.)

In *A Trolleycar Named Desire*, Imogene (as Magnolia) parodies the character of Blanche DuBois. "Mah, mah, mah! Ah thought ah nevah would get heah! That *terrible* ride on the *terrible* dusty ole train, an' . . . ah had to wait hours for a streetcar! . . . So this is your little place. Mah, mah, mah!"

Imogene was the most theater-oriented member of the cast, and despite her innate shyness and ever-present stage fright, the most disciplined. Her singing and dancing skills enabled her to lead the company of dancers and singers through musical numbers from country hoedowns to Wagnerian operas. Routines about bygone eras were often performed, such as *Tickle Toe* (a 1918 dance craze) and "Everybody Step" (about the 1920s flapper craze).

"As a dancer, she'd try anything and she could do anything," said James Starbuck, the show's choreographer.

Their ballet excerpts from *Afternoon of a Faun, Sleeping Beauty*, and *Giselle*, among others, were authentically performed, though delicately exaggerated. Of all her ballet interpretations, perhaps the funniest was *Swan Lake*, in which she became dizzy from spinning around, profusely shed her feathers, and ended up caught on a wire above the stage. She also danced in her lovable tramp numbers, which were both joyous and poignant.

As a comedienne, Imogene was equally adept at doing mime, slapstick, or dramatic takeoffs. One of her recurring roles was a low-voiced chanteuse à la Marlene Dietrich. Straddling a chair or leaning seductively against a lamp post while singing her passionate pleas, she was hilarious.

Portraying a narcissistic fashion model showing off everything from hats to shoes, Imogene's talent for spoofing high fashion knew no bounds. In one popular version, she modeled a succession of mangy, shedding fur coats, all the while ecstatic over their magnificence. "Aren't the skins simply divine? They're so beautifully matched."

The Radio and Television Editors of America honored her for her solo work on the show by naming her the best comedienne in TV for 1951. She also was named "Tops in TV" in a *Saturday Review of Literature* poll and was nominated for an Emmy that same year.

Together, Sid and Imogene performed brilliantly in many different types of sketches, but audiences especially identified with them in the roles of Doris and Charlie Hickenlooper. Diminutive Doris longed for new social and cultural experiences, and had to drag hulking Charlie along against his will. Content to dine on meat and potatoes at home, he hated the gastronomical adventures Doris was so fond of.

In one sketch, he was forced to accompany her to a health food restaurant where, perplexed by a menu offering such health food tidbits as "yeast extract" and "low sodium manganese salad," he sarcastically ordered "a broiled elm tree on toast." And so it went, whether attending the opera, a party, or an antique auction. Charlie balked and ranted, but the little woman always had the final say. Their arguments centered around his poker games, her car accidents, forgotten birthdays, jealousy — the usual things most married couples fight about.

"I don't forget these things, you know," she lectured him, after waiting on a street corner for four hours. "You're gonna suffer for this! For every minute I was out in that cold, you're going to have one hour of utter misery!"

The couple's continuing warfare struck a nerve in viewers who wrote in, saying how much they enjoyed the Hickenloopers' quarrels.

After the show's fourth season, reviewers began finding fault with it, saying it was no longer fresh and imaginative. Network management decided that Liebman, Caesar and Coca should break up, and continue in television individually. Though she knew the show would soon end, and a new show of her own had been discussed, Imogene was totally unprepared when she was called from a dance rehearsal one day to join the others in a room jammed with reporters. While cameras filmed their reactions, the demise of *Your Show of Shows* was made official.

"I made a fool of myself, crying and carrying on," she later said.

On the final show on June 5, 1954, Imogene and Sid performed a Hickenlooper sketch, the company did a spoof on both a French movie and a silent film, with Imogene playing "Bertha, the Sewing-Machine Girl," a consumptive heroine who dies from overwork, then floats heavenward wearing huge angel wings. Musical numbers were performed by The Hamilton Trio, Bill Hayes, Marguerite Piazza, and The Billy Williams Quartette. Bambi Lynn and Rod Alexander danced.

Imogene's final solo routine was her "Wrap Your Troubles in Dreams" tramp routine in which she danced with James Starbuck playing a stuffy doorman. Instead of dropping cigar ashes in his hand as they had rehearsed, she flung herself on him, hugging him and crying until the camera pulled away. Most of the cast were near tears when they assembled on stage at the end of the show. Weeping, Imogene could manage only a few words of thanks to the audience.

The three principals of *Your Show of Shows* immediately began work on their new projects. Sid headed the cast of *Caesar's Hour* with many of the same people, though he added Nanette Fabray for his female lead. The show ran for three seasons, but could not hold its own against ABC's *Lawrence Welk Show*. Max Liebman produced spectaculars for several seasons. The *Imogene Coca Show* lasted only one season, for reasons no one ever fully understood.

Imogene was widowed in 1955 and returned to legitimate theater to appear in *The Girls in 509* where she met King Donovan, whom she married ten months later. They have since appeared in over thirty-five stage shows, touring in *The Gin Game* in 1984. She worked on television from time to time and on January 26, 1958, performed on *Sid Caesar Invites You*. She also worked briefly in movies and in 1962, toured with a road company of *Once Upon a Mattress*. The following television season, Imogene starred as *Grindl*, a maid who worked out of an employment agency, but the show was not renewed for a second year.

During the seventies, Imogene appeared in individual episodes of *Love American Style* (1970 and 1972), *Night Gallery* (1971), *The Brady Bunch* (1972), ABC's special *The Emperor's New Clothes* (1972), and ABC's *Wide World of Mystery* (1975). She began working in television commercials and took a continuing role in *As the World Turns*. Nearly twenty years after her final show with Sid Caesar, Imogene was interviewed by *Esquire* magazine.

"You know what I wish for most in the world? That Sid and I could work together again," she admitted. "I'd run twenty miles in sheer joy if I'd hear that we would be able to go back on again. It was the most fulfilling time of my life."

A little later, her wish was granted in a small way when she and Sid appeared in one-minute commercials for AT&T. Fortunately, Max

Liebman had the foresight to carefully store away the kinescopes of *Your Show of Shows*, so that today much of the Caesar-Coca work is preserved in the Museum of Modern Art film vaults. Both in her illustrious and hilarious collaboration with Sid Caesar and her amazing solo performances, Imogene's comic genius was evident. There may never be another comedienne so gifted in the affectionate satire that was the Coca trademark.

Lucille Ball

It's been said that Lucille Ball's face has been seen by more people worldwide than the face of anyone else who ever lived. Whether disguised as a grape stomper, matador, statue, or ballerina, her comedic perfection and unceasing energy have earned her millions of fans. Her shows have been dubbed in different languages and shown in nearly eighty countries.

In honor of Lucy's seventy-second birthday in 1983, local television stations ran *I Love Lucy* marathons of the show's episodes back-to-back. The indefatigable performer also received *TV Guide*'s Life Achievement Award. During her career, she had graced the cover of the weekly magazine twenty-four times, including its premier edition.

Her comedy series from television's "golden age" is now entertaining a third generation of American audiences through year-round reruns. Even though Lucy has retired to her home in Beverly Hills, everyone still loves her. Fans pose for pictures in front of her mansion, ring her doorbell and run, steal her house numbers, and dig up her lawn.

Blue-eyed Lucille Desiree Ball, of mixed Irish, English, French and Scottish ancestry, was born in Celoron, New York, on August 6, 1911. After her father, Henry, died when she was 4, she became extremely close to her grandfather, whom she would later credit for passing on to her his work ethic. She accompanied him to vaudeville shows and movies in Jamestown, then would go home and act out the comedies and serials. DeDe Ball encouraged her star-struck daughter by supplying her with makeup and costumes.

The girl never wavered from her desire to be an entertainer, even after she realized how much hard work was involved. When her high school was presenting a production of *Charlie's Aunt*, she not only played the lead, but cast the other players, made the posters, sold tickets, and hauled furniture and props to the school.

Upon turning 15, Lucy enrolled in the John Murray Anderson-Robert Milton Dramatic School in New York City but could not make the adjustment, so she returned home after six weeks. Later attempts to conquer Broadway (under the name of Diane Belmont) led to a few rehearsals but no substantial parts, so she turned to modeling at Hattie Carnegie's salon and freelancing as a model for photographers and magazine illustrators. Life in New York was lonely.

"I didn't have any friends," she said years later. "I didn't go out. I had a very dull existence."

Then at the age of 17 she was stricken with rheumatoid arthritis. Having no money, she was sent by her boss to a specialist whose experimental medication helped combat the disabling disease.

"I was laid up for three years," she recalled, "and had to work pretty hard to walk again."

After she had regained her health, Lucy landed the job as the Chesterfield Cigarette Girl, a stepping stone to becoming a last-minute replacement for one of the twelve Goldwyn Girls in the Eddie Cantor movie *Roman Scandals*. The fortunate incident took place in New York on a sweltering day in the summer of 1933. The shapely model was approached on the street by a woman offering her six weeks of work in California. "I'd go anywhere to get out of this heat," she told the woman.

So she went to Hollywood and never came back. Work in over a dozen movies followed but her unrewarding early celluloid career consisted mainly of unbilled showgirl parts showing off her shapely legs. Unlike the other beauties, however, Lucy was willing to do physical comedy like wearing mud packs and falling into pools.

"I said I'd *love* to do the scene with the crocodile," she later explained. "I didn't mind getting messed up."

She finally got her first screen credit and a brief speaking role in 1935, and a second lead in *That Girl from Paris* (1936). That exposure led to a leading role in the musical play *Hey Diddle Diddle*, which never made it to Broadway.

Along the way Lucy decided that perhaps comedy was where her future lay. During the late 1930s she worked on radio as a featured comedienne on Jack Haley's *Wonder Bread Show* and Phil Baker's show. But she was still dependent on Hollywood for her livelihood. The persistent actress made twenty-two films over the next six years, becoming known as "Queen of the B's." She worked with comedy legends Buster Keaton, the Marx Brothers, and Laurel and Hardy.

It was during the filming of *Too Many Girls* in 1940 with Richard Carlson and Ann Miller that Lucy met Cuban musician Desi Arnaz, who was making his film debut as a football hero-bodyguard. Admittedly intrigued by his playboy reputation, she married him six months later. "Everybody gave it about a year and a half," she later recalled. "I gave it six weeks ... it was the most daring thing I'd ever done."

For the first ten years, the couple spent a lot of time apart because of their separate careers and later because Desi was drafted into the Army.

Playing a crippled nightclub singer in *The Big Street* in 1942, Lucy earned good reviews and the attention of MGM bosses who transformed her into a "strawberry pink" redhead and signed her for several starring roles. However, when CBS offered her the role of Liz, the dizzy wife of a bank executive in the radio show *My Favorite Husband* in 1948, she accepted and stayed with the comedy series until it went off the air in 1951.

Lucy's reputation as a first-rate comedienne prompted Bob Hope's request to costar with her in Paramount's *Sorrowful Jones* and *Fancy Pants*. Leads in other films followed, including *The Fuller Brush Girl*, but she lost out to Judy Holliday for the plum role in *Born Yesterday*.

The Arnaz's became parents of a daughter in 1951. Years and fortunes later, Lucy would claim this event to be her greatest achievement. "When you have the first baby at 39, that's got to be the biggest," she says of Lucie's birth. "My life started when my children were born."

Lucy was curious about the popular new medium of television so she and Desi did a guest spot (she played Cleopatra and wore a black wig) on Ed Wynn's trail-breaking, half-hour comedy show. When CBS wanted to use the concept of *My Favorite Husband* for television and offered Lucy the part, she insisted that Desi play her husband. The studio balked at the idea of a Latin who specialized in babalu-type numbers in the role. They also felt the couple weren't "Hollywood" enough.

"No, no Hollywood couple," she insisted, wanting to have all the trials and tribulations that most people could identify with in the Lucy show. "People told us that we were crazy, that we were committing career suicide," she later said. "I didn't listen."

To prove to CBS executives that a comedy team of a home-grown redhead and a Cuban bandleader could be accepted by American audiences, Lucy and Desi took their act on an extensive vaudeville tour, then made their own pilot on film. With reservations, the studio gave in. Within six months after the debut of *I Love Lucy* on October 15, 1951, the show was rated number one. The antics of Lucy, Desi, Vivian Vance, and Bill Frawley are now history.

Lucy dolls were manufactured, followed by comic books, aprons, and even bedroom suites. The half-hour situation comedy influenced television programming for years to come. Each episode was filmed with a revolutionary three-camera technique while being performed in sequence before a live audience. Having a sudden hit, Lucy and Desi ("a born businessman," according to Lucy) were able to sell rerun rights to CBS, enabling them to form their own producing company, Desilu, and acquire the former RKO lot for their studio.

I Love Lucy garnered five Emmys, over 200 awards, and became one of TV's all-time hits. The Ricardo family made such an impact on American audiences that when Lucy and Ricky's fictional son, "Little Ricky," was born, forty-four million viewers tuned in to *I Love Lucy*, surpassing the number of people who watched the inauguration of President Dwight D. Eisenhower. Through advanced filming, that television birth coincided with the birth of Lucy's son, Desi, Jr. The original *I Love Lucy* ran until 1957 when it became the *Lucille Ball-Desi Arnaz Show*, which aired monthly until the famous couple's divorce in 1960. That was a dark period for the family-oriented entertainer who also regretted that her decision to end the marriage "disappointed millions of people."

Lucy's dream of Broadway success was fulfilled in December of 1960 when she opened in the musical comedy *Wildcat*. She worked for months with vocal coach Carlo Menotti in preparation for the show, which enjoyed a standing room-only run.

In 1961 former stand-up comedian Gary Morton became her husband and executive producer. Lucy bought out her former husband's shares in Desilu Productions and embarked on another project.

She portrayed widowed Lucy Carmichael on *The Lucy Show* from 1962 to 1968, then sold Desilu Productions to Gulf and Western Industries for $17 million. She formed Lucille Ball Productions and presented *Here's Lucy*, in which she played widowed mother Lucy Carter. Her own son and daughter played the two children in the show, and have since gone on to careers of their own. That series ran from 1968 through spring of 1974.

Through the years of her daughter's fame, DeDe Ball regularly attended the filming of Lucy's shows. Her laughter can be heard on nearly every sound track.

Lucy's periodic returns to Hollywood resulted in several later movies including *The Facts of Life, Critic's Choice, Yours, Mine and Ours*, and Lucy's last film, *Mame*, which she made the year after she broke her leg in a skiing accident. It turned out to be her favorite film role, the kind that provided audiences with wholesome diversion instead of what she considered "violence, sex, muck and mire on the screen."

In 1972 Lucille Ball passed up signing another five-year contract for *Here's Lucy* in favor of retirement, saying she was starting to feel "a little alone out there, at my age, acting silly." However, she continued to appear in television dramatic shows and many specials featuring top personalities like Jackie Gleason, Steve Allen, Dean Martin and Lillian Carter, President Carter's mother.

Among Lucy's favorite comediennes, Carol Burnett tops the list. "That girl can do anything," she says of Carol. Goldie Hawn, Nancy Walker, and Bette Midler also win her praise.

A staff of twenty people were eventually required to handle Lucy's business affairs. In 1980 she appeared in a television special "Lucy Moves to NBC," which marked the beginning of her position as consultant to that network on new comedy properties.

One day in the early eighties, Lucy looked in her closet and said to herself, "My God, I'm outliving my henna." Early in her career she had imported from Egypt fifty pounds of henna, a dye which gave her hair its distinctive red color. When her plight became public, a man from Jordan appeared with fifty-five pounds of Egyptian henna for Lucy, thus ending her henna crisis.

On March 4, 1984, Lucille Ball was inducted into the newly formed Television Academy Hall of Fame for her valuable contributions to the television industry. Other recipients were Milton Berle, Paddy Chayefsky, Norman Lear, and the late Gen. David Sarnoff, Edward R. Murrow, and William S. Paley.

Son Desi, Jr., was on hand to thank his mother for making his birth a media event. He once told Johnny Carson on TV that while he was growing up, "every five or six minutes, a tour bus would go by." Daughter Lucie sang a tribute to "my mother the star," via video tape from New York where she was appearing on Broadway in *The Guardsmen*.

Carol Burnett told of a visit from Lucy after her second performance in the Off-Broadway show *Once Upon a Mattress*: "I was a wreck," she told the audience. "Lucy saw the show and came backstage to my dressing room. She spent a whole hour talking to me, giving me advice, encouragement, and friendship. She called me 'The Kid.' I still say that if I could be anybody in the world, I'd like to be half the woman she is."

Accepting the honor, Lucy acknowledged the many talented and creative people who had surrounded her through the years. "We never do anything alone," she managed to get out between quiet sobs. "This night has got to top them all. I'm grateful to all of America and in awe of this occasion. I love you all very much."

Soon after, the Museum of Broadcasting in New York opened a six-month Lucille Ball Exhibition featuring seventy hours of half-hour programs and a 1949 Ed Wynn show on which Lucy first appeared with Desi Arnaz. During one interview, she spoke of Vivian Vance, who played Ethel Mertz: "She was priceless. She quit a couple of times and we had to beg her to come back, and she did. She was right there by my side."

One of the famous redhead's most pertinent quotes over the years sums up her philosophy: "The days in my life that stand out most vividly are the days I've learned something."

Besides appearing in nearly eighty movies and dozens of television specials, Lucille Ball performed in 179 episodes of the original *I Love Lucy*, 156 of *The Lucy Show*, and 144 of *Here's Lucy*. Her belief in positive thinking combined with an instilled work ethic has made her a show business legend who admits to being nostalgic about her Lucy character.

"I miss her," she says. "I miss working in front of an audience. . . . the fun of taking a script from the beginning and watching it come to life. . . . It's not the same."

Martha Raye

A world-famous comedienne known for her rowdy style of comedy, Martha Raye is also remembered for being an excellent vocalist and tap dancer (with great-looking legs). She proved herself to be a genuine trooper through her attempts to lift the spirits of others, as evident in her many visits to American GIs overseas during three different military conflicts. She is described by author and fellow-comedian Steve Allen as "one of the minority of comedy performers who can be funny without a script."

Margaret Teresa Yvonne Reed was born August 27, 1916, in the charity ward of a hospital in Butte, Montana, where her touring vaudeville parents (billed as "Reed and Hooper") were stranded. By the time she was 3 she was included in the family comedy act *The Red Hooper Revue*. A few years later Margie and her younger brother Bud were dressed as a tiny bride and groom in the act. Her father, Pete, did a song and dance while her mother, Peggy, played the piano. Later on she and Bud drew favorable audience response with an act billed simply as "Margie and Bud."

"I must have been hypnotized by the spotlight," she later said. "I can't imagine being anything but an entertainer."

Young Margie attended school sporadically along the way between carnival or vaudeville engagements. When the act was no longer in demand and they were down to one-night stands, the family often ate and slept in the car.

Years later the performer told reporters that even though all the family's energy was spent just making a living, she had happy memories of those days on the road. She hadn't been aware of her deprived childhood and lack of home life, though they had indeed taken a toll. "Maybe that's why I'll always be insecure," she allowed.

Martha was 15 when the act got stranded in Cleveland just before

Martha Raye

Christmas. The country was going through the Depression and her father couldn't find work of any kind. She looked up orchestra leader Paul Ash, who remembered her from the Midwest circuit, and he gave her a job singing with his band. Changing her name to Martha Raye, a name she found in a telephone book, she began working and traveling on her own, sending home money to help her struggling family. For extra income, the attractive auburn-haired singer worked as a nurse's aid in a hospital.

She later was part of the Benny Davis Revue, the Ben Blue Company, and Will Morrisey's act. The young entertainer made her Broadway debut in 1934 appearing in Lew Brown's *Calling All Stars* and appeared next in *Earl Carroll's Sketchbook*. Singing engagements took her to Chicago, New York, and finally the West Coast where Paramount Pictures producer Norman Taurog noticed her comedic potential and offered her a contract.

Martha was not only quite pretty, but a competent singer with a natural sound which lent itself to jazz singing. Jazz pianist Mary Lou Williams years later recalled that young Martha stopped in Kansas City on her way to Hollywood. She became so enamored of the music she heard in the clubs and so enjoyed "singing like mad, night after night," that she barely made it to California for her next job.

At 19, already a veteran of the stage and nightclubs, she broke into films, first performing in short subjects. In 1936 Martha was given a lead role in her very first feature film, *Rhythm on the Range*, in which she played opposite Bing Crosby and introduced "Mr. Paganini," a song that fans would associate with her for years to come.

A boisterous comedienne with an elastic mouth and forceful lungs, she enlivened films with her zany antics. In *Double or Nothing* (1937) Martha plays an ex-stripper who keeps regressing to her past occupation. Her costars were Bing Crosby, William Frawley, and Andy Devine. In *The Big Broadcast of 1938* she sang and danced in a specialty number on the deck of a ship. Her amorous intentions caused one man to scream, "I've been kissed by a tunnel!" In 1940 she costarred with Al Jolson in the musical revue *Hold on to Your Hats*.

Her marriage to make-up artist Bud Westmore in 1937 lasted but a short time, as did her next marriage to composer David Rose. At one point Hollywood studio executives tried to capitalize on Martha's good figure and pretty features by molding her into a glamorous romantic heroine, but audiences wouldn't accept her new look. However, she was hired to endorse beauty products.

Millions of radio fans became familiar with Martha's voice as she appeared on leading radio shows with Al Jolson, Bob Hope, and Eddie Cantor. She appeared in 1941 with the comedy team of Olsen and Johnson in *Hellzapoppin*, a movie that is recommended viewing for today's vintage movie fans.

In 1942, shortly after the Pearl Harbor attack, Martha entertained Americans in uniform before the USO was even formed. She went to England with Kaye Francis, Mitzi Mayfair and Carole Landis to entertain the troops. From there they went on to North Africa, where the other three were taken ill. Martha stayed on for several months until she contracted yellow fever and was sent home. Undaunted by the experience, she later continued her missions and became known for her morale-boosting excursions with the USO into the battlefronts. Of the Fox film *Four Jills in a Jeep*, based on the tour of North Africa and England, one critic wrote that Martha had never been more "raucous, rough and pleasing."

Of the forty films Martha worked in, her most notable film perform-ance was in Charlie Chaplin's sardonic "comedy of murders" *Monsieur Verdoux* (1947), in which she plays an indestructible intended murder victim. As a daffy ex-tart who has won a lottery, Martha is the target for a gold digger who passes himself off as a sea captain. His hilarious en-counters with the fruit-hatted Martha while trying to kill her were called the highlight of the film. Reviews of the movie noted that her "bull-in-a-china shop personality" perfectly contrasted with Chaplin's preciseness.

By 1945, Martha's third marriage, to hotel executive Neal Lang, had ended in divorce and her brother Bud had died of tuberculosis. She mar-ried dancer Nick Condos, and in spite of her performing schedule and trips to the war zones, the union lasted almost ten years and produced a daughter, Melodye. When they split up, Nick stayed on as her business manager.

In the fifties, Martha made rare film appearances but performed in leading nightclubs and found her way to the television screen. After a series of guest appearances with Milton Berle on his *Texaco Show*, she became alternate host for *All-Star Revue*. That officially became *The Martha Raye Show*, airing every Tuesday night. Her show included a lot of physical humor, with Martha roughing up the guest stars and her sidekick, former boxer Rocky Graziano.

Martha held her own for three television seasons with such golden age luminaries as Bob Hope, Sid Caesar, Red Skelton and Milton Berle, and was considered by many to be the country's top comedienne. She became a frequent and popular guest on Steven Allen's NBC comedy series and worked in summer stock productions of *The Solid Gold Cadillac, Annie Get Your Gun, Wildcat, Bells Are Ringing, Call Me Madam*, and *Everybody Loves Opal*. She also found time to put on telethons to raise money for charity.

When the Korean War broke out, Martha once again left the com-forts of home to entertain American servicemen. Short vacations were spent deep-sea fishing in Florida, where she had her own nightclub in Miami, the Five O'Clock Club. Her next two marriages, to actor Ed Begley and policeman Robert O'Shea, also ended in divorce and Martha swore never to marry again. "My career is my whole life," she admitted. "I'll always work."

She moved back to California in 1962 and returned to the screen, costarring with her old friend Jimmy Durante in *Jumbo* for MGM and working in Las Vegas clubs.

During the Vietnam conflict she traveled to Southeast Asia to enter-tain troops for four months of every year. Called "Boondock Maggie" by the grateful troops, she was the only woman authorized to wear the uniform of the Green Berets. Martha endured the heat, mud, and danger of enemy fire to visit troops in remote rice paddies and jungles. She was lifted to safety by a helicopter just minutes before the Viet Cong attacked the Plei Me outpost. During one of her five trips to Vietnam, Martha served as a nurse in a field dispensary near the DMZ, helping overworked medical personnel take care of incoming wounded. For her efforts she later received presidential recognition and a special Academy Award (the Jean Hersholt Humanitarian Award) in 1969. She was the first woman ever presented with this honor.

Back home, Martha became the third Dolly Levi when she replaced Ginger Rogers in *Hello Dolly* on Broadway. She next replaced Ruby Keeler and Patsy Kelly in *No, No, Nanette*. Winning an Emmy nomination for her guest role on a *McMillan and Wife* segment titled *Greed* in 1975 led to regular appearances during the following season. Her most recent film was *Airport '79: The Concorde*. In 1982 the tireless performer toured the country in the musical production of *Four Girls Four* with Helen O'Connell, Teresa Brewer and Rosemary Clooney.

Martha's Bel Air home is dubbed "Maggie's Team House," and Vietnam vets who wish to visit her are always welcome. Martha's considerable financial gifts to charity and her numerous appearances in homes for the elderly and orphanages never received as much publicity as her personal affairs did. In spite of her raucous slapstick style of entertaining, Martha Raye is surprisingly serious and soft-spoken away from the spotlight. "Few people actually know me, or take me seriously," she once said.

The veteran entertainer shows no signs of retiring. Besides touring in shows such as *The New Four Girls* (Kay Starr replaced Teresa Brewer) and making television movies and commercials, she played Mel's mother, Carrie, on the popular show *Alice*. One episode centered around Carrie's lifelong dream of being a professional singer, instead of playing bridge with "boring Brooklyn biddies." Viewers were treated to a sensitive rendition of "Embraceable You" and a rousing climax in which she and Alice (Linda Lavin), dressed in short funky costumes, sang and did a dance routine to "Do You Think I'm Sexy?" Her eyes were never bluer nor her voice better. And the legs were still terrific! In mid-1984, she began a pre–Broadway, cross-country tour in the role of Miss Hannigan in the popular musical *Annie*.

Martha's unselfish nature and her eagerness to do anything for a laugh have made her one of the best-loved women in show business. No one has worked harder to bring others happiness. Through the years she has remained an original and endearing comedy artist.

Carol Burnett

"I love to zero in on characters, their foibles or quirks. That's the most fun for me in comedy."

Carol Burnett was born in San Antonio, Texas, on April 26, 1934. Life was insecure for the older daughter of movie theater manager Jody Burnett and Louis Creighton Burnett. The alcoholic couple was continually separating and reuniting. While still a toddler, Carol was left in her grandmother's care when her parents moved to California. Grandmother Mae White was a fervent Christian Scientist who raised Carol in a one-room apartment in Los Angeles where she too decided to live. Years later, Carol would tug her ear to let Mae know that all was well before millions of television fans every week.

At Hollywood High, the slim red-haired girl was a good athlete as well as editor of the school paper. After her graduation, she attended the University of California on a scholarship where she planned a career in journalism until a playwriting course required her to get up on stage. She got her first laugh and changed her major.

"That was it," she later said. "I was in heaven. From that moment on I was hooked."

During her junior year in college, Carol and some other students entertained at a party in San Diego. One of the guests, a building contractor, was so impressed by the young woman's performance in a scene from *Annie Get Your Gun* with fellow student Don Saroyan, he gave them each $1,000. The money was to help them go to New York to break into show business. They were expected to pay back the loan within five years, and when they became successful, to help others who were struggling to get started. Carol paid back the loan and later established scholarships at Emerson College in Boston and at UCLA. Their benefactor wished to remain anonymous and he does to this day.

Upon her arrival in New York, Carol moved into the Rehearsal Club, a well-known hotel for aspiring actresses. Her part-time job as a hat-check girl in a restaurant paid her room and board ($18 a week) and other expenses, and left her time to make the rounds of theatrical agents.

"Get a part-time job," she later told aspiring performers, "so when you go to see a producer, you don't have that desperate, starved, 'I'm going to kill myself' look."

The agents Carol contacted all told her the same thing: They couldn't give her a job until she had experience. So the enterprising young woman organized an audition show at the Rehearsal Club to solve the dilemma she shared with so many others. They got enough money together to hire a hall, talked writers into furnishing them with material, and invited every agent they knew. The experiment paid off. Martin Goodman, an important Broadway agent, was so impressed with Carol's spoof of Eartha Kitt doing a sexy number in a shabby robe and hair curlers, he signed her. Her first professional job—in summer stock— quickly followed.

Carol and Don Saroyan, a cousin of writer William Saroyan, were married. During the mid-fifties both of Carol's parents died, so she took over the responsibility of raising her younger sister Christine.

Carol first appeared on television on Paul Winchell's children's show on NBC. For thirteen weeks, she played the girlfriend of the ventriloquist's wooden dummy Jerry Mahoney. A stint on the short-lived television series *Stanley* as comedian Buddy Hackett's girlfriend came next. "It was the era of mugging, so I became known as 'The Mugger,'" she explained. "I thought that's what they wanted."

In October, 1956, Carol first auditioned for Garry Moore's morning show on CBS. Those weekly auditions were responsible for initiating many careers, among them those of George Gobel, Jonathan Winters, Don Knotts, Kaye Ballard, and Don Adams. Auditions were held in the CBS studio on East 52nd Street where Arthur Godfrey did his radio show. When the folding chairs were removed, it seemed very large and deserted to nervous auditioning performers.

Carol walked over to the microphone and faced her judges in the glassed-in control room. Her special material had been written by her accompanist Ken Welch who, a few bars into the piece, hurled himself into a series of dazzling arpeggios. When his fingers finally came to rest, Carol walked over to the piano and exclaimed, "O-o-oh, That's *won*-der-ful!" Garry Moore came out of the control room to tell her she was booked for that week's show, an exception to the rule. Newcomers who were hired usually waited weeks to get on.

"Most women are obsessed with an outmoded sense of modesty," Carol told Pete Martin while discussing the scarcity of good comediennes during those years. "They are afraid that being funny is unfeminine. Most men seem to have the same idea about comediennes. They laugh at us, but they're wary of us...."

In addition to performing frequently with Garry and his gang, Carol filled guest spots on many other programs, including the *Ed Sullivan Show* and the *Dinah Shore Show*. She was also in demand for club work. It was during Carol's first nightclub engagement at the Blue Angel that she introduced an unlikely torch song, "I Made a Fool of Myself Over John Foster Dulles." The number, written by Ken Welsh, generated stints on Jack Paar's *Tonight* show and Ed Sullivan's program.

Carol Burnett

Three years after first appearing on Garry Moore's morning program, Carol was welcomed into his evening show lineup. Her knack for goofball slapstick and her grating Tarzan yell quickly became familiar with viewers. She usually portrayed a half-dozen characters on each show, running the gamut from slob to snob. Critics and audiences loved their "new first lady of television," and Carol was recognized wherever she went. Twenty-five years later on a national television show, Carol still referred to Garry Moore as her "spiritual father."

Carol's show was family fare so censorship was seldom an issue. She still tells her favorite story about the TV censors in those days: In one sketch Carol was in a nudist colony being interviewed by Harvey Korman, a reporter standing outside the fence. She was explaining their Saturday night dances to him and he asked how they danced. "Very carefully," was her reply. The censors objected to the line. When pressed for a better one, they came up with "Cheek to cheek!" That broke up everyone within hearing distance.

Carol's dream of performing on stage came true in 1959 when she landed the lead in the Off-Broadway musical comedy *Once Upon a Mattress* playing a rowdy princess. When they were forced to evacuate the theater for a previously scheduled play, Carol organized the cast to picket for the right to continue the show at another location. They were soon working in a Broadway theater to a packed house.

"I'd love to do musical comedies for the rest of my life," she said of the experience.

Carol's theory about the beginning of comedy concerns a caveman describing a dinosaur he had seen to his friends. They all laughed. Then the inhabitants of the next cave paid him some beads to tell *them* the dinosaur story. Thus was born the first stand-up comic. Another caveman said, "Listen, at the cave down the road, I can get you ten beads for the dinosaur bit, if you give me one." He was the first agent.

In 1962 *TV Guide* named Carol the favorite performer on television for the second time and she won her first Emmy award for her work on the Garry Moore Show. That's also the year her seven-year marriage to actor Don Saroyan ended. Carol then married Joe Hamilton, the Moore show's producer and the father of eight children, the following year and he became the force behind her career. The ambitious team also became the parents of three daughters—Carrie, Jody and Erin.

After starring on Broadway in *Fade Out, Fade In* (the show quickly closed) and trying several other television projects, Carol and Joe hit the jackpot in 1966 with *The Carol Burnett Show*. A phenomenal success, it established Carol as Imogene Coca's replacement in television variety and would eventually win its participants twenty-two Emmys.

"Comedy has multiple layers that make it funnier and more real," she explained of her desire to make the show's comedy more three-dimensional.

Whether playing a haughty glamour puss, a shrieking housewife, or a devious girl scout, Carol broke up her fans (as well as other members of the cast) every week. She gave devastating impersonations of Joan Crawford, Bette Davis and other movie legends as well as her favorite comediennes Bea Lillie, Lucille Ball, and Fanny Brice. Carol's cleaning woman with mop and bucket became the symbol of the long-running show which featured first-rate performers Tim Conway, Harvey Korman, Dick Van Dyke, Lyle Waggoner and Vicki Lawrence (who later starred in her own show, *Mama's Family*, on which Carol guested from time to time). Carol usually sang at least one ballad on every show, and often joined her guest star in a vocal duet or song-and-dance routine. She also headlined with good friend Jim Nabors at Caesars Palace in Las Vegas in 1970.

In the British tradition of comedy, Carol prefers working from the outside in, using costumes and props to achieve a feeling for the part: "If I know what I'm gonna look like, it helps me develop the character."

It was in the mid-seventies that Carol realized that she no longer needed to mug and put herself down to get laughs. "... I was a mature woman who could still be funny without crossing my eyes all the time," she reasoned.

She went on being just as funny without the contortions until finally in 1978, Carol folded the show. It was immediately scheduled for reruns. "We had our turn," she said of the decision, "and I wanted to leave before we ran out of new ideas completely."

During the summer hiatus between the show's fourth and fifth season, Carol had made her legitimate theatrical debut in *Plaza Suite* at the Huntington Hartford Theatre in Los Angeles opposite George Kennedy. The play broke box office records as did both her subsequent summer appearances in *I Do! I Do!* and *Same Time Next Year*.

When *The Carol Burnett Show* ended, its star was ready to try movies. Her dramatic breakthrough came in the film *Pete 'n' Tillie*, for which she was nominated for Best Actress for her portrayal of a bereaved mother. "I was frightened," she said. "It was my first big movie."

She next held her own in Robert Altman's star-studded *A Wedding* and Billy Wilder's *The Front Page*. She also starred in *The Tenth Month* and CBS-TV's *The Grass Is Always Greener Over the Septic Tank*, adapted from Erma Bombeck's best seller.

Her role in the television movie *Friendly Fire* as the mother of a boy killed in Vietnam was an acting triumph, and *The Four Seasons* resulted in praise for her part as Alan Alda's magazine-editor wife. Between movies she found time to do television specials with buddies Julie Andrews, Beverly Sills and Dolly Parton. *Julie and Carol at Carnegie Hall* won Carol another Emmy.

In 1980, Carol said she'd finally acknowledged her need for solitude, and no longer made up excuses in order to spend time alone. She even furnished a third-floor room in her home to serve as a private oasis. She also began relying on her own decisions concerning her career and became quite vocal in her support of women's rights.

When daughter Carrie conquered her problems with drugs, both she and Carol decided to let others know about it, in the hope it would help other young people. Carol was equally candid about the chin surgery she later underwent to improve her appearance. She also fought hard and won her well-publicized libel case against the *National Enquirer*, who had reported that Carol, who neither smokes nor drinks, had appeared intoxicated in public.

In 1982, Carol separated from Joe Hamilton after twenty years of marriage. "I've never understood the notion that you're half a person without someone else," she said during the transition. Within a short time, she was hard at work portraying the harridan Miss Hannigan in the film *Annie* and shooting *Between Friends*, an HBO premiere movie costarring Elizabeth Taylor. Carol likes to work with people she considers better than herself, so she therefore welcomed the chance to work with movie veteran Elizabeth Taylor.

"That's how I learn," she said.

In *Between Friends*, Carol plays a single parent and real estate agent who saves the life of an "ex–Jewish princess" (Elizabeth Taylor). Though admittedly somewhat of a prude, Carol's frank portrayal of a menopausal woman hit the mark. "I just had my big Hawaii Five-O birthday," she said, "and here I am, a sex maniac...."

Off camera, Carol and Elizabeth got along fine, playing tricks on each other and sharing their common passion of watching soap operas. The show received good reviews. "... I feel terrific.... I love being fifty," she said at the time.

Carol was a most fitting host on *Here's Television Entertainment*, a two-hour tribute to thirty-five years of comedy-variety shows in late 1983. She hosted the segment on the history of the Emmy, something she knows quite a lot about since she's personally won five herself. She opened 1984 with another television special titled *Burnett Discovers Domingo*, in which she and opera star Placido Domingo sing and clown their way to the finale, then portray two gone-to-seed performers recalling their show biz glory days by singing a medley of numbers from the musical *Follies*.

"If I had my show now, I would be doing a takeoff on *Dynasty*," she says. I try to get an audience to recognize a certain thing ... that maybe they hadn't consciously seen."

Besides her five Emmys, the comedienne-actress's numerous awards and honors include six Fame awards, six Golden Globe awards, five Photoplay Gold Medals, four Entertainer of the Year awards, The Variety Club Award, four People's Choice awards, The Jack Benny Humanitarian Award from the March of Dimes, and an honorary degree from Emerson College in Boston. She was named one of the World's Ten Most Admired Women by *Good Housekeeping* and the International Radio and Television Society presented her with the Gold Medal Award for her contributions to television. In 1985, she was inducted as the youngest member in the Television Academy Hall of Fame.

Dividing her time between New York, Los Angeles, and Hawaii, Carol is eager to get on with life. She hates to cook, exercises a lot, and looks terrific. Her plans include acting and singing lessons and more stage work. In early 1985, her movie *The Laundromat* premiered nationwide. A Home Box Office project, it was filmed in Paris under the direction of Robert Altman. Carol describes her character as "a very closed and extremely lonesome woman," and admits that's partly what drew her to the role.

"I've had problems opening up what's inside me," she says.

There was a time when Carol readily agreed with those saying how "lucky" she was, but she gradually came to realize that years of hard work had more to do with her success than luck. "You have to work for it," she says, "but anything you visualize is possible."

A few years ago, Carol decided to record the events of her early life, up until the time she entered show business. She wrote a few pages every day about her parents, whose own problems left them little time for their daughter, and her grandmother, with whom Carol shared a one-room apartment for fourteen years. Mae accompanied the girl to eight movies a week and later became a "stage grandmother." Making entries in her journal helped her realize that they all loved her and did the best they could at the time.

"I'm doing it for my three girls," Carol said at first. "I think they should know what my roots were and what it was like growing up in Hollywood and being on relief. I'm feeling a whole bunch of memories pouring out. . . . It's almost self-therapy."

As she continued to exorcise the painful ghosts of her past through the writing process, Carol made the decision to publish the material as her autobiography, titled *One More Time*.

Despite her many achievements, Carol insists success hasn't taught her a thing. She continues to strive for order within herself so she knows where she's going. "I have always grown from my problems and challenges, from the things that don't work out, that's when I've really learned."

Mary Tyler Moore

Of the hundreds of women appearing in comedy shows since the beginning of television, perhaps none are more warmly remembered than Mary Tyler Moore, cocreator of Mary Richards, the main character on the *Mary Tyler Moore Show*. Just when American women were trying to break out of their stereotypes, along came Mary Richards — an attractive and competent career woman who fought for equal pay, silenced chauvinistic coworkers, and enjoyed a full life without marriage. Viewers fell in love with her, making the show one of the most successful ever. Off camera, the comedienne's sunny optimism and self-discipline became legendary.

Mary was born in Brooklyn on December 29, 1937, the oldest of three children of George Tyler and Marjorie Hackett Moore. As a small child, she loved visiting her grandparents' country home in Virginia. When she was 8, the family moved to Los Angeles where her father became an executive with the Southern California Gas Company. Her mother worked on a radio program called *Pet Exchange* and answered calls from people who were willing to adopt stray dogs rescued from the pound. One day she brought home a beagle named Jeff, and he became Mary's pet.

Young Mary studied dancing while attending St. Ambrose Grammar School and later, Immaculate Heart High School. Her love of ballet has never diminished — she still takes classes on a regular basis. Though she went through the usual rebelliousness during her teen years, Mary once told a reporter for the *New York Times* that she'd had a happy childhood and had never felt neglect or a loss of love.

"I know that everyone successful in this business is supposed to have some neurosis that provides that extra push," she said. "In that area I guess I am deprived."

The day after graduating from high school, Mary got her first job — an uncle and aunt with connections in show business helped arrange it. She was hired to be a singing and dancing pixie in a Hotpoint television commercial. "Nothing can surpass the thrill when I saw myself on television," she later recalled.

By the end of that year, she had earned $10,000 making commercials. She was also married, at 17, to a 27-year-old salesman named Richard Meeker, and became the mother of a son, Richard. Though she admitted the marriage was a mistake from the beginning, it was eleven years before it was legally terminated.

Her exposure on commercials led to other television assignments such as chorus work on the *Eddie Fisher Show*. Then in 1959 she was chosen to play the sultry-voiced secretary to the private detective (David Janssen) in the *Richard Diamond* series. That first dramatic role was a bittersweet accomplishment in that, while it was on a network show, only Mary's hands and legs were visible.

However, it wasn't long before Mary's wholesome beauty in toto was evident in *77 Sunset Strip*, *Hawaiian Eye* and other popular series. She auditioned for the role of Danny Thomas' daughter in *Make Room for*

Daddy, but was turned down because of her pert nose. "With a nose like yours, my darling, you don't look like you could belong to me," Danny Thomas told her.

A few years later, when Thomas and Carl Reiner were casting the *Dick Van Dyke Show*, he sent for "the girl with the three names and the smile." Mary won the female lead part of Laura Petrie, wife of writer Rob Petrie. Rounding out the cast were Morey Amsterdam, Richard Deacon, and a funny woman who'd spent her entire life in show business, Rose Marie. (Baby Rose Marie was radio's first child star, singing on her own coast-to-coast show at the age of 6.) From its debut in 1961, the show was an immediate hit and Mary was cited by reviewers not only for her girl-next-door beauty and ebullience, but her marvelous comic timing. Her extraordinary popularity with women (as well as men) viewers was said to be because of her portrayal of a warm, likeable, yet fallible housewife.

During the filming of the pilot, Mary met Grant Tinker, an NBC executive. On June 1, 1963, they were married and settled down in Beverly Hills with her son, Richard Meeker, and three dogs. She admitted not liking housework or cooking, and left that to her hired help. Their weekends were spent at a seaside apartment where Mary could enjoy swimming, water skiing, and walks on the beach. "I like the outdoor life," she said.

The *Dick Van Dyke Show* was a winner from the beginning and remained high in the ratings. Emmy awards were received for outstanding writing, directing, and acting. In 1965 Mary received the Emmy for best actress in a regular television series and the Foreign Press Golden Globe Award. When the show ended in 1966 because of Dick Van Dyke's decision to pursue a movie career, it was syndicated for reruns around the country.

For the next three years, Mary's career got off the track. She starred as Holly Golightly in David Merrick's production of *Breakfast at Tiffany's*, a musical stage version of Truman Capote's novel. The show closed after four preview performances. Following the Broadway fiasco, Mary went to Hollywood to appear in a series of movie roles for Universal Pictures. None of them were memorable: Julie Andrews' prissy roommate in *Thoroughly Modern Millie*, a would-be novelist in *Don't Just Stand There*, a hippie in *What's So Bad About Feeling Good?*, and a nun in *Change of Habit* with Elvis Presley.

In addition to her professional disappointments, Mary's personal life took a downturn as well. Her pregnancy ended in miscarriage and it was then discovered that she was diabetic. From that time on, she's had to adhere to a strict diet and administers her own insulin shots twice a day.

"I was at the lowest point possible when I got a call from Dick Van Dyke," she said of that period.

Dick invited Mary to team up with him for a nostalgic television special, a show which drew unbelievable ratings and turned Mary's career around. TV executives were so impressed by the talented, striking brunette with the wide smile, all three major networks offered Mary her own series.

She accepted CBS's offer, a multimillion-dollar contract stipulating part ownership and her own creative contributions to the new production. Her collaboration with producer-husband Grant Tinker and writers James Brooks and Allan Burns resulted in the *Mary Tyler Moore Show*, with Mary playing Mary Richards, an assistant-producer of a Minneapolis television news show.

American audiences took to perky Mary Richards in a big way. Small-time office politics, sex, friendship and fun were all present in Mary Richards' life. Her superb supporting cast included Ed Asner as her crusty boss, Ted Knight as an egocentric anchor man, his girlfriend Georgia Engel, Valerie Harper, Mary's rad-lib neighbor, their landlady Cloris Leachman, newswriter Gavin McLeod, and Betty White, the station's cooking show hostess. Many of the supporting performers developed followings of their own, and later had their own shows.

The *Mary Tyler Moore Show* was filmed on the site of Mack Sennett's "Fun Factory" with three cameras and a live audience. Mary drove to work every day in her white Mercedes. From its premiere on September 19, 1970, the show got good reviews and good ratings. Once again, Mary's flawless sense of timing impressed the critics who were also pleasantly surprised by a television heroine who was "over thirty without being either a widow or a nurse." The creators and writers of the show were congratulated for presenting Mary Richards as a positive female role model.

"I'm proudest of the show for giving women the opportunity to choose what they want to do with their lives by emulation," Mary stated. "Marriage is wonderful for some people . . . but it's not the end of the world for Mary Richards if she never gets married. She has a rich, full life . . . and that's good."

> Mary Richards: I think you're asking a lot of personal questions you have no right to ask.
> Lou Grant: You know you've got spunk? I hate spunk.

The camaraderie and enthusiasm among the cast members became widely known. Ed Asner once said they never got bored on the set because "the scripts are too good."

Though Mary was considered by many the most self-disciplined person they had ever met (despite her tight schedule, she found time to work with a ballet instructor several times a week), she didn't pull rank. Instead she considered herself a part of the ensemble whose goal it was to turn out a first-rate show every week.

Perky, ever cheerful, and efficient both on camera and off, Mary became television's sunniest personality. "Couldn't you just slap my face for being so positive and optimistic?" she once asked a reporter. Though no one looked more smashing in evening clothes, she preferred casual dress, calling herself, "essentially a white-ducks-and-sneakers person."

The *Mary Tyler Moore Show* was a critical and financial success for Mary and her husband, who began adding other shows to their Mary Tyler Moore Enterprises. When not in front of the camera, Mary was learning the television industry business. Her parents, George and Marjorie Moore, still lived in Los Angeles and attended nearly every weekly filming.

Valerie Harper eventually departed from the show to star in her own show, *Rhoda*, a MTM production in which talented former stage comedienne Nancy Walker played her "Ma" (she also appeared on the series *McMillan and Wife* and later starred in ABC's *The Nancy Walker Show* in 1976). Later Valerie reminisced about days on the set and a pumpkin-shaped cookie jar which stagehands kept stocked with Oreos and Lorna Doones.

"Mary with her diabetes and me with my weight problems, we used to love to open that jar and just sniff the sugary smell. We'd say, 'Oh, wow!' then put the lid back on."

After five years as Mary Richards, Mary Tyler Moore decided to wrap up the show. During rehearsals for the final episode, she explained her reasons: "Creative people need challenges," she said, "and when they get comfortable, that's the time to say, enough! It's not right to sit back and say, okay, I know all the tricks now, it's just a matter of shuffling them around. I miss struggling and worrying and proving myself . . ."

When the show ended, Mary thanked her talented coworkers for teaching her about comedy, friendship and trust, and hoped she had set a good example for them with her self-discipline. Asner and the others all had work lined up, so Mary's decision didn't put anyone out of work.

"They're all good, and they're all in demand," she said. "I've been very lucky. We want each other to succeed."

Fans of the show wore neatly lettered T-shirts that asked, "Oh God, what are we going to do without Mary Tyler Moore?" The sale of the syndication rights to the *Mary Tyler Moore Show* marked the largest deal of that type in television industry, giving the Tinkers money to finance still more television projects. Besides *Rhoda*, they created *Phyllis* and the long-running *Bob Newhart Show*, all with the MTM trademark — a strong comic idea and a stronger supporting cast.

Mary quit the show at the prime of her personal and professional life. She credits a diabetic diet for sustaining her energy and healthy appearance, saying it is "the healthiest one possible." She eagerly dove into projects close to her heart.

Her childhood interest in animals still intact, Mary joined and eventually became national chairman of the Fund for Animals, an anticruelty to animals organization. She wrote the introduction for her friend Cleveland Amory's book *Animail*, published in 1976. That same year, her article "Please Help Me to Stop Cruelty to Animals" appeared in the June issue of *Good Housekeeping*.

Departing from her patented TV personality, Mary took on heavy dramatic roles. In 1978 she appeared in a TV movie based on Betty Rollin's autobiography, *First, You Cry*, in which she portrays a TV commentator who discovers she has breast cancer. The movie was called one of the best made-for-TV films of the decade.

Mary went on to play equally serious roles both on stage in *Whose Life Is It Anyway?*, playing a quadriplegic paralyzed from the neck down, and in the Robert Redford-directed film *Ordinary People*. Her role as a bereaved mother encompassed by grief earned her an Oscar nomination. Mary doesn't see why her dramatic success surprises others so much, claiming that comedy prepared her for more serious parts. "As a comedienne, I'm an observer of life and people," she explained. "That's what enables me to do dramatic work."

Mary has periodically sought psychiatric help for problems of insecurity and her lack of assertiveness. Saying her first separation from Grant Tinker was because of her need for "breathing space," she also told one interviewer, "I was too dependent on Grant . . . I leaned on him too much." These admissions remind one of Mary Richards' lament to Lou Grant on the show. "You don't know what it's like being a perky cute person. No one realizes what's bubbling underneath — the doubts, fears, worries, tensions."

The life of Mary Tyler Moore seems to alternate between long periods of extreme happiness and fulfillment and periods of disappointment and tragedy. Since the final episode of the *Mary Tyler Moore Show* in 1975, she has had to call upon her inner resources of courage to transcend the private agony that has befallen her. Her youngest sister, Elizabeth, died from a drug overdose, her seventeen-year marriage to Grant Tinker came to an end, her son, Richard Meeker, died of a self-inflicted gunshot wound, and both her parents became ill. She embarked on an extensive European trip with her convalescent parents as soon as they were able to travel. One of the highlights was a private audience with the Pope. On a *Barbara Walters Special*, Mary talked about her determination to go on in spite of suffering enormous personal pain.

The lithe performer has always continued her dancing classes wherever she lives (she once had a huge dance studio built at her Bel Air home in California). In November of 1983, Mary married cardiologist Robert Levine and the couple honeymooned in Hawaii. With his encouragement, she began working on the television movies *Heartsounds* (ABC) and *Finnegan Begin Again* (HBO), and accepted the chairmanship of the International Juvenile Diabetes Foundation for 1984. She also spent five weeks at the Betty Ford Center to end her habit of drinking two martinis every night. (Diabetics who consistently drink run the risk of permanent hypoglycemia.) At the 1984 Academy Awards, Mary looked radiantly lovely as she presented Jack Nicholson with his Oscar for best supporting actor, and two months later helped present the thirty-eighth annual Tony Awards.

Later that year, Ron Alexander of the *New York Times* wrote about a late-night cult of Mary Tyler Moore fans in the New York area. Over 150,000 strong, they watched reruns of three successive episodes of the show from 1:30 to 3:00 a.m. every night, some setting alarms to catch the shows. At the end of ten weeks, the original show with Mary Richards moving to Minneapolis, getting a job, and meeting her coworkers began a new cycle. Those interviewed said the shows were "soothing" and "relaxing," and that they caught different nuances each time around. All agreed that Mary and the rest of the cast were like "old friends" with whom they enjoyed spending their time.

All the time Mary was working on serious movies and plays, she was itching to return to comedy, but had to wait for the right script to come along.

"I'd much rather do comedy," she said. "I'd love to make people laugh again."

She got her chance when her new CBS television series *Mary* made its debut on December 11, 1985. She portrayed Mary Brenner, a divorced fashion writer who lands a job as a consumer columnist for a sleazy Chicago tabloid. In the series, she was again surrounded by oddball coworkers, this time played by James Farentino, Katey Sagal, John Astin, David Byrd, and Carlene Watkins. And she conducted her lunch-break ballet classes as before. However, her new character was more assertive than the old Mary Richards.

"Mary Brenner, like me, has grown, has experienced all kinds of things ...," she says. "We now have a little tougher shell."

While television audiences will never forget the old Mary, they definitely love the new Mary. She's more mature, sassier, but as endearing as ever.

Chapter Six

Familiar Faces

Many comediennes have worked their way into the limelight over the past three decades and are instantly recognized as notable stage, film and television performers. No one method propelled these funny women to success. Some got their start by working with improvisational companies, well known for providing a training ground for fledgling comics; some were singled out from the casts of television comedy shows or theater productions for their unique qualities; some originally integrated their musical and comedic talents into an act which brought immediate response; and some worked their way up through the clubs, delivering jokes as a stand-up.

A successful comedienne needs an inner direction which gives her the courage to be true to herself, instead of just following trends. That distinctiveness makes others take notice. Television talk show hosts have been responsible for introducing many struggling comediennes to national audiences, and the exposure has often led to return guest spots and offers for work from directors or producers seeing the show. One performer may prefer to concentrate on a single area of show business, while another would rather test the waters in media beyond her launching point.

Once in demand, a promising comedy star must prove her ability to consistently please audiences and build up a following of fans. No longer able to rely on the same "safe" material that initially brought her recognition, she must stretch toward new goals and incorporate new material or characters into her repertoire. Ideally, her experimentation will produce a comedic essence which no one else can duplicate. With talent, persistence, and luck, she will achieve that goal.

Joan Rivers

Joan Rivers has never even considered analysis: "It would straighten me out — and there goes the act." She's been called the bitchiest woman in America, and one of the sharpest wits in comedy. Her outrageous humor and raspy voice are familiar to millions of her fans, who pack the clubs or tune in their television sets to watch her deliver her rapid-laugh routines. Her trademark icebreaker, "Can we talk?" lets loose a barrage of jokes about the royal family, gynecologists, stewardesses, or celebrities of her choice (finger in the mouth — "barf, barf, barf").

Joan firmly believes that television should be gossipy and unpredictable. When she hosted the *Tonight Show*, the Wicked Witch of the Night wasted little time on superficial conversation with her guests, quickly skewering them with personal questions.

"You're sleeping together, right?" she once asked Olivia Newton-John and John Travolta, to get the interview rolling.

Joan Sandra Molinsky was born in 1933 in Brooklyn, the second child in an upper-middle-class family ("... my mother took the test in the *Reader's Digest*, and that's what we were"). Her father was a doctor, an internist, whom she proclaims was "just as good as a lot of those men with degrees."

The family later moved to Larchmont, New York, and Joan attended Barnard College, where she studied English and wrote for the school newspaper and participated in dramatic productions. She graduated Phi Beta Kappa in 1954. Persuaded by her parents not to follow her plans for a career in the theater, Joan instead became a fashion coordinator.

"I tried it their way," she said later, "and none of it worked." Even her marriage to "the right man," a retail clothier, lasted but six months and was, in Joan's words, horrible. "But that marriage gave me courage to go into show business," she said.

Her parents so adamantly disapproved of show business as a métier for their daughter, they refused to help her in any way. Determinedly setting off on her own, Joan stayed with friends and lived in run-down motels, getting by on what she earned doing part-time secretarial work. During the early sixties she landed parts in the Broadway revues *Talent '60* and *Talent '61*, then replaced Barbara Harris in another revue, *From the Second City*. For three months she joined a USO troupe in the Pacific.

While making the rounds as an actress, she tried to get closer to the receptionists by joking with them. They all told her she was funny enough to make it in comedy, so she went to work at six dollars a night. Taking her tape recorder from one seedy bar to the next to test the decibels of the

Joan Rivers

laughs, she worked in Greenwich Village clubs, Mafia strip joints, and toured the borscht belt. She suffered the humiliation of often getting fired after her first show and heard one club manager yell over the loudspeaker, "Get her off!" She now jokes that her agent's business card had two masks on it . . . "both tragedy."

When in the Village, she went to see Lenny Bruce every night, and credits him for the healthy state of comedy today (she also admires Lucille Ball for her marvelous timing). Gradually working her way into intimate Village clubs where her esoteric humor went over well, she ventured into comedy writing, eventually writing sketches for *Candid*

Camera and material for Phyllis Diller, Bob Newhart, Zsa Zsa Gabor, and Topo Gigio, the puppet mouse popular with viewers of the *Ed Sullivan Show*. She did a short stint with a comedy threesome, Jim, Jake, and Joan, before returning to solo performing. Finally the struggling performer got a shot at national television, but her big chance to appear on the *Jack Paar Show* ended in failure. Paar thought she was terrible.

"Even my agent told me, 'You're too old. It's not gonna happen,'" she says.

The following week, though she'd already been turned down several times, Joan auditioned again for the *Tonight Show*, was accepted, and finally appeared with Johnny Carson.

"Bless him," she says of that first appearance in 1965 when she went over big with her jokes about her hairdresser and her parents' latest gimmick to marry her off with a big sign: "Last girl before Thruway."

"Nobody thought I was funny until he put his arm around me and said 'you're gonna be a star. . . .' He's the best and most loyal friend any person can have. . . . In another life, I'm sure we were a vaudeville team."

Television producer Edgar Rosenberg (born in Germany, raised in South Africa, and educated in England) saw her television debut and hired her to rewrite a Peter Sellers comedy script. In an interview years later, Edgar recalled that when he first met Joan, she was so overwhelmed by stage fright, she feared electrocution if she touched the microphone with her perspiring hands. She admits she still gets frightened and stutters at times.

"Edgar and I married four days after we met," she says. "I think he realized I would make his life fun."

Soon after settling down in their New York apartment, Edgar became Joan's manager and the couple collaborated with Lester Colodny in writing *Fun City*, a Broadway show in which Joan starred. Next came a serious cameo role in the film *The Swimmer* (1968), starring Burt Lancaster. Better club dates resulted from the national exposure on the Carson show, with Downstairs at the Upstairs her homebase in Manhattan. She also made her first recording, *Joan Rivers Presents Mr. Phyllis and Other Funny Stories*.

A few years after Joan's marriage to Edgar, daughter Melissa was born. That experience gave Joan more material for her act and prompted her to write her first book, *Having a Baby Can Be a Scream*, relating her experiences during pregnancy and childbirth. For one year, she hosted *That Show*, a daytime television talk show on NBC. After opening the loosely formatted program with a monologue, she vivaciously chatted with her guests and the audience. Television critic Jack Gould of the *New York Times* found Joan to be "quite possibly the most intuitively funny woman alive," and Ed Sullivan stated, "she is unique — there is a great quality of warmth in her work." When the show ended in late 1969, the entertainer made her Las Vegas debut at the Riviera Hotel to favorable reviews.

Though Phyllis Diller was the first woman to host the *Tonight Show*, Joan was the first to take over the show for a full week, back in 1971. In recent years, she has sometimes drawn a bigger rating than Carson himself.

"He's a master," Joan insists. "He can make anyone look witty and charming. I'm more of a gossip.... I really love to get bitchy ladies — Victoria Principal, Joan Collins...."

Joan received $2 million for her one-year contract with Caesar's Palace in Las Vegas, $1 million for a comedy album, and $250,000 for nine weeks' work as Johnny Carson's replacement on the *Tonight Show* during the 1983–1984 season. However, she has never forgotten the poverty she endured those first seven years while trying to break into the business, and still worries about becoming poor again. The successful comic can still name the clubs where she bombed in the sixties, and admits that when she leaves a hotel suite, she takes with her all the soap, packets of coffee, and tissues.

"Each night I say, 'What if I'm not funny in the morning?'"

It's been said she inherited her fear of destitution in part from her Russian-born mother, Beatrice, whose wealthy Jewish family lost everything during the Russian Revolution. Though Dr. Meyer Molinsky provided his wife and their two daughters (Joan's sister Barbara is a Philadelphia attorney) with a comfortable life, she always yearned for more.

Joan admits to getting rid of a lot of hostility through her routines. Much of her humor deals with her unhappy childhood as a girl so fat, "I was my own buddy at camp.... In my class picture, I was the whole front row." However, her mother told interviewers that her daughter never had a serious weight problem. "Puberty was not very kind to me," Joan once claimed. "I had no boyfriends and was never popular."

In a published photo of her at a high school prom with her date and another couple, Joan appears to have been an attractive, slim teenager, and over the years, old classmates have mostly spoken well of her. For unknown reasons, she has instructed her alma mater, Barnard College, not to release her 1954 yearbook to anyone.

Joan, who has said she truthfully thinks of herself as sexy, conceals those feelings when she struts out on stage to perform her angst-filled act. She presents herself as so undesirable that when she ran through the room naked, Edgar asked, "Who shaved the dog?" Nearly every performance includes grotesque jokes about her body: "My body is falling so fast, my gynecologist wears a hard hat."

Her failure at being a good wife also generates jokes about a television show about her cooking called "That's Inedible." Also, the roaches leaving her home wipe their feet on their way *out*.

"I take all the hang-ups that people are afraid to talk about and let them know they're not unique in their pain," she explains.

Her harping on physical attractiveness in others has drawn criticism, but Joan defends her sometimes vicious jokes about other celebrities: "If I thought I hurt anybody, I'd go crazy. That's why I pick on the biggies — they can take it. . . . Comedy should also be on that very fine line of going too far. . . . Otherwise it's pap. . . ."

A few of her targets are Nancy Reagan, Jimmy and Rosalyn Carter, Eleanor Roosevelt, Sophia Loren, Jane Fonda, Yoko Ono, Bo Derek ("so dumb that she studies for her Pap test"), and Elizabeth Taylor ("a very dear friend. . . . I'm part of the reason she lost weight. She ought to thank me").

Joan's bitchiest gossip usually concerns her fictional friend and hometown tramp, Heidi Abromowitz: "She had more hands up her dress than the Muppets." After Joan moved to California, she acquired a new imaginary friend to ridicule in her act, rich Desirée Nussbaum. Joan's nightclub routines have to be toned down for television, but she thinks it's all relative.

"If you've seen Richard Pryor . . . Robin Williams . . . and Bette Midler, I'm very mild," she says. "If you've only seen Danny Thomas and Bob Hope, then I am very dirty."

Joan says black humor can be a catharsis and considers only deformed children, religion, and death taboo subjects for her act (too depressing), though she thinks it's time people started dealing with the subject of death. She claims she got through her mother's death "by doing joke after joke."

The frenetic performer equates being a comedienne with being an improvising jazz musician. In recent years, Joan has preferred not to appear in front of an all-male audience, because she feels men can better relate to her through the women to whom she freely gives advice.

"Marry rich," she tells them, citing Jackie Kennedy Onassis as an example. "Buy him a pacemaker, then stand behind him and say 'boo.'"

When hosting the Carson show, she often pelts a woman sitting down front with poisoned barbs ("Oh, grow up," she admonishes when anyone gasps at her cheekiness), then graciously presents her with the floral arrangement from Johnny Carson's desk.

Joan didn't feel welcome when she ventured into films by making *Rabbit Test* (1978), a comedy about the first man to become pregnant. Even though the critics panned the film, which cost less than $1 million to make, it has paid off ten-fold for its investors.

When she tries out new material at "workouts" in small clubs, Joan often tapes a series of cue cards on the floor. As she paces back and forth, she delivers her zingers on "Housework," "Mean nurses," "Gloria Vanderbilt," "Having your period," and so on. After one such rehearsal in Los Angeles, a fan made off with her cards. "I love to do clubs," she says. "They keep you fresh."

It took two years for Joan and David Brenner to convince others they should work together and that having two comedians on the same stage was a good idea. (Traditionally, comics are teamed with musicians, acrobats, ventriloquists or magicians.) David has been a fan of Joan's before he ever considered giving up his career as a TV producer in Chicago and becoming a comedian. "I had never seen anyone better than she was onstage," he remarked, "and I had seen a lot of comedians."

Since their initial 1981 appearance together at the Diplomat Hotel in Hollywood, Florida, David and Joan have broken many attendance records on the comedy circuits. "Not only did the chemistry between Joan and me work.... I have the fun of working with . . . one of America's real screwballs," he says.

Joan pushes herself at a grueling pace, spending forty weeks a year on the road. An exercise enthusiast and fanatic about her weight (around 110 pounds), Joan often attends dinner parties, but declines to eat. She has talked candidly about the plastic surgery done on her nose and eyes. One of her trademarks is the fashionable clothing she wears — she made nine changes during the 1984 Emmy presentations. On the Carson show, her ensembles are designed by the likes of Arnold Scaasi and Calvin Klein, delivered by courier from New York and returned the following day.

The most wickedly funny woman in America has confessed to being shy. "At parties I hide myself," she once said. "It's very difficult to just let go."

Soft-spoken Edgar, in recent years a real-estate developer, lends a solidarity to their marriage of nearly twenty years. "He's much nicer than I am," Joan concedes.

They live in Beverly Hills in a home decorated with French and English antiques. ("If Louis XIV hasn't touched it, I don't want it.") When Joan is on the road, she calls home many times a day to chat with Edgar and Melissa. She suffered two miscarriages before Melissa was born, and considers herself a very conservative mother. Proficient in horseback riding, Melissa often participates in riding competitions. Joan (who is afraid to ride) jokes that each show ribbon Melissa wins costs $95,000, but says the expensive sport has been a healthy outlet for the teenager.

From her beginnings as a stand-up in dives during the sixties, Joan has made a steady climb to become the first lady of comedy. Her one-woman show at Carnegie Hall was sold out, she has played to packed houses in Las Vegas, a twelve-city tour was an instant sellout and her comedy album, *What Becomes a Semi-Legend Most?* disappeared from the record stores shortly after being shipped. As cohost of the 1984 Emmy Awards show with Eddie Murphy, she stirred up controversy by insulting James Watt and using profanity. In 1984, Joan was chosen for the "Woman of the Year" award by Harvard's Hasty Pudding Theatricals. She accepted the honor, acknowledging that her trademark opener, "Can we talk?" should perhaps be grammatically corrected. With everything going so well, Joan routinely pauses to reflect on the magnitude of her success: "Every time I go on stage, I say, 'Thank you, God.'"

Joan considers herself a writer first and writes ninety percent of her own material. She has pads and pencils stashed all over her house to jot down ideas for the act, and frequently rifles through twelve drawers of jokes on cross-indexed cards under such headings as Face Lifts, Drugs, etc. Much of her humor is based on the articles about celebrities she reads in the *National Enquirer*.

Her latest book, a best seller, is titled *The Life and Hard Times of Heidi Abromowitz* (Delacorte Press, 1984). Other projects include a movie about television titled *Situation Comedy* and a series of greeting cards with untraditional messages. After not finding just the right card one day, she decided to go into the business.

"We sat down one night and wrote out all these funny lines," she said of her humorous spin-off. (Example: *Happy birthday*. Inside of card: *You always looked old*. Or: *I wanted to buy an appropriate gift for your birthday. . . . But Tiffany's doesn't sell vibrators*.) Joan's fans await her autobiography *Enter Talking* which chronicles "my early exciting tramp days to my first *Tonight Show* appearance."

The hottest comedienne in the country tells hopeful female comics: "Stop talking about it, and do it! Work anywhere . . . get started."

Joan realizes that her career may cool off for periods of time, but feels she can always "go back and open for Barry Manilow." Going back to her first Carson show, she says, ". . . I was the hot girl in town. Now, I'm the hot woman in town. I figure it happens to me every sixteen years. Next time I'll be the hot old lady in town."

On October 18, 1984, Joan's husband, Edgar ("my best friend in the whole world"), suffered a massive heart attack and underwent quadruple heart bypass surgery, barely surviving post-surgery complications. The comedienne canceled all appearances and moved into UCLA Medical Center to keep a bedside vigil. Between pacing and crying, she forced herself to talk and make jokes, hoping to get through to the comatose patient. "Humor is our shorthand for saying, 'It's okay,'" she says.

After two weeks of hanging precariously on to life, Edgar came out of the coma and said, "Joan, stop trying to run the hospital." Get-well messages poured in and Elizabeth Taylor sent him flowers. "Isn't that classy?" Joan acknowledged the next day. "Isn't that lovely?"

With Edgar's recovery underway, Joan resumed her career, but says the experience of nearly losing "my best friend in the whole world" changed her focus: "I already see the change in myself — getting down to basics, simplifying, as though scraping away the old barnacles . . . all the things I find don't actually matter."

By March of 1985, Joan had completed taping *Joan Rivers and Friends Salute Heidi Abromowitz*, a Showtime special for television. She was also considering movie offers and preparing for her first live appearance in England, where she's been offered top money to play the Palladium and other prestigious theaters.

Joan Rivers is indeed a successful funny woman who is likeable and flamboyant. She has made it big and has brought much publicity and glamour to stand-up comedy. Her humor, which packs a punch and stirs up controversy, keeps her in the news. She once attempted to explain her phenomenal success: "Comedy is relief," she said. "Life is very sad and tough. That's what my act is . . . it's therapy."

Kaye Ballard

"I always knew I wanted to be an entertainer," Kaye says, after nearly forty years of ups and downs in show business. Though the comedienne with the mile-wide smile is known for her outrageous mugging, she claims she is really shy. Gloria Katherine Balotta was born in Cleveland on November 20, 1926, and desired a show business career from the age of "three hours on." The daughter of first generation Italians (her father was a cement finisher), she was named for Gloria Swanson. At the age of 5, she'd pretend she was Bette Davis and emote while doing the dishes. "I'd borrow my father's hat and do Maurice Chevalier," she says.

She learned to play the flute and was a natural at singing and telling jokes. A Cleveland burlesque house hired her at 16 to play a straight woman in a comedy act, unusual in a time when most women in burlesque were hired as strippers. She toured on the burlesque circuit in the South, traveling in a bus called the Blue Goose. "We had a five-piece band, two strippers and comics," she later recalled. "I did impressions of Betty Hutton and Judy Garland."

That led to a job with Spike Jones' wacky band. Kaye gave that group credit for changing her life in regard to satiric comedy. While in New York with the band, a ticket broker gave her tickets to see Ethel Merman in *Annie Get Your Gun*. That provided the motivation she needed. "Then I knew what I wanted to do," she said.

One of her early impressions was that of veteran Sophie Tucker. Kaye's appearances on the nightclub circuit became a blur: "They just rearranged the drunks and I was on again." The talented performer put together *A Tribute to Fanny Brice* for the prestigious Blue Angel nightclub in New York. She appeared in roles both on and Off Broadway in *Carnival*, *Top Banana*, and *The Golden Apple*, a turn-of-the-century American *Iliad* and *Odyssey* in which Kaye sang the show's hit tune "Lazy Afternoon."

She was honored when she was chosen to replace her idol Beatrice Lillie in the *Ziegfeld Follies* in 1957. Kaye next went on to steal the show in *The Decline and Fall of the Entire World as Seen Through the Eyes of Cole Porter, Revisited*. Her television debut in 1952 on Mel Torme's show introduced the fresh nuttiness of Kaye Ballard to viewers at home and led to more work in the expanding medium. For two years she was a regular on Perry Como's show. One of her "big numbers" was "I Just Kissed My Nose Goodnight."

Back on Broadway in 1961, she played Rosalie, the raucous mistress, in *Carnival*. That experience was one of the high points in her career. During the late 1960s, Kaye appeared in the revue *Cole Porter Revisited* and costarred with Eve Arden in the television series *The Mothers-in-Law* (1967–1970). They played next-door neighbors whose son and daughter had married.

Through the years, the versatile entertainer has performed in cabaret revues across the country and frequently done guest spots on *The Love Boat, Fantasy Island*, and other television series. She's chalked up over fifty guest appearances each on the Merv Griffin and Johnny Carson shows. In 1974, Kaye played Molly Goldberg in *Molly*, an unsuccessful musical version of *The Goldbergs* radio show. Her film credits include the musical *The Girl Most Likely* (her debut in 1956) and more recently, *Freaky Friday* (1976) and *In Love Again* (1980).

Kaye's Manhattan apartment is filled with mementos of her career. Theater posters and photos of other performers abound, and on display in a glass case are two tiny black hats given to her by Bea Lillie. Like Bea, she has a penchant for poodles and dotes on her three, named Punky, Pockets, and Big Shirley.

All of Kaye's show business experiences (and the emotional peaks and valleys they evoked) were recently compiled for a one-woman show called *Hey Ma . . . Kaye Ballard*. It opened Off Broadway on March 5, 1984.

Good friend and pianist Arthur Siegel, her accompanist for many years, again provided musical backup for the nostalgic evening with the comedienne who, if she had the chance, would do it all again.

Ruth Buzzi

When Ruth played in a stock production of *Auntie Mame*, her directions for playing dowdy secretary Agnes Gooch were to "schlump in." So Ruth learned to schlump, later accentuating Agnes' careless posture and frumpy clothes to transform herself from an attractive, cheerful woman into Gladys Ormsby, the sourpuss resident of TV's *Laugh-In*, who opened every skit by shuffling towards a park bench. With her eyebrow-hugging hairnet, out-of-shape cardigan and baggy stockings, frowning Gladys seemed the least likely target for Tyrone, a lecherous little old man played by Arte Johnson, who tried to sidle up to her. Outraged by his indecent proposals, she always ended up pummeling him with her purse, and leaving him in a heap on the ground.

The zany brunette comedienne was born July 24, 1936, in Westerly, Rhode Island. Her father was a gravestone salesman whom she has claimed taught her "the fine art of sandblasting." She attended Pasadena Playhouse, and for a while supported herself working in a perfume factory and then as a maid. Ruth later joked about walking down Sunset Boulevard "with a spaghetti mop over my shoulder."

Her acting debut was in *Jenny Kissed Me* in 1956 in San Francisco. From there she went to New York to appear in *Misguided Tour*, an Off-Broadway revue, and shortly thereafter was hired for the part of the good fairy in *Sweet Charity* on Broadway. Venturing next into television, she worked on the popular series *The Monkees* (premiering in 1967) and then became a regular on *Laugh-In*, which ran from 1968 to 1973.

Ruth played many recurring characters on the hit show in addition to Gladys Ormsby. Among them were "Busy Buzzi at Tinseltown" who brought viewers "hot flashes" from Hollywood, a klutzy Shirley Temple singing and tap dancing in corkscrew curls and miles of ruffles, Flicker Farkle of the Farkle family, and a hilariously funny, frowsy barfly who chomped on a dill pickle while getting pie-eyed with her buddy Dick Martin. She portrayed a trilling opera singer overcome by a laughing jag in the midst of her aria and a Cockney woman mistaking Dick Rowan for Fred Astaire from America. Her contribution to the series of chicken jokes: "How do you cook a one-and-a-half ton chicken? Bring Lake Erie to a boil and add a pinch of salt."

During the seventies, Ruth appeared in episodes of *That Girl*, *Love American Style*, and *Emergency! Medical Center*. Her credits also include performances on children's television and over 200 TV commercials.

In late 1983, the versatile entertainer attended a Beverly Hills party to celebrate the tenth anniversary of *Laugh-In's* last show and its beginning as a syndicated rerun that will allow more viewers to be entertained by Ruth's antics. She loves to make people laugh, but hopes to work in every area of show business so she can become "a female Alec Guinness."

Lily Tomlin

She's been acclaimed as one of the most eccentrically original minds of our time. While most women get laughs with funny lines or stories (either in or out of character), Lily Tomlin tends a different garden. Respected for bringing dignity and compassion to women's comedy, she has invented a repertoire of unique and endearing characters while keeping the fragile balance between grotesqueness and humor. ". . . I do them all with love," she once said. "After all, in private we're all misfits."

Mary Jean Tomlin was born in 1937 in Detroit, Michigan, shortly after her parents had moved there from Paducah, Kentucky. Her brother, Richard, was born a few years later. Their mother, Lillie Mae, was not much of a disciplinarian. Their father was a hard-drinking man who worked at the Commonwealth Brass Company and often brought home new machine parts he'd made to show his daughter. He also encouraged her at the age of 5 to sing for his friends at his favorite hangout. Lily later said that he was a drinking, gambling man who would invite Jehovah's Witnesses in for a beer. He brought home the family's first television set when she was 10, and she quickly became a fan of Bea Lillie and Imogene Coca.

The willowy girl with brown eyes and hair attended Detroit's Crossman Elementary and Hutchins Junior High. She and Richard often practiced mimicking their neighbors and country cousins in Kentucky whom they visited every summer. Lily often said that growing up in a blue-collar neighborhood that still had remnants of the upper-class area it had once been influenced her approach to humor.

"There were still . . . residual people hanging around . . . who clung to the idea that we were living in a very chic apartment building," she said. "In that building was every kind of person. . . . I soon learned that not one of them was really different from any of the others in human terms.... There was so much humor and beauty in all those different kinds of people. And I've always been able to draw on it ... I love them...."

Years later, while naming people she'd most want with her on a desert island, she listed Mrs. Taitelbaum, Mrs. Creek, and Mrs. Valone, all women from her old apartment house.

Lily was a cheerleader in high school—"possibly the best white cheerleader Detroit has ever had," until she was asked to leave the squad for being "too vulgar." Her "semi-hood" stage involved membership in a girls' club of Scarlet Angels, who wore pegged skirts, ballet shoes, and red angel decals on the backs of their blouses.

As a part-time usherette at Detroit's Avalon Theatre, impressionable 14-year-old Lily became star-struck and tried to make herself up to look like Audrey Hepburn, Brigitte Bardot, or whoever was starring in the movie that week. Speaking of the celluloid fantasies sold in those days, Lily said years later, "Either Hollywood was concocting dreams of the ideal woman that the average woman in 'real life' could not live up to, or they were concocting dreams, wet dreams at that, of the hot, scorching, sinful, seamy, slithery side of feminine nature according to the popular mythology of the time.... For sexual awakening, there was *nothing* like a bad woman B-Movie."

Comparing dreams manufactured in Hollywood with cars manufactured in Detroit, Lily said both should be recalled for obvious errors. "Parts are missing, like Reality and Probability," she said of movie illusions.

After surviving "Bardot Damage," "Audrey Hepburn Damage," and "Jeanne Moreau Damage," Lily entered Wayne State University as a premed student because she liked biology and "I'm a Virgo and most of them are hypochondriacs." During her second year there, she auditioned for *The Mad Woman of Chaillot*, and got a walk-on part, which she tried to stretch by improvising. That's when it hit her that she'd like to make people laugh. "I thought, 'Gee, it would be great if I could make a living doing this!'" she later said.

Soon after, she appeared in a college variety show and introduced Mrs. Earbore the Tasteful Lady, now familiar to American television viewers. She then began to entertain in a coffeehouse near campus, often for no pay, and appeared on local radio and television shows. By the end of her second year, she decided to quit school and go to New York, where she studied mime with Paul Curtis for a short time before returning to Detroit. She had been disenchanted by the humorless "people who were so dedicated and so involved ... they subjugated themselves to the art...."

Lily worked in hometown clubs and coffeehouses for a few years

Lily Tomlin

until 1965, when she returned to New York. Between occasional tryouts at the Improvisation (which also spawned Richard Pryor, Robin Williams and the late Freddie Prinze), she worked in an office and as a waitress in the theater district. On impulse one day, she announced over the restaurant PA system: "Attention, diners. Your Howard Johnson's waitress of the week, Miss Lily Tomlin, is about to make her appearance on the floor. Let's all give her a big hand!" She doubled her tips that day and got her walking papers.

Lily's next assignment was totally distasteful to her but it paid the bills—she began doing television commercials. She moved from the Lower

East Side to an apartment in Yonkers and bought an eighteen-foot boat. At night, she would circle the city, then drop in at the marina for a beer with the boat people.

Her major break came in 1966 when she made a series of appearances on Garry Moore's show. After more club work and guest spots on Merv Griffin's show, she was signed by a talent agency.

The comedy documentary style of Elaine May inspired Lily, but she was most influenced by the material of a comedienne from nearly a half-century earlier. When she heard Ruth Draper's monologues of different characters on recordings at the New York Public Library, "I just started jumping up and down and screaming." Soon she was developing her own stable of characters and her own following of admirers. After she appeared at Manhattan's Upstairs at the Downstairs, Vincent Canby wrote in the *New York Times* that Lily Tomlin "was headed for the big time."

She joined the cast of Emmy-winning show *Laugh-In* in 1969, and became a forerunner of the type of performers whose countercultural comedy became popular in the seventies. On one of her first shows, nearly 40 million viewers were introduced to Ernestine, Ma Bell's snorting, powermad switchboard operator who helped serve everyone from "Presidents and Kings to the scum of the earth." Within weeks, the lines "Is this the party to whom I am speaking?" and "One ringy-dingy, two ringy-dingies," were becoming catch phrases around the country.

"Mr. Veedle? Mr. Veedle?" Realizing that she's talking to Gore Vidal, the author of *Myra Breckinridge*, Ernestine lambasts him for his "trashy . . . vulgar degeneracy" and sneers, "I'll bet your mother's proud of *you*!" He complains to her that he's been overcharged on his telephone bill. "Overcharged!" she says, "I'd say that's pretty obvious from the books you've been writing."

The following year, Lily was made an honorary member of the California telephone operators' union and presented with the "Cracked Belle Award." When the Bell System offered her $500,000 to make a series of Ernestine commercials, she turned it down, preferring to keep artistic control of the character.

In spite of a lawsuit against *Laugh-In's* producers in 1972 that declared her the original creator and sole owner of all her characters (the Tasteful Lady, fifties pompom girl Suzy Sorority, the Fast Talker, and devilish 5-year-old Edith Ann), Lily has good memories of *Laugh-In* and says she really developed on that show.

In addition to the series work, she performed at leading clubs, took Ernestine to London to appear in the Royal Variety Show, and did guest spots on shows such as *The Electric Company* and the *Dick Cavett Show*. She walked off the latter in protest when a fellow guest talked about the pets he owned: "I have three horses, three dogs, and a wife." (She also would never do jokes on *Laugh-In* that she felt were sexist or racist.)

Comedy albums came next. Her first LP, *This Is a Recording* (1971), featured Ernestine and won a Grammy for the year's best comedy recording. The following year, she collaborated with writer Jane Wagner to present Edith Ann's sassy repartee on *And That's the Truth* (Polydor).

When *Laugh-In* went off the air in 1973, Lily appeared in the *Lily Tomlin Show* on CBS. The one-hour show was written by Lily and guest Richard Pryor, among others. A good Nielsen rating and mixed reviews led to her second special, *Lily*, later that year.

Lily's cast of endearing characters continued to grow. The mother of a crippled child suggested the character of Crystal the Paraplegic to Lily. She even gave her a line to use: "At an amusement park, a little kid asked me if I was one of the rides." Lily took it from there and created a humorous, but not pathetic, character who hang glides and during her monologues, tries to enlighten "walkies" about the handicapped.

Tess the Bag Lady hawks hotpads she made when she was "inside" and explains that since the budget slash, officials have decided she wasn't crazy after all. Rummaging through her tattered shopping bag, she talks about her extraterrestrial visitors and other subjects to anyone who will listen.

Lily's first male portrayal was Rick, the singles bar stud. She later added Tommy Velour, a phony Vegas-type singer. Whether portraying country-western singer Wanda Wilford, lounge organist Bobbi Janine, preacher Sister Boogie Woman, or the world's oldest beautician, Lupe, Lily captures the humanity of her subjects.

Fans wonder why their comedy idol has never had a weekly show on television. Her Emmy-winning TV specials were actually pilots for a weekly show, but they were never picked up for a series. "I'm not ready for a weekly show," she's said. "There isn't that much material."

Others agree that Lily's comedy material (finely polished over a period of time) often doesn't depend on jokes and is too special for weekly exposure.

Lily scored a triumph on Broadway in her one-woman show *Appearing Nightly*, which earned her a special Tony and grossed around $2 million at the box office after a five-city tour of sold-out performances. Her New York fans remember the many nights she passed out coffee to those waiting in line to see the show.

Moving on to films, she got off to a good start. Her sensitive portrayal of a white gospel singer in the film *Nashville* (1975) earned Lily an Academy Award nomination. ("I'd never dreamed of that.") In 1977, she played the dizzy sidekick to Art Carney's seedy private eye in the well-received film *The Late Show*.

The following year, she appeared in the highly publicized *Moment by Moment*, playing the older woman in John Travolta's life. The movie was panned by critics and ignored by moviegoers. Lily later admitted that the reviews (John Simon's vitriolic remarks about her, in particular) took a long while to get over. However, her next two films were quite successful — *Nine to Five* with Jane Fonda and Dolly Parton and *The Incredible Shrinking Woman* with Charles Grodin and Elizabeth Wilson. Lily kept the oversized blue wing chair used in the latter film.

Lily, the girl from Detroit, is still in awe of Hollywood stars, forgetting that she is now one of them. When spending an afternoon getting acquainted with Jane and Dolly before starting *Nine to Five*, she told them, "I feel just like the high school senior who's won the contest — spend the day with your favorite heroines." The trio's friendship continued long after the film was completed and another collaboration is in the works. A few years later, Jane Fonda was asked about Lily: "When I saw her one-woman show . . . I wanted to work with her. . . . Lily's comedy *synthesizes* the American female experience. . . . I value my friendship with Lily and Dolly more than I can say."

Dolly Parton, a fan of Lily's since *Laugh-In*, said, "No matter what she says, she's creative . . . we'd do the same scene over and over and Lily could do it differently every time. . . . Lily was so giving and caring . . . a true sister and friend."

When she returned to television to host *Saturday Night Live*, Lily talked about the national debt and conserving plastics, warning that "vinyl leopard-skin is becoming an endangered synthetic." She also worried that "the person who invented leisure suits will tell us what to do with our leisure time." As a prim housewife sampling her way through a supermarket (a few grapes, sample slices of bologna and cheese, potato chips from a torn bag), she slyly ripped a wing off the chicken on the rotisserie in the deli section, and after savoring it, finally left via the checkout without one item. Besides appearing as Edith Ann, who named all the little boys "who will show you their penis if you ask," Lily portrayed the "Messiah of Love," a male singer oozing charisma.

Comedian Steve Allen feels there is a "poetic content . . . detectable in some of Lily's work," as when Edith Ann describes getting angry: "First your face gets just like a fist . . . your heart gets like a bunch of bees, flies up and stings your brain . . . your blood is like a tornado and then you have bad weather inside your body."

In late 1983, the old *Laugh-In* crew had a reunion to celebrate the syndication of the series' reruns, which will consist of 130 half-hour shows taken from the original 130 hour-long shows. Lily attended to see her old friends and watch Judy Carne, the "sock it to me" girl, get a glass of water in the face, a token of the drenching she received every week on the show.

Over the years Lily has often performed at ERA fund-raising benefits and for other women's causes. Accepted by many as an unofficial spokesperson for the women's movement, Lily's observations are right on target.

"Everytime I see a yield sign on the highway, I feel sexually threatened." Among her "Lies My Mother Taught Me," she quotes, "Whatever makes you happy, makes me happy." She once said that if it hadn't been for the women's movement, people would call her career "her hobby." According to critic Clive Barnes: "She is woman's eye view of madness. She defines herself and her times."

Lily lives in a pink stucco 1920s house in Hollywood (the former home of W.C. Fields) and takes her high school girl friends on studio tours when they visit California. She still claims to enter "some sort of cinematic Zen-state" when she settles down to watch a favorite movie. Not much of a partygoer, she prefers getting together with non–show business friends she's made over the years. Her fondness for clothing from the past takes her into secondhand boutiques featuring vintage fashions. The slender comedienne-actress swims and works out to stay in shape. A hearty eater, she has a special fondness for soul food. "I eat pretty much as I want, and then one day, health foods and juice are what I want. You kind of let your body tell you."

In 1984, Lily teamed up with Steve Martin in the comedy film *All of Me*, which quickly became a box office hit. Steve plays Roger Cobb, a lawyer who finds himself sharing his body fifty/fifty with deceased heiress Edwina Cutwater (Lily). That same year, Lily's Ernestine won an Emmy nomination for a *Flashdance* parody on the NBC miniseries *Live . . . and in Person*. Lily showed up at the awards ceremony in the persona of Ernestine and pouted when she lost.

Ernestine helped welcome in 1985 when she teamed up with Andy Williams to host *CBS's Happy New Year, America*, televised from Times Square and New York's Plaza Hotel. Then Lily and Jane Wagner got together to develop and refine a one-woman show titled *The Search for Signs of Intelligent Life in the Universe*. For months they moved across the country, trying out material on small audiences in motels and storefronts in Seattle, Portland, Houston, San Diego, Atlanta, Denver, Aspen, Lexington and Boston. Finally in September, the two-and-a-half hour show opened on Broadway to standing ovations and glowing notices. Critics welcomed Lily back to New York, calling the show "a brilliant work," "a marvel," "a full tragicomic play."

Using only a few simple props, Lily embodies more than a dozen quirky characters, most of them new: Teen punkster Agnus Angst who wears so many chains and zippers that garage doors flap open when she passes, feminists Lynn, Edie and Marge who review fourteen years of the women's movement, Kate the socialite who is boring herself to death, two prostitutes—black Tina and white Brandy, and all the members of a down-home Indiana household. Lily weaves them all into a rich tapestry of humor and insight. She has never been better.

The performer says she works on each character until she finds the "little key" that reveals its essence. Then she gets her important message across to her audiences: "We are all alike in the important ways . . . we all feel the same."

Fannie Flagg

The Southern charm of Fannie Flagg has graced the American television screen since her debut on *Candid Camera* in the mid-sixties. The comedienne with a thick Alabama drawl has demonstrated what a person can accomplish through hard work and the willingness to explore one's potential.

Born in 1942 in Birmingham, Alabama, Frances Flagg was an only child whose childhood was tumultuous. "Alcohol caused a lot of comings and goings in my life," she has said. "It's hard to forget."

When she was old enough to qualify, the redhaired, blue-eyed young woman began entering Alabama beauty pageants. Fannie earned the title of runner-up in several of the contests. Her career as an entertainer started out when she was hired as a $50-a-week talk show host and "movie girl" in Birmingham. She proceeded to New York where she got a job performing her own comedy skits at the Upstairs at the Downstairs nightspot. Allen Funt, the *Candid Camera* prankster, caught the act and hired her to write for his show. One day, she replaced an actress who was ill, and from then on, Fannie was a regular member of the cast. It still pleases her when people associate her with the show.

"I like *Candid Camera* the best of anything I've ever done," she says. "I got to do all kinds of crazy things and I never had to learn a script."

That exposure gave her the boost she needed, and soon she was regularly invited to appear on *Laugh-In* and top talk shows where she cashed in on her ability to impersonate two Southern political wives in the news—Lady Bird Johnson and the late Martha Mitchell. The popularity of her biting impressions made hits of both her record albums, *Rally Round the Flagg* and *My Husband Doesn't Know I'm Making This Phone Call*. Now looking back, she says she no longer enjoys doing that type of humor.

"I found that in doing those kinds of impressions, you really have to be cruel to be funny." The syrupy-voiced performer appeared in the movie *Five Easy Pieces* (1970) and spent a year on Broadway playing Miss Mona in *The Best Little Whorehouse in Texas*. An ardent spokeswoman for ERA, Fannie added speaking engagements to her busy schedule in 1979. Her next assignment was as Barbara Eden's sidekick in NBC's sitcom *Harper Valley*, premicring on January 16, 1981, and ending the following season.

Fannie has become a writer of fiction in recent years, squeezing in time to write whenever she can. Her first book, *Coming Attractions*, published in 1981, is a comic memoir-novel about her Southern girlhood. It won critical acclaim, being compared to *The Catcher in the Rye*.

Between acting assignments (such as starring roles in *The Supporting Cast* at Burt Reynolds' Florida dinner theater and Erskine Caldwell's *Tobacco Road* in hometown Birmingham) and game show appearances (*Match Game/Hollywood Squares*), Fannie is working on a second book. Set in Georgia in 1918, her tale unfolds through the Depression and World War II. Fannie lives in Santa Barbara, California, with her cat Roots and is so busy she doesn't have time to think about what lies ahead, but says it doesn't matter. "In this business, you wait for somebody else to call you to work."

Bette Midler

Bette calls herself "the last of the truly tacky women," who do "trash with flash and sleaze with ease." She regales audiences with her unrestrained wit and brings lyrical magic to any ballad she sings. She's been called "a superstar of superstars," who inspires other entertainers to impersonate her and avid fans to dress up in funky clothes when coming to see her. The small performer (five feet one, 110 pounds) with lively eyes, full lips, and reddish-blonde hair exudes merriment and optimism in her bizarre acts (mermaid tails and wheelchairs are often used during performances). Baudy Bette insists that "a good laugh is one of the most important things in the world."

Born in Honolulu on December 1, 1945, she was named by her mother, Ruth, an avid movie fan, after Bette Davis, whose name she thought was pronounced the way it looked. Her mother sold lingerie before Bette was born, and later went into real estate. She always encouraged her three daughters to be ambitious, and was happy when Bette became an entertainer. Her father, Fred, "a bit of a curmudgeon," was less encouraging.

Bette grew up in rural Aiea, near the U.S. naval base where her father found work as a house painter for the Navy after moving his family from Paterson, New Jersey. "More like Harlem" is her description of her birthplace, where they were the only Jewish family in a Philippine neighborhood. Overweight, full-breasted and lonely, Bette dreamed of becoming a performer, and entered amateur shows all through her school years. "I never felt like I belonged," she told Gloria Steinem in an interview for *Ms.* in December, 1983.

After one year at the University of Hawaii, her best friend from high school died in a car crash. Bette didn't return to her studies, but decided to pursue a theatrical career. To support herself, she worked in a pineapple factory and as a radio station secretary.

In 1965, she got a break when she was hired for the bit part of a seasick missionary wife in the movie *Hawaii*. When the cast returned to Hollywood for further shooting, Bette was invited to go with them. For six months she earned $300 a week plus her living expenses. She managed to save enough so that when the filming ended, she could leave for New York, where she got along by living in an inexpensive hotel and holding down a series of jobs as a typist, saleswoman, and go-go-dancer.

The determined young woman made the rounds and took any minor parts she could get. She performed in children's theater and Catskill revues before landing a chorus job in the hit musical *Fiddler on the Roof*. She also understudied the part of Tzeitel, the eldest daughter in the play, and was asked to try out for the part when the girl playing Tzeitel decided to leave the show.

Bette won the part (in spite of the casting woman's attempts to dissuade her from auditioning) and played Tzeitel for three years. However, that episode and other offstage rivalries and jealousy of her success dampened her fervor for theatrical stardom. It was also during the run of *Fiddler* that tragedy struck. Bette was waiting for her sister Judith, who had moved to New York a few months earlier. On her way to meet Bette at the theater, Judith was killed in a traffic accident. Stunned by her grief, Bette sought help in the form of psychoanalysis.

By listening to a friend's extensive collection of recordings of Bessie Smith and other early singers, Bette became familiar with black singers' recordings of the blues and gospel music.

One night at the Improvisation (where performers were not paid but hoped to be discovered), Bette sang three songs, and during the third song, something happened. She later told Al Rudis of the Chicago *Sunday Times* of that milestone: "I suddenly knew what the song ("God Bless the Child") was about," she said. "I had an experience, some kind of breakthrough . . . I knew I had to do that. For as long as the trip would be, I had to live it out."

Her appearances at the Improv led to television guest shots with David Frost and Merv Griffin. In 1969 Bette left *Fiddler* and was studying singing and acting when she heard that the Continental Baths, Manhattan's subterranean gay mecca, needed a singer on Friday and Saturday nights.

She was paid $50 a night to entertain male homosexuals, who were clad in bath towels. Bette's onstage wardrobe recalled earlier decades: gold lamé gowns, garter belts, toreador pants, and platform shoes. She wore low-cut dresses with high slits.

"My field of expertise is brassieres," she'd claim, recalling that she was 11 when she got her first, "a D-cup!"

Bette's clowning and strutting delighted the gatherings. Campy renditions of songs from the thirties, forties, and fifties, often imitating the original singers, soon had crowds of both men *and* women coming to the Baths. Her young accompanist, who also composed music and sang, was named Barry Manilow. Offers of club enegagements and television appearances followed shortly.

"My career took off when I sang at the Continental Baths," she later explained. "I was able to take chances on that stage . . . I was freed from fear by people who, at the time, were ruled by fear."

Under the tutelage of her manager and lover, Aaron Russo (now a Hollywood producer), Bette rapidly rose to stardom. She was such a hit on Johnny Carson's *Tonight Show* that she was called back many times over the next year. After playing dates at leading clubs like Mister Kelley's in Chicago and the West 56th Street Downstairs at the Upstairs (where she was held over from two weeks to ten), Bette returned to the Continental Baths in 1972 for a farewell appearance. Rex Reed commented on the frenetic performer's astounding popularity: "In a city where nightclubs are shutting down . . . there are 3,000 people waiting to get into the Continental Baths to see the freaky Miss M."

"The Divine Miss M." next teamed up with Johnny Carson for an engagement at the Sahara Hotel in Las Vegas, then played the Bitter End and Carnegie Hall in New York. Though she appeared to be having the time of her life doing her comedy material and songs, Bette suffered excruciating bouts of nervousness. Cold sweats and vomiting before going on were common occurrences.

Her first album, *The Divine Miss M.* (Atlantic), which she dedicated to her sister Judith, included the Andrews Sisters hit "Boogie Woogie Bugle Boy" and "Chapel of Love." It was a smash, selling more than 100,000 copies the first month. The reviews were so good, one critic was prompted to say they "could have been written by her mother."

Producing the ten songs on the album had taken ten long months. Instead of recording one of her concerts live, Bette worked in the recording studios with four producers, four arrangers, and dozens of horn players and singers to get the desired effect.

The electrifying song stylist was in demand from California to New York, where she easily filled concert halls with sold-out audiences. "She's given camp back to women," novelist Rosalyn Drexler proclaimed.

Bette gave two performances at Lincoln Center's Philharmonic Hall, where at the stroke of midnight on December 31, 1972, she appeared on stage in a diaper and vinyl sash with "1973" written on it.

"The crowd went insane," one critic wrote. "I can't stand to think that any of you . . . missed it." Another was impressed by "a gaiety and sweetness one seldom finds in a comic, man or woman."

Later that year, she received the *After Dark* Ruby Award for Performer of the Year. She also won a Grammy and a Tony. "Pits" (meaning awful) and "hot" (meaning fantastic) were her favorite expressions around that time. Her parents still lived in Hawaii and had not seen any of Bette's live performances. She told one reporter that she felt her father would be shocked by her costumes, gestures, and language, and her talks of weighing her breasts on a mail scale. "I won't tell you how much they weigh," she tells her audience, "but it costs $87.50 to send them to Brazil."

Often compared with her contemporary Barbra Streisand, whose vocalizing is highly stylized, Bette says of her own loose emotional singing style, "I'm a compulsive performer."

TV specials, a triumphant *Clams on the Half Shell Review*, and grueling concert tours during the next few years left her drained, but led to one of the highlights of her career. She was chosen to star in the film *The Rose* (1979), a fictional account of a rock singer à la Janis Joplin. For her work in that film, she was nominated for an Oscar. The theme from the movie has become her signature song. "People identify with "The Rose," she explains. "I wanted a ballad everyone could relate to. It touched people."

That same year, Bette parted company with Aaron Russo and took over control of her own business affairs. She opened on Broadway in *Bette! Divine Madness*. Then her mother died of cancer. Bette had just returned from Australia when she got word—she missed her mother's death by one day. "I felt I should have been there . . . but I wasn't," she said. "I was working."

Following her split with Russo, Bette entered other romantic liaisons, but none ever led to marriage. Her raunchy, funny memoir, *A View from a Broad*, was published in 1980. The following year she received the Grammy for best female vocalist of the year and made the movie *Jinxed*, which prophetically bombed at the box office. Unhappy during the entire filming, she worked with a producer and costar who were quite outspoken about their dislike of her. When the ordeal was finally over, Bette admitted feeling "completely alone and worthless." Her internal picture of herself as unconventional but attractive was shattered when "they started calling me names." She again visited an analyst.

A gentle, calm woman in private, Bette is usually unrecognized as she strolls the streets of New York studying people. She compares herself to a squat, hardworking tugboat and insists that sometimes on stage she surprises even herself. "Who *is* that person?" she wonders, feeling no connection to her brash persona.

An avid reader, Bette has a passion for books on art and the theater, especially "stuff that has gone on before—circus acts, bubble dancers, fan dancers," she says. Her favorite was the Frenchman Le Petomane. "He farted the 'Marseillaise' in tune."

She spends her private time either in her Manhattan loft or her Mediterranean-style house in Beverly Hills. Admitting that there was a time when she felt the need for drugs, she says "but not anymore. I can't stand that overwhelming sense of paranoia and helplessness you get."

Bette admires comedian Richard Pryor because he moves people socially. She constantly looks for new characters to assume, and prides herself on her ability to find new accents and tricks. The quality in herself that she's most proud of is her "heightened sense of the ridiculous, lampshade on the head quality" which influences even her album titles (*Thighs and Whispers*).

Bette for a time was doing a Sophie Tucker character, but "the jokes got so vile, that to save Sophie's memory, I stopped telling Sophie Tucker jokes."

Her character was a vulgar woman who didn't see the harm in having a good laugh and her boyfriend was Ernie who once asked, "Soph, how come you never tell me when you're having an orgasm?" Sophie answers, "Well, Ernie, you're never around."

Another time Soph meets a woman on the street with her breast hanging out of her dress. She says, "Clementine, your left breast is hanging out of your dress." Clementine says, "Oh my God, I musta left the baby on the bus."

While doing a summer concert of *De Tour* (which embodied every emotion anyone could ever expect from one performer) near Detroit in 1983, Bette collapsed from a combination of the 104-degree weather, her run-down condition and a gastrointestinal ailment. "I felt panic-stricken and couldn't stop crying," she later admitted.

After a brief hospital stay, she had recuperated enough to continue the tour. "I'm a bouncer-backer," she says.

Many of the dynamic performer's coworkers have been with her for ten years, and she feels their productions are better than ever. And Bette has just recently had enough confidence to trust her ability to write most of her own material. Her act is still hard physically but emotionally easier. No longer sick before going on, she says the vomiting and cold sweats are finally over.

For her ninth album, *No Frills* (which featured the song "Beast of Burden"), Bette found songs to record from a pile of 2,000 tapes sent in. "I found some great songs," she said. One was from a young all-girl band in Wichita, Kansas. Bette liked in particular one called "Alien Love," but never recorded it. "They didn't have a phone. They didn't have a manager. I couldn't reach them, so I couldn't cut the song."

Though she considered the songs "out-to-lunch" and by 14-year-old girls, "I did flirt with the idea of cranking out a teeny bopper album," she said.

In late 1983 Bette's second book was published and she set off on an exhausting eleven-city tour ("flogging myself into a stupor"), from Manhattan to Miami. *The Saga of Baby Divine* (Crown), came to Bette in a vision that she would write a children's book about a baby. "She'd have red hair, high heels, and say just one word: 'More!'"

Admittedly autobiographical, the poetic tale deals with an outrageous baby who shocks her parents, and the insecurity and alienation with which the author is so familiar. Plucky Baby Divine's message of living life to the fullest appealed to adults as well, and the book became a best seller. It returned to press for a second printing of 50,000 copies shortly after it was published, and was made into an animated television special using the author's voice for the main character.

Bette can keep smiling through hours of book signing, and enjoys a sassy repartee with her fans, who often bring her gifts. Always decked out in a hat from her collection of sequin-and-veil creations (one has a Baby Divine doll in a basket, another a tiny black typewriter swathed in white veiling), she autographs her books in gold ink.

"Any author worth her salt always wears a hat for the public," she says.

In Miami especially, she was mobbed by fans because of her song "Only in Miami," a lament of a young Cuban refugee who misses her homeland. "I like to deal with basic themes," she says of the recording. "This song is about alienation and loneliness and homesickness ... and terror too."

Bette's fans were surprised to learn of her marriage to Martin von Haselberg, a German commodities trader and performance artist. The couple was married by an Elvis impersonator at 2 a.m. during a private $45 ceremony at the Candlelight Wedding Chapel in Las Vegas on December 16, 1984.

Since then, she has appeared in *Down and Out in Beverly Hills* with

Richard Dreyfuss and Nick Nolte, her first movie in four years. (Her next is *Ruthless People*.) Her first all-comedy album, *Mud Will Be Flung Tonight!*, was recorded live in Los Angeles. On the record, she defends her breast obsession, saying everyone needs a specialty: "Do they dump on the Pope 'cause all he ever talks about is God?"

Bette celebrated her 40th birthday and first wedding anniversary in December, 1985. Looking back, she says, "I wish I hadn't been so mean to some people in my name-calling days and I wish I had been a better friend." She also made peace with her father, who still lives in Honolulu. Now contemplating motherhood, Bette thinks she and her husband will be good parents.

"We're both old-fashioned," she says. "In your young life, you rebel against values you think are square. After a while, you realize they are good values and there's a reason they've been around for thousands of years."

Though she is settling into a more tranquil private life, it is likely that Bette will continue to present her unique combination of audacity and vulnerability when performing. Her book *The Saga of Baby Divine* ends with the advice to just be "very enthusiastic." "And I have," says the woman whose motto is: "Cherish forever what makes you unique. You're really a yawn when it goes."

Goldie Hawn

The word "irresistible" is often used to describe the spirited blue-eyed entertainer who tickles the funny bone in fans of all ages. Her trailer on a movie set is usually crowded with friends, family, and dogs. Peers find her a joy to work with. "Absolutely no temperament," "most gifted," "a natural comic talent," they say of one of the few major female stars to successfully cross over from television to films. She now commands $2.5 million per movie, and according to some critics, is the best film comedienne since Carole Lombard.

Goldie Jeanne Hawn was born on November 21, 1945, in Takoma Park, a Maryland suburb of Washington, D.C. When she was 3, her mother, Laura, arranged for her to take tap dancing and ballet lessons at the Roberta Fera School of Dance. The girl expanded her repertoire to include jazz and modern dance by the time she was 12. She took voice lessons from her father, Edward Rutledge Hawn, a direct descendant of Edward Rutledge, the youngest signer of the Declaration of Independence and governor of South Carolina. Goldie says her dad had "a great sense of humor." He was a professional musician who played the clarinet, saxophone and violin with orchestras providing music for the Capitol city's society events. "I get a lot of good things from my mother too . . . a strong woman," she says.

She remembers being "always uninhibited" and enjoyed a happy home life and family support when she decided to pursue an entertainment career. During a 1983 television interview with Barbara Walters, Goldie spoke of her closeness with her father, whose death in June of 1982 affected her deeply.

"I remember almost all of my childhood," she once said, "and all the memories are pleasant."

Seldom invited out on dates, young Goldie was a late bloomer and remembers spending lots of time in the ladies' room at school dances. As a teenager attending Montgomery Blair High School in Silver Spring, Maryland, she concentrated on cheerleading, swimming on the school team, her dancing and dramatic productions in school and the community. Jerry Lewis movies cracked her up. "I would laugh so hard . . . they would kick me out of the theater."

In the absence of a much-hoped-for romance, Goldie directed all her energies toward a career. After a year of teaching dancing and attending drama classes at American University, she moved to a cheap apartment in Manhattan where she scrimped to get by. Within a short time she was involved in a serious auto collision on the West Side Highway. While it left no physical scars, Goldie suffered deep anxiety for months after the accident.

The entertainer's first jobs were as a dancer in summer stock and at the World's Fair Texas Pavilion. Following was a stint doing four shows a night on the go-go dancing circuit in New York and Las Vegas (". . . I worked some *dives*"), where she learned what it was like to be regarded as simply a sexual object.

"It was grim and hard . . . ," she later said of that unhappy time. In response to one offer for success "the easy way," she replied, "If I have to make it that way, I won't go."

Goldie met dancer Gus Trikonis, who was also born on November 21, during musical tent-show productions of *Guys and Dolls* and *Kiss Me Kate*. They married and though broke, they were happy with each other and their circle of friends in New York.

While working in the chorus of a 1967 Andy Griffith television special, Goldie was spotted by an agent who arranged for her to play Sandy, the dizzy neighbor of two disc jockeys in the short-lived CBS-TV situation comedy *Good Morning World*. Around the same time she landed a dancing job in a Disney movie, *The One and Only Genuine Original Family Band*.

Shortly after joining NBC's 1967 hit television show Rowan and Martin's *Laugh-In*, a hodgepodge of sight gags and one-liners, the pixie blonde in the bikini blew her lines at rehearsal. The resulting infectious giggles of embarrassment captivated the producers, so from then on, cue cards were switched and off-camera pranks were used to make her fluff lines and giggle. Her guileless quality intrigued viewers and she quickly became the popular "ding-a-ling" who introduced a guest as Jill Street John and talked about her Street Bernard puppy.

"The character was my creation . . . my sense of humor that enabled me to laugh at my mistakes," she explained. "You had to be 'on' all the time. . . . I had to delve down deep . . . and bring that kind of excitement way up from my insides."

Almost overnight Goldie's life changed — she felt insecure about her new status, the move to California, and her marriage. She has often referred to that time as her life's "toughest period."

George Schlatter, who worked again with Goldie a few years later on a special titled *Goldie and Liza*, admitted that Goldie was much brighter than she was given credit for, another example of how an entertainer's image often works against her.

The comedienne's movie debut was playing Walter Matthau's lover in *Cactus Flower* (1972), while she was still working on *Laugh-In*. The director of the film, Gene Saks, praised her performance: "Never has a girl in her first film been so professional." Critics singled her out, the *New York Times* reporting that her character gave the picture luster and substance, and Judith Crist called Goldie "an intelligent and sensitive performer." Her peers in Hollywood agreed by voting her the recipient of an Oscar for best actress in a supporting role, and the National Association of Theatre Owners presented her with the "female star of the year" award.

Lily Tomlin, her *Laugh-In* coworker and lifelong movie aficionado, once said, "I have this inner-outer theory of what makes charisma. Goldie has an inner glow and an outer twinkle. You can't beat that combo."

Goldie next played opposite Peter Sellers (and refused to play a scene in the nude) in *There's a Girl in My Soup*, then starred in *Butterflies Are Free* with Edward Albert and Eileen Heckart.

Her television special, *Pure Goldie*, in 1971 prompted *Variety* to report that Goldie's talents were four-fold as "Goldie the Beautiful Blonde, Goldie the Comedienne, Goldie the Singer, Goldie the Dancer." Especially noted was "her built-in sense of presence and timing." The large number of viewers tuning in gave the show the highest New York Nielsen rating for that time slot, topping even *The Carol Burnett Show*.

Unfortunately, Goldie's phenomenal success took its toll on her marriage to Gus (who was struggling with his own career) and they separated. To deal with her problems, she began a seven-year process of psychoanalysis. Friend and comedienne Ruth Buzzi remarked, "Goldie's really a one-man woman . . . in need of a serious relationship."

More movies followed: *The Sugarland Express* (1974), a comedy-drama in which she played a witless mother trying to save her baby from adoption, and *The Girl from Petrovka* (1974), the story of a Russian girl who loves an American journalist. Hal Holbrook acknowledged his costar's "total trust in her intuition." Goldie portrayed a dippy hooker with bank robber Warren Beatty in *Dollars* (1971), and again was Beatty's girlfriend in *Shampoo* (1975), a movie which resulted in a flood of publicity for her. *Foul Play* (1978), with Dudley Moore, Chevy Chase and Marilyn Sokol was a comedy thriller set in San Francisco.

Goldie has always described herself as "old-fashioned" and a "very middle-class person" who wanted a nice house and children. Her intense yearning for motherhood was finally satisfied after she married Bill Hudson, already an established performer with the pop-rock group Hudson Brothers. Son Oliver Rutledge Hudson was born in 1976, and Goldie abandoned superstardom to settle into contented domesticity in a sprawling Pacific Palisades house crammed with antiques.

"Being a mother," she said happily, "has made me feel as if I've found a missing part of me."

However, the entertainer couldn't resist the chance to produce and star in *Private Benjamin* after reading the script. She considered it a chance to express some of her views about women. Though conspicuously pregnant again, Goldie took the script around to the offices of studio heads herself. "The time had come for me to become a businesswoman," she said.

Because *Foul Play* had made over $50 million by then, she had some leverage in persuading studios to accept her in the provocative role of a woman who finds independence on her own terms. She was warned by some executives that she was making a big mistake.

After Warner Brothers signed a contract and a suitable director was hired, Goldie, as executive producer, became involved in every aspect of the production from script revisions and casting to choosing the promotion close-up of Private Judy Benjamin's exasperated but determined face. She even read with those who were auditioning, a chore most stars wouldn't consider. Goldie not only managed to protect her own interests in a male-run industry, but gained everyone's respect while charming both those who agreed and disagreed with her ideas about the film. "I just stuck to my guns," she said, ". . . and this was hard for me because I didn't want people to see me as a bitch."

Judy Benjamin in *Private Benjamin* is a Jewish-American "princess" who finally leaves the domineering men in her life to forge an independent existence. Goldie was attracted to the script because she related to Judy's girlhood dreams of marital happiness. She also wanted to prove a point.

"There's a correlation between Judy Benjamin and my *Laugh-In* character," she later said of her own battle to gain acceptance as "a person who has a brain.... I'm smarter than people give me credit for."

Already committed for *Seems Like Old Times*, Goldie's time was dispersed over the making of two movies and her family responsibilities, which included new daughter Kate. *Private Benjamin* costar Eileen Brennan remarked of the juggling act, "What Goldie did was incredible!" Nevertheless, conflicting time schedules and pressures led to her separation and subsequent divorce from Bill Hudson.

"I'm 35, and now I'm gonna have to learn to *date* again!" she said during an interview with *Rolling Stone*.

Goldie worked hard to promote *Private Benjamin* after its release. The feminist comedy was 1980's top comedy film, a $175 million hit at the box office and Goldie was nominated for best actress. When *Private Benjamin* became a television series, Eileen Brennan again played her original movie role. The two women remained good friends and, in October of 1982, while leaving a restaurant in Venice, California, where they had met for lunch, Eileen was struck by a car and critically injured. Goldie cradled her friend in her arms until paramedics arrived to rush her to the hospital. She agonized over the tragedy of her buddy whose recovery and long, valiant rehabilitation took many long months. Eventually, Eileen was able to work again, beginning with television guest appearances.

Charles Grodin, who played Goldie's husband in *Seems Like Old Times*, explained Goldie's popularity. "She's got a good spirit, which comes over on the screen. She loves to laugh."

The actress's new contract with Universal Studios included provisions for office space. "Goldie Hawn has offices at Universal," she exclaimed. "Isn't that insane?"

The comedienne-producer has become recognized as a shrewd investor and has since produced and starred in *Swing Shift*, a romantic drama set in an aircraft plant during World War II (she plays a Rosie the Riveter character during the mass entrance of women into the American work force), and *Protocol*, a comedy about the U.S. government. Returning to the likeable, goofy gamine role that her fans love, Goldie plays a cocktail waitress who becomes a congressional candidate. The movie, which was compared by critics to *Mr. Smith Goes to Washington*, was dedicated to her father. In her latest movie, *Wildcats*, a sports comedy, Goldie plays a football coach who is assigned to a tough Chicago ghetto team (one student is six feet, five inches tall and weighs 410 pounds). She has to overcome their blatant chauvinism and locker room language before whipping them into shape.

Goldie retains her "basically middle-class" values and is content to be no longer considered the sex symbol of *Laugh-In* fame. Mostly shunning glittering Hollywood parties, she frowns on the promiscuity and drugs so prevalent in the industry. Though she has matured and is accorded respect, Goldie admits to feelings ranging from klutzy to sophisticated. "Sometimes I wonder exactly what propelled me out into the world to seek fame and fortune," she has mused.

Her difficulty in balancing a professional and private life is not an uncommon problem among women today. She has a "terrible guilt about work" and tries to compensate for being away from her children by spending her free time cooking and caring for them at their Malibu beach home. Never expecting to find herself a single parent, she considers her responsibility awesome, though she and Hudson share custody and are on friendly terms. Since making *Swing Shift*, she and costar Kurt Russell have had a close romantic relationship.

"There are values and traditions I've had since I was a kid, and plans and hopes about how the future would turn out," she says. "A lot of dreams didn't come true."

Goldie appears much younger than her years, dresses simply, and likes comfortable surroundings. Early American primitive paintings and folk art have always been a penchant, reflecting her "naive idealistic attitude toward life." However, she's worked hard to change that, too.

"If there's one thing I've learned in life, it's not to expect too much.... Whatever I get, I'm happy for."

LaWanda Page

Born in Cleveland, Ohio, on October 19, 1920, LaWanda Page spent many years in show business, taking small parts and making little money, before she became established. Her big break came when she was cast as sharp-tongued Aunt Esther on the hit television series *Sanford & Son*. Since then, the witty comedienne has often been invited to participate in television "roasts" of celebrities and has no trouble holding her own with the likes of veterans Don Rickles and Milton Berle.

LaWanda joined the popular comedy show *Sanford & Son*, in which Redd Foxx starred as the 65-year-old proprietor of a Watts junkyard, in 1973. As Aunt Esther Anderson, sister of Fred Sanford's late wife,

Elizabeth, she bickered and feuded with Fred (and most everyone else) for the next four years. Esther owned the Sanford Arms, a run-down rooming house next to his junkyard, so their paths crossed regularly. Her verbal lashings could inflict welts on Fred from across the room. Fred's friend Grady once joked that he kind of liked having her around because "she makes the junk look so pretty." Self-righteous Esther, who said she needed both hands free to preach some gospel into Fred's heart, carried a Bible and chastised Fred for his shifty ways. "Thou shalt not steal — that's in the Top 10!"

While gaining national exposure on the show, LaWanda's home life demanded a great deal of her time and energy. Not wanting to put her 82-year-old mother in a nursing home, she took care of the woman herself. She later spoke of juggling her responsibilities and a television career: "By the time I had success, she was very sick and senile," LaWanda said. "I'd go to work and leave her with a nurse.... It was pretty hard."

Wanting to show her mother that she had finally made it in show business, the performer plugged in a television set near her mother's bed so the woman could watch an episode of *Sanford & Son.*

"I got her glasses and she sat up for a minute and looked real hard ... and she said, 'LaWandoo' — that's what she always called me — 'La Wandoo, you shouldn't hit on old Fred Sanford like that.'" LaWanda's mother died in 1976.

When Foxx couldn't iron out his differences with NBC in 1977, he quit the show. Then *Sanford Arms* took its place and Aunt Esther was left in charge of Fred's property. Fred and his son, Lamont, supposedly had retired to Arizona. The show, which starred Theodore Wilson and kept most of the same supporting characters, was short-lived.

In the meantime, Redd Foxx became the host of his own comedy-variety show on ABC. The hour-long, black-oriented show was titled *Redd Foxx.* LaWanda was Fred's guest several times during its five-month run. In 1979, LaWanda became Charlene Jenkins on *Detective School*, a summer show which ran from July to November. She also appeared as "Ma" on a hot-rod police show titled *B.A.D. Cats* the following year, but it was cancelled after a short time.

It was also in 1980 that Redd Foxx decided to bring his junkyard back to television in a resurrected format titled *Sanford.* LaWanda was again called upon to do battle with Fred in the persona of Aunt Esther. But before she agreed to show up for work, the producers of the show had to meet her asking price.

"I wasn't going to take a step backwards because I've stayed down too long as it is," she said. "I just won't take any jobs that are not going to pay my price.... Because you stay in this thing long enough, you know what you're worth."

LaWanda in recent years has joined a growing number of black performers protesting that blacks, even those who star in television series, are underpaid as compared to other performers. Their complaints about the scarcity of parts and their struggles for equal salaries and residual rights have sometimes resulted in boycotts and lawsuits.

The new *Sanford* show had programming difficulties. After jumping from one time slot to another, the series went off the air in May of 1981. LaWanda continued to play guest roles on shows such as *Diff'rent Strokes*. She told *Jet* magazine that she supported Gary Coleman's decision to hold out for a bigger share of syndication profits.

"I did a *Diff'rent Strokes* with him and I played a long-lost cousin," she said. "The night that we were taping the show, my brother died. That little boy remembered all of my lines. If it hadn't been for him, I never would have made that show 'cause I forgot every line. That little boy is definitely the star of that show!"

When she's not in front of a camera or out-zinging her contemporaries at celebrity roasts, LaWanda attends premieres and parties. She loves dressing up. One of her wilder costumes includes a pair of shoes with plastic heels that flash on and off with a built-in electronic light. Those set her back $2,000!

Gilda Radner

Many well-known funny women have emerged from Chicago's Second City and its Canadian counterpart in Toronto. Elaine May, Anne Meara, Valerie Harper, Madeline Kahn, Barbara Harris, and Mary Steenburgen were followed by a second wave of comediennes: Andrea Martin, Catherine O'Hara, and Gilda Radner. A newer crop of graduates includes Mary Gross, Betty Thomas, and Shelley Long. All are bright, ambitious, and willing to take a chance.

Gilda was one of the original troupe of stand-up satirists on NBC's tremendously successful *Saturday Night Live*, which debuted in 1975. Her portrayals ran the gamut from klutzy Lisa Loopner to regal Baba Wawa. An ability to play funny people in a funny way prompted one critic to compare her to Peter Sellers. Another, in 1979, described her as a "33-year-old woman who appears to have a Band-Aid on her knee."

"This Jewish girl from Detroit," as she describes herself, was born on June 28, 1946, into a suburban Detroit family with one older brother. Her mother named her after the Rita Hayworth character in the movie *Gilda*. She knew early on that she wanted to tell jokes and be funny. She once described herself as "a very fat child," who realized that she'd never "make it on looks."

Gilda's father was enamored of show business and owned a hotel that periodically housed road company actors. With the complimentary tickets they gave him, he and his young daughter often attended their shows at the Riviera Theatre. Gilda was just 14 when he died, but by then his love for show business had been instilled in her.

"My dad was real funny . . . he loved to sing . . . and tap dance . . . I feel that some part of my father is back alive in me, back doing what he always wanted to do," she later said.

Gilda feels that she may have also inherited some humor from her mother's side of the family, especially from her maternal grandmother, who was known as a marvelous story teller. When Gilda finished fifth grade, she transferred to the Liggett School for Girls where wit was more appreciated than looks. "I was a cutup and silly and well liked for that reason."

Her first role came at age 12 when she played the innkeeper in a Christmas play at school. Her loud voice drew the faculty's attention, and she was included in other productions from then on. Pleased that her comedy reflects the transition of women's roles, she says, "During the fifties, when I was in school, being funny wasn't considered attractive in a woman, but today it is."

After high school, Gilda attended the University of Michigan off and on, majoring in dramatics. She also made a trip to Europe, worked in a record store, a china shop and a hamburger place. In 1969 she quit school for good to follow her boyfriend, a metal sculptor, to Canada. While working in a Toronto theater box office and playing minor roles in plays, she heard about auditions being held for a Toronto production of the Broadway religious rock musical *Godspell*. She walked in off the street, auditioned, and got the part.

"A lot of people think you have to have show business connections, but I've always maintained that all you have to do is keep working at it," she insists. "If it's meant to happen, it will."

After a year with *Godspell*, Gilda joined the improvisational company Second City on Lombard Street — Toronto's offshoot of the original in Chicago. She impressed Second City's founder Bernard Sahlins who found Gilda "the same offstage and on. She has the same vulnerability."

It was at Second City that the newcomer met the future producer of *Saturday Night Live*, Lorne Michaels, and her colleagues Dan Aykroyd and Bill Murray. When one critic told Gilda that she was nice looking and didn't need to be gawky or have a bag over her head to be funny, she took his advice. "I concentrated on being more attractive *and* funny."

Gilda returned to the United States for a one-line part as a chanting Buddhist in the film *The Last Detail* (Columbia, 1973). The next year she appeared on the *National Lampoon Radio Hour*, and in the Off-Broadway revue *The National Lampoon Show*. In the latter, she played "Rhoda Tyler Moore," a blind girl trying to make it in New York. Trying to escape her sadistic boyfriend (played by John Belushi) she tripped over things and ran into walls. Gilda got laughs, but she also got bruises.

"I'm not afraid to do anything comedically," she has said. "I don't worry about femininity. I see that being funny . . . frightens some men. But . . . it just won't shut me up."

NBC's *Saturday Night Live* premiered on October 18, 1975, and was an enormous hit, eventually reaching 10 million viewers. Lorne Michaels' idea was to produce a show that was different, so he chose New York instead of Los Angeles, went live, and took chances. The Not Ready for Prime Time Players, a group of zanies he hired for the show, included Chevy Chase, John Belushi, Bill Murray, Dan Aykroyd, Laraine Newman, Jane Curtin, Garrett Morris, and Gilda, whom he signed before all the others.

"I felt there was a remarkable quality to her, a goodness which came through whatever she was doing," Michaels said.

For the next couple of years, Gilda's life revolved around the show. She even spent her off hours in her office and dreaded vacations. Her dedication and talents didn't go unnoticed. ". . . she doesn't let you down," Michaels explained. "If you're a writer, she'll take what you do off the page and make more of it than there is — she always makes you look good."

Though no one player was meant to shine brighter than the others, Chevy Chase dominated the show from the beginning. When he left, John Belushi gained the popularity edge, and Gilda later took his place. Gilda (all 105 pounds of her) with the frizzy tangle of hair and tippy-toe walk became recognized by her fans wherever she went.

Her characters also became familiar: bratty 8-year-old Judy Miller, brash newscaster Roseanne Roseannadanna who liked to talk about unappealing topics like armpit hair and "somethin' stuck in your teeth and you don't know what the heck it is," gum-cracking Jewish princess Rhonda Weiss, punk rock star Candy Slice, and 80-year-old Emily Litella, the dotty little woman who expounded her beliefs about "Violins on Television" and "Soviet Jewelry." Besides reporter Barbara Walters, Gilda's numerous impersonations included Lucille Ball's Lucy Ricardo and Olympic gymnast Nadia Comaneci.

In 1978, Gilda was honored by the television industry when she was awarded an Emmy for "outstanding continuing performance by a supporting actress in music or variety." During her years at *SNL*, Gilda depended greatly on Lorne Michaels when she had to make decisions such as when she turned down the $850,000 offer to play Olive Oyl in Robert Altman's movie *Popeye*.

Gilda has always been lavish in her praise for the writers of the show. She credits them with not only collaborating in the creation of certain characters, but actually giving her off-camera coaching during the telecast. Writers Alan Zweibel and Rose Shuster helped develop "Roseanne Roseannadanna" (Roseanne's "It's always something" was inspired by Gilda's father), and Marilyn Miller collaborated on "Judy Miller." The first time Gilda (then 32) did Judy, she hurt her ribs badly in dress rehearsal and had to be taped up. She insisted on keeping the skit in the show.

"Gilda is able to use her body in ways that haven't even been tapped yet," Marilyn said at the time. "She's fearless."

A habit of getting louder and more boisterous when she senses the audience's loss of interest earned her the name "Kamikaze Radner" on the set of the show. Singing alone when she did punk rock star Candy Slice was a turning point for Gilda; she then was ready to test herself in other areas. "I intend to do everything that frightens me," she said.

After polishing her acting skills in summer stock, in 1978 Gilda bounced off to Broadway with her *personae*, singing, tap dancing, and gymnastics in a one-woman show *Gilda Radner—Live from New York*. It was produced by Lorne Michaels and directed by Mike Nichols. From the opening song, *Let's Talk Dirty to the Animals*, Gilda wowed audiences and critics. A recording based on the show was later done, as well as a motion picture in 1980 titled *Gilda Live*.

When Gilda left *SNL*, she received offers for her own series and specials. She finally signed a contract with NBC stipulating that she would be paid a considerable sum just for not signing with any other network. She went to work in a movie in which she plays the 28-year-old presidential daughter in Buck Henry's farce *First Family* (Warner Bros.) with Bob Newhart and Madeline Kahn. The daughter's attempts to date are continually thwarted by the Secret Service, who keep bringing her back to the White House. Gilda and Buck met when he hosted *SNL*. "I used to tease him to write a movie, so I could be in it," Gilda stated.

Mike Nichols also directed her in Jean Kerr's Broadway comedy *Lunch Hour*, which opened in late 1980. (At Nichols' insistence, Jean Kerr saw the movie *Gilda Live*. Gilda's nostalgic song at the end, "Honey, Touch Me with My Clothes On," convinced her that the comedienne was right for the part.) In the play, Gilda and costar Sam Waterson portray two people conspiring to end the affair of her husband and his wife. Before the show opened, Gilda had second thoughts about appearing in a Broadway play. She said her biggest fear was coming out on stage and hearing someone in the audience yell, "Hey, Gilda! Do Roseanne Rose-annadanna!" Though she worried about the critics, the reviews were generally favorable.

In the spring of 1980 Gilda married G.E. Smith, a 28-year-old, boyish-looking rock guitarist who had played in one of the skits in her Broadway show. The evening of their wedding day, they celebrated at a screening party for the film of *Gilda Live*. The marriage was short-lived.

Gilda, who wants to concentrate on making films, is aware of the dangers of celebrity status and doesn't like being a product or "brand name like Scott Towels." She feels that maintaining that special "spark that made you get where you did in the first place" is more important than audience adoration. On occasion she even denies being Gilda Radner when fans spot her. "When I'm grocery shopping, I'm not Rose-anne Roseannadanna," she says.

She is also on guard against taking herself too seriously, and tries not to theorize about comedy, saying simply that "My comedy is an obser-vance of life."

Roseanne and Emily are Gilda's best-known characters. Emily Litella is based on a much-loved servant named Dibby who helped raise Gilda. She joined in when young Gilda did skits at the tea parties they put on. Dibby taught Gilda to see things in a comical light, and to laugh at herself first, before others had the chance.

While promoting her book *Roseanne Roseannadanna* on the *David Letterman Show* in late 1983, Gilda called Dibby, then 90 years old, at her home in Canada. At the end of their conversation, she good-naturedly said "Never mind," for Gilda, David and the audience.

"She's wonderful," Gilda told him. "We'd call her up to get her voice intonation and see what she had to say before we'd write the Emily Litellas."

In September, 1984, Gilda married actor Gene Wilder in a private ceremony in southern France, following the showing of *The Woman in Red* at the American film festival in Deauville. Gilda plays his lovesick secretary in the movie. The couple had earlier costarred in *Hanky-Panky* (1982).

Over the years, Gilda has been compared to Gracie Allen, Zasu Pitts, Judy Holliday, and Beatrice Lillie, but remains her own in-congruous combination of slapstick and innocence. She is known for her kindness and thoughtful deeds and is not temperamental. Though she loves being a woman and feels she's aging well, Gilda admits that she'll probably never learn to relax. "I just never let go of my child self. Being a child is being impulsive. Keeping that part of me alive is very useful in comedy."

Jane Curtin

Jane Therese Curtin was born in Cambridge, Massachusetts, on September 6, 1947, the daughter of John and Mary Farrell Curtin. Her father was an insurance executive and her mother Boston's first female probation officer. An upper middle-class upbringing included Catholic boarding school and a proper Boston debut. After earning her A.A. at Elizabeth Seton Junior College in 1967, she briefly attended Northeastern University before heading for New York to pursue a career.

Soon after her arrival, Jane joined the cast of *The Proposition*, laying her comedic dexterity on the line every night as the company of comic improvisors performed skits based on suggestions by the audience. The show enjoyed a run of 1,109 performances. In 1973, Jane toured with the road production of *Last of the Red Hot Lovers* and the following year, wrote and performed in the Off-Broadway revue titled *Pretzels*.

Jane married producer Patrick Lynch in 1975. The couple had met on a blind date. A short time after their wedding, she tried out for NBC's *Saturday Night Live* at an open audition and landed a job. The reserved young woman, thrust overnight into one of the nuttiest and most rambunctious casts in television history, quickly became familiar to the millions who viewed the program every week. One of Jane's recurring characters was a no-nonsense newscaster, whose patience was tried by the circuitous ramblings of Roseannadanna, played by Gilda Radner. "That's disgusting," she'd hiss at the frizzy-haired guest who always managed to offend her host's sensibilities. Jane says the funniest thing she ever did on the show was "ripping open my blouse on *Update*." She later said she didn't fit in very well at *SNL*, though she got along fine with the other cast members: "Here I was, this nice Catholic girl, and suddenly I'm this rock 'n' roll cult figure. After the show I'd just go home to bed, while everybody else kept partying."

Upon leaving *Saturday Night Live* a few years later, Jane had no trouble finding work in films and television. She appeared in the film *How to Beat the High Cost of Living* (1980) with Richard Benjamin and Susan Saint James. Costarring with Joanne Woodward, she also appeared in the television presention of George Bernard Shaw's comedy *Candida*, and the HBO special *Bedrooms* with Renee Taylor and Louise Lasser.

In 1984, after considerable reluctance about being cast in a maternal role, Jane again teamed up with Susan Saint James in the prime-time television sitcom *Kate & Allie* on CBS. They portray two divorced women, Allie Lowell and Kate McArdle, who live together with their three children in Greenwich Village. As strong, intelligent women, they don't have to "jiggle" to keep viewers interested. Both in their thirties, Allie (portrayed by Jane) stays at home and efficiently looks after the house and children, while Kate goes off every day to work in a travel agency. Earning high marks for portraying independent women determined to succeed, the show was renewed for the following season, and Jane won an Emmy for best actress in a comedy series.

"I have no idea what I am saying," she said upon winning. "I always felt that I was a bridesmaid in this year's race."

Jane and her husband, who live in a 50-year-old house in Connecticut, became parents of a daughter, Tess, in 1983, so the idea of a steady job with regular hours appeals to her. "I wanted to be near my husband and to give my children the structure I had as a kid," she says.

Her image as a cult figure has faded and Jane is now settling into a role in which she feels more comfortable. ("This isn't like work, it's play," she says.) If high ratings and good reviews are any indication, it looks as though her perfect setup may last quite a while. And television viewers will reap the benefits.

Catherine O'Hara

She has been called "the funniest woman on television." Blonde and shapely with a throaty voice, Catherine O'Hara possesses chameleon-like powers when doing her impeccable incarnations of both celebrities and her own make-believe personalities.

Catherine was born the fifth of seven children in 1954 in Toronto, Ontario, Canada. After attending Catholic grade schools, she switched to a public high school where she became a cheerleader, but never attended the prom. Though she entertained thoughts of becoming an actress, it never occurred to her that humor might be a part of her future. "It wasn't supposed to be ladylike for a girl to joke," she says.

Following high school, Catherine lived at home, worked in a fabric store and occasionally ventured out to auditions, which she dreaded. Nothing happened until her brother Marcus, a waiter at Toronto's Second City comedy club, got her a job there as a waitress. Eventually they were both hired by the Second City touring company, and then Catherine became Gilda Radner's understudy. When Gilda left for *Saturday Night Live,* the newcomer took her place and blossomed on her own.

The next three years prepared Catherine for her big break in 1976. Two women were needed for the new *Second City Television Show* and

Catherine's talents as a first-rate mimic landed her a job. She and Andrea
Martin made up the female counterpart of the company of loonies known
as *SCTV*, an improvisational comedy show filmed in Toronto for Canadian television and syndicated in 1977 in America, where it captured a
cult of viewers and really hit its stride. The show-within-a-show that
spoofed television became an instant classic. Critics showered praise,
calling it "superb" and "uproariously funny."

The show was set at the mythical Second City television station,
Channel 109, in Mellonville, Canada. Its premise was that the performers, fed up with the fare TV had to offer, decided to do something
about it and began their own station. The parsimonious station operator
beamed his shows off a satellite fashioned from a rotating hot-dog spit.

The cast introduced their own character creations and delivered the
most acerbic send-ups of celebrities home viewers had ever seen. Besides
Catherine and Andrea Martin, the cast included John Candy, Eugene
Levy, Joe Flaherty, Hårold Ramis, and Dave Thomas. At first, Catherine
and Andrea felt left out because all the writing was done by men. "They'd
write a fifty-page scene where the girls had two lines.... After a while,
we started writing for ourselves."

When the show later won an Emmy for writing, Catherine was
among the eighteen writers who trooped onstage to accept the awards.
Catherine was a natural for glamour-puss roles such as her own creation
of pouting, finger-snapping songbird Lola Heatherton, who wore pink
lipstick and long bangle earrings. At the slightest provocation, Lola
threw her head back and laughed—"Haaa ha ha ha."

Everyone at SCTV was wary of Lola. After all, she had once had
a nervous breakdown on the air and made disparaging remarks about
certain coworkers' love-making skills. "Wait till I shake your tree, boy,"
she threatened one admirer. "I'll break those Christmas balls."

Catherine's impersonations of wisecracking Lucille Ball, smirking
Rona Barrett, Meryl Streep, and Katherine Hepburn (with sprawling
postures and palsied trembling) were right on target. Her stable of
characters grew to include Faye Dunaway, Diane Keaton, Brooke
Shields, and many others.

"I think the success of my work stems from being truthful," she said
during an interview with *Rolling Stone*. "... when I pretend to be someone else, I go to the depths of nothingness. The more I do that—become
nothing—and the more I let the character take over, the more I feel like
that person. When you become the person, nothing is contrived."

Television critic James Wolcott reported that "Catherine O'Hara is
funny and squeezable and sane, and yet tantalizingly vague, leaving
scented wisps of enigma in her wake.... Satiny-svelte as she is, (she) contains multitudes ..."

In early 1982, the show (which had been moved to Edmonton), was extended to ninety minutes and renamed *SCTV Network*. For the cast, eighteen-hour days became the norm. In spite of being hailed as a brilliant comedy performer, Catherine decided to leave *SCTV* in June of that year, returning from time to time to appear in guest spots.

"People thought I was nuts," Catherine says of her decision to exit when she was doing so well. She felt that the long filming sessions in Edmonton, four hours by air from Toronto, left little time for anything else. "It just wasn't fun anymore," she explained.

She also feels that she has paid a price for losing her own personality so completely in her impersonations—"... that makes *me* hard to remember." Fans often tell her how much they enjoyed all the girls on *SCTV*, not realizing that there were only two—Catherine and Andrea. Because of a scarcity of good parts and her aversion to auditioning, Catherine turned to writing. ("I'd like to write a nice, relaxed funny film ...") The performer was sorely missed every week. In addition, the show that many called "the funniest show on the air," couldn't survive the Friday after-midnight time slot on NBC and was subsequently cancelled.

In 1984, Catherine again took on other *personae* on the short-lived television comedy program titled *The New Show*. In a Naughty Lady episode, she portrayed a harried mother (in bathrobe and curlers, nervously chain-smoking), doing the ironing and yelling at her two bratty kids. Putting down her iron to answer the phone, her shrill voice changed to a sexy purr. Interrupting her erotic tête-à-tête from time to time, she held her hand over the phone to scream at her son Billy. Then she sweetly murmured to her gentleman caller: "Why don't you take off some of your clothes?" just as her husband came home with the news that he'd got his raise and she could give up her job as the Naughty Lady. She happily hung up on the panting caller, who was eagerly awaiting further instructions.

Catherine's characters are provocative, arrogant, and very, very funny. She does some celebrities better than they do themselves, and seems destined for a long career as a funny woman — as long as it doesn't interfere with her personal priorities. The comedienne, who has been teased by her coworkers for being a "non-swinger," loves the city of Toronto and enjoys being close to her family.

"I believe in family. I also have a basic belief that God takes care of me," she says. "I want it all. I want to get married, have kids and do good films to make people laugh and cry at the same time."

Andrea Martin

Andrea, who considers herself an "instinctive" performer, was born in 1947 and raised in Portland, Maine. Feeling she didn't fit in because of her background and appearance, the young Armenian girl used comedy to get attention. Performing in school plays and working on skits in dancing class led her to studying dramatics, and she later moved to Toronto, Ontario, Canada, where she felt more accepted.

In her first professional job, Andrea toured the United States in *You're A Good Man, Charlie Brown*. That led to being hired for parts in *Private Lives, Candide* and *Godspell*. While appearing as several different characters in the revue *What's a Nice Country Like You Doing in a State Like This?*, the tiny performer with enormous brown eyes was invited to join Toronto's Second City. "I was scared because there wasn't a script. . . . But I loved it. . . . It was all my own expression," she later said.

Andrea soon became a charter member of *SCTV*, the hilariously irreverent Canadian television series about a fictional television network set in Melonville, Canada. The show premiered in 1976 and quickly generated a fanatical following of American fans when it was syndicated the following year. Critics touted the show as being "sophisticated satire" and "smashingly funny . . . needlingly accurate."

Shows were taped in Toronto so the productions wouldn't be part of the scene in New York or California, home bases for the programs being spoofed. The skits were written from the cast's own ideas, then taped and edited, and finally polished for production. Andrea eagerly attended the weekly creative free-for-alls with the male writer-performers of the show — Joe Flaherty, John Candy, Eugene Levy, Harold Ramis, and Dave Thomas. However, some of her original ideas that she instinctively *knew* were funny got a cool reception from the men. So she began writing and performing her own one-woman skits on the show, soon becoming one of the least inhibited performers in the troupe.

Andrea did send-ups of Liza Minelli and Indira Gandhi, but with her own special touch of dementia. She also helped write and performed in *SCTV*'s takeoffs on movies and fake commercials, often difficult to distinguish from real ones, because of the cast's brilliance at satire and their sharp attention to detail.

The olive-skinned brunette (who has been turned down for certain roles because of her looks, not a lack of talent), immediately hit it off with blonde, blue-eyed Catherine O'Hara. Their collaboration (Catherine usually outlined a scene and Andrea would add the character) resulted

in many hilarious skits. In one titled "Only for Women," Catherine
played an unhappy divorcée being interviewed by a militant feminist
(Andrea) who bragged, "Who needs men? . . . I love cooking for one . . .
waking up with the blankets on me in the morning." But gradually worn
down by her sniffling red-eyed guest, Andrea concluded the interview by
wailing, "No marriage, no proposal, not even a cheap one-night stand.
Oh, my God I need a man." Both women were sobbing as the skit ended.

"I enjoyed working with Catherine," Andrea later said. "The pieces
I liked the most are the ones I did with her."

While with the show, Andrea met *SCTV* writer Bob Dolman. They
married and became parents of a son named Jack, who at the age of three
months made a brief appearance on the show. In December, 1982, Andrea
(expecting her second child), expressed her concern that she no longer
could devote so much time to the show. "Maybe it's all in my head," she
said. "Maybe I always thought that my work can only be really good
when it encompasses my entire life."

Saturday night viewers looked forward to Andrea's caustic imita-
tions, which ran the gamut from Cher to Mother Teresa. As deadpan sex
therapist, repressed Dr. Cheryl Kinsey, she started twitching every time
she talked about sex. One of her Kinsey skits almost went too far. Dr.
Cheryl coached women on how to fake an orgasm with lines such as,
"Make me a woman, big boy," and "You're so good." She concluded that
". . . nine out of ten males will believe anything, especially if it confirms
their virility." Her lines made network executives jumpy, but they were
finally allowed to be aired.

"Andrea is really refreshing, because she has no inhibitions at all,"
joked Dave Thomas. "You can drop your pants in front of Andrea and
Andrea will go, 'Good, dear. So that's what it's like, huh?' Catherine will
be down the hall and out the door, will have ordered a cab and got *into*
it before the belt hits the ground."

Not liking to analyze her comedy, Andrea has said she not only
observes others, but delves into her own personality to create original
characters (she also finds costumes and props helpful). She then does the
character for a friend or family member and relies on them to tell her if
it works. She says she can't watch any television without thinking,
"Could I parody that?"

Andrea's fans, who can still enjoy *SCTV* reruns, grow nostalgic
when her name is mentioned. Who can forget her babushka-clad Pirini
Scleroso, eagerly repeating English phrases, but dismally failing to even
come close; or Libby Wolfson, host of the *You're So Beautiful Show*,
neurotically whiffing her underarms when she thought she was off-
camera.

Best remembered among Andrea's stable of characters is boisterous

Edith Prickley, Melonville's television station manager, who was always rounding up her "pals" to join her in a madcap adventure. Lewd-mouthed Edith was convinced that every male she met had lustful intentions toward her. After all, what red-blooded man could resist that vision in a leopard-spotted coat and pillbox hat, that charmer who wore rhinestone-studded glasses and snorted when she laughed? Edith did have her moments of glory, however. She once danced wildly with Pierre Trudeau at Studio 54. When Trudeau whispered, "We're very much alike, Edith," she brightened and said, "Don't tell me you get cramps, too."

Mary Gross

She seems the epitome of sweetness—the demure manner, tiny voice, wide blue eyes. Even her handwriting is ladylike, the perfectly formed letters bringing to mind childhood memories of spelling words carefully written on a blackboard. Therefore, audiences are completely caught off guard when this *adorable* person viciously cuts down another character in a skit or goes into a tirade. Though she still can't believe she's getting paid for what she does on television every week, Mary Gross is on her way.

The lanky brown-haired comedienne was born in Chicago in 1953. She has early childhood memories of family get-togethers where her mother's side of the family donned funny clothes and hammed it up (her father was more reserved). At the time, Mary had no idea she had inherited the same wackiness that made family parties so riotous. "I felt *so* embarrassed," Mary recalls of her mother's flamboyant behavior.

Now she proudly admits that she incorporates many of her mother's traits into the characters she plays. Mary's first taste of performing occurred when she was "an enormous hit" in a history club production at Madonna High School in Chicago. Wearing a tutu, pink tights and a wig of cotton balls glued on a paper bag, she played Louis XIV.

"I was very shy and probably didn't talk until I was in my teens," she says. "I had decided to become a writer and was majoring in English at Loyola University when I did a very daring thing—I answered an ad for a comedy workshop."

Attending only with the intention of learning about writing comedy sketches, Mary was in for a surprise. The director of the workshop (The Reification Company, an improvisational group) ignored the newcomer's timidity and shoved her on stage. She flopped dismally. But her pride

Mary Gross

made her return and after several weeks she got the hang of *reacting* to a funny situation instead of trying to *act* funny. Though she still had stage fright, she was soon appearing in the company's comedy reviews. "It only took a few times on stage and something clicked," she says. "Getting laughs gave me a special power over people that I didn't have before."

Her first roles were in studio productions at the Victory Gardens Theatre: playing a mute in "Peppermints," and the Statue of Liberty in "East Liberty, Pa." After two years with The Reification Company, Mary replaced Audrie Neenan, who was leaving Chicago's Second City, an institution in the Windy City's night life.

The comedienne occasionally worked with original *Saturday Night Live* performers John Belushi and Bill Murray. Making her Second City debut in the company's revue *I Remember Dada*, she portrayed a college student who had to confess to her parents that her obsession in life was to become a mime.

Critics were immediately impressed with Mary (who also worked in the resident company's revues *Freud Slipped Here* and *Live from the*

Second City), and predicted great things for her. In Second City's sixtieth revue, *Well, I'm Off to the Thirty Years' War* or *Swing Your Partner to the Right*, she worked with Jim Belushi, Danny Breen, Meagen Fay, Bruce Jarchow, Lance Kinsey and Rob Riley. *Variety* chose that production as one of the best revues for the cabaret theater.

Mary came into her own for a "landmark performance" of her portrayal of a girl in a Fotomat booth who lives vicariously through her customers' photographs — gradually her fantasy world revolves around an affair with a man who drops off his film for processing. "I based her behavior on a girl I knew who told outrageous stories to get attention," she admits.

Other sketches which had the audience howling: Mary as the mother of James Joyce (Bruce Jarchow), Mary and Meagen Fay as a pair of chillingly inept nurses in charge of a comatose patient, and Mary and Rob Riley playing Marilyn Monroe and Albert Einstein trying to figure out the theory of relativity on a date. Einstein wonders what happens when the atom is *schplit*. "Maybe when the atom is *schplit*," Marilyn theorizes in a breathy hypothesis, "mass is converted into energy . . . it's just a wild thought." Einstein goes into ecstacy.

The neophyte was awarded the Joseph Jefferson Award for the best principal actress in a revue that year. Within a short time, she had blossomed into a company pro, a transition for which she always has given her coplayers plenty of credit. There were nights when Mary had doubts about recreating something funny she'd originally done spontaneously, but most of the time everything worked.

When approached by the producers of *Saturday Night Live* about becoming a regular on the show, she was astonished. "I didn't think I had paid my dues yet," she says in that familiar wonder-filled voice.

Figuring she would make some good contacts and get national exposure during the thirteen-show stint, she agreed to join the cast of one of the few "live" shows on television (NBC had completely revised the original *Saturday Night Live* show for the 1981–1982 television season. The talented cast was younger than their predecessors and the humor more thought-provoking). She remembers her first *SNL* show: "In the middle of the first sketch, I went blank and had to look for the cue cards."

Mary soon realized that what worked on stage didn't always work for television — things like running all over the set and ad-libbing, both of which drive cameramen crazy. And it didn't take long for the show's writers to realize that Mary was a dream to write for. "You're aware that when you're writing for Mary, she can get away with anything," one said. "Whatever she says, it sounds like it has pink and blue flowers all over it."

Critics applauded the new *SNL* show, saying it was better than the original, and one columnist considered Mary Gross to be a reincarnation of Gracie Allen! Viewers took to the "ditsy" yet sometimes profound entertainer. When she later returned to Chicago to visit her family and boyfriend Jay King, she was invited to appear on *Today in Chicago*, and Irv Kupcinett's show. "It had been my fantasy to do his show," Mary said.

What surprises Mary the most about show business is the competitiveness among the actors, herself included. "That's the thing I like least about myself," she says. "We find it very hard to be happy about each other's triumphs if we think we were equally qualified for the part. Network politics and the importance of ratings is often discouraging too."

Over the years Mary's roster of impersonations has grown to include Eleanor Roosevelt, Mary Richards (the character from Mary Tyler Moore's show), Marilyn Monroe, Suzanne Somers, Ann Landers, Alfalfa of the Our Gang comedies, sex therapist Dr. Ruth Westheimer, and more recently Pee Wee Herman.

"My method for learning impersonations is to view a videotape of the subject," Mary says. "The more exaggerated the person's gestures or voice, the easier it is."

Among the characters who have evolved from Mary's imagination are the ethereal housebound poetess Ariel Feeley, and Irish radio show host Siobhan "Juicy" Cahill.

"New characters are often based on different facets of my mother's personality. I do not mean to suggest that she is schizophrenic. Twenty years from now I'll be behaving exactly the way my mother does now, but dressing in 2005 fashions."

Other characters are modeled after schoolmates, relatives or casual acquaintances. Mary feels her improvisational background has often helped to inspire new characters. "You are thrown into a strange situation and must quickly come up with the best choice of character for the highest comic effect," she explains.

Since joining the *SNL* show, the performer has written comedic material, earning her writing credits not only for *SNL*, but as cowriter (as well as principal actor) in two as-yet-unaired television pilots.

"I find it difficult to write dialogue for myself," she admits, ". . . to produce a sense of spontaneity at the typewriter. It's easier to write for other people and not have so much ego involved in the project."

Mary often brings her camera on set to photograph and take portraits of the cast, crew and guests of *SNL*. For relaxation away from the studio, she reads classic novels and show-biz biographies and plays her new Irish harp ("I just purchased it after thinking it over for nineteen years").

"To keep in shape, I swim in my own limited fashion and ride my terribly chic mountain bike," she says.

Mary's goal is to maintain her career and eventually do stage and film work. She also thinks of going back to school to study classical theater.

"I'm not sure I even know the difference between high and low comedy," she allows, "though I have a suspicion that I'm much more familiar with low comedy."

Along with legions of other performers, Mary finds it impossible to calm down after the cameras are turned off and the audience leaves after the end of every telecast. Her postshow behavior follows a predictable pattern.

"If I've had a *good* show and introduced a new character or was in a sketch I was proud of, or a mediocre sketch that got laughs anyway, then I'm hyperactive until 4 a.m." she says. "If I've had a bad show, but have managed to be good-natured about it, I'm only hyperactive until 3:45 a.m. Then I'm very bitter for fifteen minutes until I decide to go to sleep."

Chapter Seven
Writers and Directors

A great deal of contemporary comedy is developed from written material. Good editing is crucial to successful comedy, so it follows that those who write humor are indispensable to the art of laugh-getting. They have the task of condensing material to its purest, most effective form. An economy of words and impeccable sense of timing are essential for the material to hit the mark.

Many of today's comedy stars, when first trying to break into the business, sold jokes to established comedians. Now that they are established and in search of more new material than they have time to write for themselves, they rely upon others, and so the cycle continues. Television appearances, in particular, use up enormous amounts of material, so good writers are always in demand.

Each play, movie, radio program and television show usually depends on the collaborative efforts of a team of writers. Women writers have played an important part in many of the most successful comedy projects in entertainment history and more are entering the field every year.

Directing is also a form of editing the comedic presentation. The director pares the actors' lines and integrates them with specific movements until the performance is as perfect as possible.

Women are involved in contributing and shaping comedy material for stand-up routines, plays, books, humorous commercials, and radio, movie and television scripts. Whether they jot ideas on a scrap of paper, put in long days at the typewriter, engage in a chaotic writing session, or direct others in a production, the desired result is the same — laughter.

Selma Diamond

Selma Diamond of "the corduroy voice" and short, chopped hairdo was born in London, Ontario, Canada (she would never say exactly when), and raised in Brooklyn. After graduating from New York University, she sold fiction and cartoons to a number of magazines, including *The New Yorker*. One of her early experiences in show business was playing the lead in Noel Coward's *Private Lives* on the borscht circuit. The intrinsically funny woman turned to writing comedy and soon worked for top entertainers, becoming a forerunner for other female comedy writers.

The droll newcomer was usually the lone female on a writing staff. In the late forties she wrote for Groucho Marx, who introduced her to Goodman Ace of *Easy Aces* fame, then a writer for NBC's *The Big Show* on radio (1951–1953). The program starred Tallulah Bankhead and featured top entertainers of the day, such as Fanny Brice, Fred Allen, Bea Lillie, and Jimmy Durante. According to *Newsweek*, the ninety-minute show was "the biggest bang to hit radio since TV started." During Selma's brief interview, Ace decided she had all the requirements to be a mass-medium comedy writer, but was surprised that she didn't ask for an hour off every day to see her analyst. "I used to imagine I was a tall, willowy blond. Now I've reconstructed my thinking," Selma said of her ability to get along without therapy.

When Ace hired her, she proved to be as adventurous as her male partners (Frank Wilson and George Foster, along with Ace) and one of her jokes was used on the very next show (this was the early fifties):

Judy Holliday: I've worn strapless evening gowns since I was twelve years old.
Tallulah: Isn't twelve a little young for a strapless evening gown?
Judy: If it stays up, you're old enough.

When the show later went to Paris (which Selma said was "like a great big motel") she wrote a joke for guest star Fred Allen:

Tallulah: I can't get used to this French money.
Fred: Yes, it's printed on the thinnest paper I've ever seen in public.

A few years later Selma joined a male foursome to write for Milton Berle's television show where she regularly contributed jokes about the frustrations of women in a man's world. She went on to create funny lines for Martha Raye, Sid Caesar, Garry Moore, and Perry Como.

It's like being Red China," she once said of working with all male writers. "I'm there, they just don't recognize me."

Actually, she made more of an impression than she thought. When one of those writers, Carl Reiner, created *The Dick Van Dyke Show* in 1961, he admitted that the character of comedy writer Sally Rogers (played by Rose Marie) was based on Selma Diamond.

In the early sixties, Selma became a popular guest on the *Jack Paar Show*. "I'm a writer," she'd say, even though Paar and the audience found her stories about men and her Jewish relatives as hilarious as those told by stand-up performers. Selma went over so big, a recording company decided to reassemble the sound tapes of her guest shots into a comedy record (Paar's lines were cut).

"I think a mike distorts my voice," she said after hearing herself on the Paar show. "I never knew I sounded anything like that." (One interviewer was convinced that her vocal chords were lodged up in her sinuses.)

Selma's comedy-writing talent afforded her a comfortable life. She lived in an apartment on New York's posh Sutton Place and wore mink coats. ("Buying your own mink coat is real mass rejection," she quipped.) Even though she'd moved up in the world, Selma made frequent visits to her old Brooklyn neighborhood. She told Paar about the time she returned after a stint of writing comedy in Hollywood and dropped into Landsman's Candy Store, wearing a stylish new outfit. Dying to talk about her trip, she waited for the proprietor to notice her. Finally Selma broke down and said, "I haven't been in this store for nine weeks. You know where I've been?" His face saddened and he said, "You been goin' across the street?"

Selma's movie debut occurred in 1963 when she provided the telephone voice of Spencer Tracy's wife in Stanley Kramer's comedy *It's A Mad, Mad, Mad, Mad World*. Twenty years later, she loaned her whiny nasal voice to a little girl in *The Twilight Zone*, a film about a group of people in a home for the aged who become children again. That led to appearances in the motion picture comedies *Lovesick, My Favorite Year* and *All of Me*.

Selma's effortless repartee made her a natural for television game shows. She also played Ted Knight's neighbor in the short-lived television series *Too Close for Comfort*. Then in 1984, she took on the role of Selma Hacker, a sardonic chain smoking bailiff, in the popular NBC television sitcom *Night Court*, starring Harry Anderson. Carl Reiner remarked that Selma's comedy style and crack timing were evident in her portrayal of the crusty court matron. "She didn't go into any long routines," he said.

"She would just walk in and drop a few plums." (When asked by someone in the courtroom if she worshipped regularly, she growled, "Honey, at my age, I don't do anything regularly.")

The same year, Selma graced the thirty-sixth annual awards evening of the Writers Guild of America, West, as a presenter of Variety Awards. She once again took a ribbing about her inimitable raucous voice.

The writer-performer said she had many women friends outside show business because her actress friends were never ready: "I always have to wait for them. It seems when you're an actress, you can't go out unless your hair is done and you've got makeup on. Now *I'm* ready all the time . . . I walk around like I did when I was a writer."

Men were always a topic of conversation for Selma. While appearing as a guest on Johnny Carson's show, she told her host that she didn't go for younger men the way so many mature women do: "I have no patience with anyone born after World War II," she said. "You have to *explain* everything to these people. . . . I don't have trouble with men. There are plenty of neurotic contemporaries of mine still around."

In the spring of 1985, Selma completed filming the last script of *Night Court* for the season. Two weeks later, it was discovered that she had lung cancer. She died on May 13 at Cedars-Sinai Medical Center in Los Angeles at the age of 64. Her untimely death deeply shocked her coworkers and fans. Selma Diamond's personality and talent were an effective force in American comedy for nearly forty years. Her rusty voice and terse wit will be greatly missed.

Lucille Kallen

Lucille Kallen, born (circa 1925) in Los Angeles, California, was the daughter of two musicians, Samuel and Esther Kallen Chernos. She attended Harbord Collegiate in Toronto, Ontario, before heading for Pennsylvania's Pocono Mountains where she joined other budding writers and performers at Tamiment, a summer resort. There she wrote material for the revues produced weekly for the entertainment of 1,500 guests. That training was to prove invaluable a few years later.

In 1949, Producer Max Liebman, familiar with their work at Tamiment, hired Lucille and Mel Tolkin to write for his first television endeavor, the *Admiral Broadway Revue*. By that time, Lucille was also a lyricist and composer. The following year, the young duo became the primary writers (along with Liebman himself) for *Your Show of Shows* with Sid Caesar and Imogene Coca. Early on, the writers had to share space with the dancers in the dressing room, so they wrote their scripts either there or in the hallway. Somehow, they managed to write enough material for a new ninety-minute show every week, forty weeks a year.

Lucille once described the hectic writing sessions in which ideas and lines were tossed back and forth with Mel Tolkin, Mel Brooks (who later joined the show as writer), and the cast.

"To command attention, I'd have to stand on a desk and wave my red sweater," she said. "Sid boomed, Tolkin intoned, Reiner trumpeted, and Brooks ... imitated everything from a rabbinical student to the white whale of *Moby Dick* thrashing about on the floor."

She equated presenting an idea to the group with tossing a magnetized piece of a jigsaw puzzle in their midst and having the other pieces racing toward it until the picture was complete.

Lucille married businessman Herbert Engel in 1952 and they became the parents of a son and a daughter. When *Your Show of Shows* ended in 1954, Lucille Kallen was a seasoned television writer, who preferred to remain in New York City when the industry moved to California.

Between 1954 and 1976, she became a novelist and playwright, also writing television scripts for *Bell Telephone Hour*, *David Frost Revue* and U.S. Steel specials. Her first book, *Outside There, Somewhere* (1964), was one of the first novels dealing with female consciousness. In recent years, she has written a series of mysteries centering around small-town newspaper publisher C.B. Greenfield, and his reporter, Maggie Rome. Her other interests center around preserving the environment and natural resources.

Though she's enjoyed a long, prolific writing career, nothing can equal those resplendent years on *Your Show of Shows*. Lucille once reminisced about writing for what was probably the best comedy show during the Golden Age of Television: "I don't know whether there are any shows today in TV where producer, performers, and writers are as tuned to each other's talents as we were then," she said. "It was a lot of fun ... being young and single and at the top of the heap...."

Anne Meara

"I have always used my humor to get along, to make people like me," Anne once said.

Anne Meara and Jerry Stiller are the best known husband-and-wife comedy team in the country. They realized the chemistry between them was right when they met in an agent's office in 1953. Since then, the couple have succeeded in every facet of show business they've entered.

Anne, born in New York City in 1929, is a tall redhead who grew up in an Irish family in the Long Island suburbs. She went straight from high school to the stage, apprenticing in stock productions in the Long Island area and Woodstock, New York. Her income was supplemented by part-time jobs such as the laboratory testing of detergents. She was paid $15 to immerse her hands in different products and return to show the results. The aspiring actress studied with Uta Hagen and found work in several Off-Broadway plays.

"First I was in a terrible Welsh play," she says, "where people . . . say things like 'Going I am out to the moors . . . ,' or 'Come to the heather over the hill with me.'"

Better parts followed in Michael Redgraves' *A Month in the Country* and *Ulysses in Nightgown*, which starred Zero Mostel and was directed by Burgess Meredith.

She met Jerry, the son of a struggling Jewish bus driver from Brooklyn, while making the rounds. He had studied drama at Syracuse University and spent his summers in stock. They married four months later, and after a few years of theater work (where Jerry usually played a clown and Anne was cast as the leading lady), they left their jobs with Joe Papp's newly formed Shakespeare company to do comedy. "Jerry always thought I was funny," she says.

They first tried out their material with the Compass Players in St. Louis, then moved on to Chicago for five months' work with the cast of "Medium Rare" at the Happy Medium. Anne dropped out of the act to give birth to daughter Amy, and sat home all winter working on comedy material. When she was ready to resume working, she joined her husband in the new comedy act of Stiller and Meara. At first the going was rough: "When I started playing clubs, I had all the guilts of leaving my baby. Amy would look at me with those big eyes. It was awful," she says.

She will never forget some of those first club dates. One owner was a bon vivant whose checks usually bounced. When Jerry demanded they be paid in cash because they needed the money, he counted out the amount in dollar bills and coins. By then, it was time to go on for the next show, so they put their salary in a paper bag and took it on stage with them. Anne also recalls playing for an all-male audience in Boston that had been drinking all day.

"Those guys were animals," she says. "Jerry wanted to leave, I said 'we're staying, and who agreed to take this job anyhow.' We had the worst fight of our marital life that night."

At a Cleveland club during the early sixties, Anne and Jerry were aware of a loud radio in the back of the room they were playing. Jerry explained that they were trying to do an act, and could someone please turn the radio off. A gruff voice answered from the direction of the club owner's table: "I won't turn it off, I'll turn it down."

Fortunately, things eventually got better. Appearances at establishments such as the Sands in Las Vegas, the Hungry i in San Francisco, and the Village Gate, Persian Room, and the Blue Angel in New York led to guest spots on the *Merv Griffin Show*, *The Tonight Show* and *Ed Sullivan Show*, where they were signed to do six shows a year, eventually totaling over thirty appearances. The couple's fresh funny sketches on their Irish-Jewish marriage, the movies they'd seen, and the absurdities of daily life became familiar to Sunday night audiences.

In 1969, Jerry Della Femina caught their act at a club in the Village and remembered them eight years later when his ad agency was looking for someone for the Blue Nun account. "Here was a funny, sensitive . . . talented team whose love for each other shows through," Della Femina said.

After their son Ben was born, Anne had been more reluctant to tour, so radio work was a welcome replacement. Anne and Jerry turned an unknown wine into a sparkling success through humorous spots confusing the wine with a real nun. When Jerry brings home a little Blue Nun to celebrate his recent raise, Anne says, "Honey, don't you think an extra dollar in the collection plate would have been thanks enough?"

The Blue Nun campaign led to sponsors such as United Van Lines and Amalgamated Bank of New York. They helped to "humanize" the moving company (in one spot the pair honeymoon in a United van) and have generated appreciative letters to Amalgamated.

The light-hearted hucksters who present the world as "plastic Americana run amok," command top money for what they do and turn down accounts that don't interest them. They write and record the advertisements, changing and polishing the material until they're satisfied. "Anne is brilliant and quick," Jerry once said. "She can write a skit sometimes in twenty minutes."

Their radio commercial for Harrah's, the Atlantic City casino, won the Big Apple Radio Award in 1983. The team also received the "Voice Imagery Award" from the Radio Advertising Bureau. "We reach a nerve in people," Meara says. "They identify with us."

Through the years, Anne has continued acting. Her movie credits include *Boys from Brazil*, *The Out-Of-Towners*, *Lovers and Other Strangers* and *Fame*. She costarred with Eugene Roche in ABC-TV's summer series *The Corner Bar* and created the role of "Bunny" in John Guare's award-winning *The House of Blue Leaves*. Anne also starred in her own short-lived series *Kate McShane* in 1975 and was a continuing guest on *Rhoda*. She has since learned to live in the present, instead of worrying about the past or planning for the future.

For three years, Anne, who hates to cook, portrayed Veronica Rooney, the caustic restaurant cook on *Archie Bunker's Place* after Jean Stapleton (who played Archie's wife, Edith) left the show. She received her fourth Emmy nomination for her final year as Veronica. Anne was brought in at Carroll O'Connor's suggestion after fifty actresses had been considered for the part, and commuted cross country from New York to Los Angeles for the tapings. Executive producer Mort Lachman said her skill as a writer was "invaluable" and that she worked well with O'Connor.

"We go back to 1958 when we worked together in a James Joyce play," Anne explained. "Carroll is shanty Irish and so am I. We understand each other."

In 1984, Anne returned to where she had started her career twenty-five years earlier—Off Broadway, this time in *Spookhouse* by Harvey Fierstein, author of Broadway hits *Torch Song Trilogy* and *La Cage aux Folles*. "It's a tragedy and it's comic," Anne says of the dark comedy about a woman trying to fight the system while living with her family above a Coney Island spookhouse.

Anne says she prefers theater audiences and doesn't miss club work and the traveling it entailed. "In a club you compete with the 25th wedding anniversary, impressing the boss. . . . You had to first get their attention, then keep them laughing," she says. "You could take the same people and have them buy tickets to the theater, and their attitude would be different."

Working together, with occasional solo commitments, seems to work spendidly for Anne and Jerry. The couple have their own production company in New York where they work as writers, producers and consultants. They appeared together in a CBS two-hour movie titled *The Other Woman*. Collaborating with writer-producer Lila Barrett, Anne also wrote the script. One of these days, she plans to add gourmet cooking to her impressive list of achievements.

"I'm going to learn to cook something other than Irish stew and oatmeal," she promises.

Elaine May

Elaine was born in Philadelphia on April 21, 1932. The daughter of Jack Berlin, an actor in the Yiddish theater, she made her stage debut while still quite young. She portrayed a boy named Bennie in one play until she was 11. "I had developed breasts, and our people do not believe in breast binding," she has noted.

After years of moving about, the family settled in Los Angeles, where Elaine went to school until she started high school. "I stopped going to school at 14," she said. "I really didn't like it."

A teenage marriage to Marvin May (whose surname she kept) produced a daughter Jeannie and ended in divorce. Later deciding to further her education, she sat in on classes at the University of Chicago. Though she wasn't formally enrolled, she attended campus events and enjoyed the benefits of student life for two years. It was there that Elaine met Mike Nichols, an undergraduate amateur actor, who was leaving for New York. Later Mike recalled that mutual friends had introduced them, insisting that ". . . she and I had the cruelest tongues on the campus."

The slender, dark-haired young woman worked at odd jobs, studied method acting and performed with the Playwright's Theatre. Her path crossed with Mike's again in 1954 when they both joined the improvisational theater group The Compass, which later became the Second City Company. The two discovered an easy rapport while doing sketches suggested by the audience.

After three years, Elaine and Mike headed for New York, where they signed with theatrical manager Jack Rollins. Soon they played the Village Vanguard and the Blue Angel, both special places for comics, as were the Bitter End and the Village Gate. These were clubs where the likes of Mort Sahl, Lenny Bruce, and Dick Gregory performed. The team of Nichols and May was an immediate hit. "The role of the writer or artist is to be the competent observer," they said, when complimented on their devastating satirical routines.

Television offers followed their cabaret success. They debuted on *The Jack Paar Show* in 1957, then went on to appear on the weekly shows of Steve Allen, Dinah Shore and Perry Como. The routines were highly original, yet exposed age-old human frailties. Elaine's motto was tested to the fullest: The only safe thing is to take a chance. "She had endless capacity for invention," Mike Nichols said of his partner.

One popular skit concerned a male patient visiting a woman doctor for the first time. In another, Elaine portrayed a haughty telephone operator who destroyed Mike by losing his last dime. They often poked fun at Jewish mothers — one woman would not eat for days for fear her mouth would be full when her son called, another called her rocket-technician son to berate him for not writing. When she had made him feel sufficiently guilty, he wailed, "Mama, let me tell you, I feel awful." "Oh, God, Sonny, if I could only believe that, I'd be the happiest mother in the world."

On May 1, 1959, the comedy duo filled Town Hall and caused critic John S. Wilson to compare the skillful interplay between them with that required of the first-rate musical ensembles usually performing there.

The following year, Nichols and May appeared on the television special *The Fabulous Fifties* to great acclaim. They were scheduled to work on the annual Emmy television award show that June, but because one of their skits made fun of home permanents (and the show was sponsored by a home permanent manufacturer) they were dropped from the lineup. In spite of frequent disagreements over their satirical material about funeral parlors ("Hello, I'm your grief lady.") and other taboo subjects, they continued to appear on television and radio where their *Monitor* spots on NBC won a loyal following. They were also among the first to make comedy recordings.

On October 8, 1960, the couple opened on Broadway in *An Evening with Mike Nichols and Elaine May*. Wishing to stay loose, they never wrote down their routines, preferring to change them from performance to performance. "We just sort of outlined it — you be so-and-so, I'll be so-and-so. . . . That was it," Mike later said.

The finale every evening was an impromptu skit with some of the lines and the style of delivery the audience's choice. A comedy album was made for Mercury Records, bearing the same title as the hit revue. Over a period of time, Mike had become fearful of relying so heavily on their improvisational material every night while Elaine hated performing the same "safe" sketches night after night, even if they did guarantee big laughs. After the revue closed, Elaine wrote a play titled *A Matter of Position* and Mike played the starring role.

"I was onstage," he later recalled, "she was in the audience . . . judging me. As soon as we weren't . . . equals on the stage . . . angers arose."

In 1962, the play closed in Philadelphia and Elaine and Mike made the painful decision to call it quits professionally and personally.

"I told Mike there was no way we could top ourselves," Elaine said after the dissolution of their partnership.

"When Elaine and I split up — that was a shattering year for me," Mike admitted. "I was the left-over half of something."

Elaine entered into two marriages but both ended in divorce after a short time ("the usual thing — we couldn't get along"). Her new avocation of writing plays resulted in *Not Enough Rope* (1962) and *Adaptation* (1969). In the meantime, she honed her directing skills on *The Third Ear*, three separate touring productions of *Adaptation*, and *Next*.

Combining her talents, Elaine wrote the script for the movie *The New Leaf* (1971), then directed and starred in it, supported by Walter Matthau, James Coco, and Jack Weston. In the film, Elaine plays a wealthy and terribly clumsy botanist pursued by a gold digger. One critic noted Elaine's direction was "perfect, never slick, always warm and slightly askew."

Elaine directed her own daughter, Jeannie Berlin, in *The Heartbreak Kid* the following year and found it a pleasure. The film starred Cybill Shepherd and Charles Grodin, but Jeannie stole the film playing a nagging young wife on her honeymoon. Mike Nichols too became a successful award-winning director of movies and plays.

In 1980, Elaine and Mike reunited to costar in *Who's Afraid of Virginia Woolf?* at New Haven's Long Wharf Theatre. The reconciliation was a long time coming, but when it finally occurred, it was between two independently successful individuals. They became very close once again. "I think now it's forever," Mike remarked in 1984.

Elaine has said that directing just came with the territory once she had written the script and that she also became proficient at discussing "budgets, schedules, meal penalties, gross, net, and distribution ." As one of a number of what Hollywood calls "hyphenates" — writer-directors, actor-directors, etc., Elaine had to choose which branch of the Academy of Motion Picture Arts and Sciences to join. She carries a Directors membership card in the nearly all-male Directors Branch. Each year at Academy Awards time, Elaine casts her vote for the director of her choice. (All members also vote for the movie they feel deserves the Oscar for best picture of the year.) She equates her methods of directing actors to methods of dealing with life: "You do anything that works . . . you describe the scene . . . you play the scene . . . with him. Sometimes you cut the scene."

Seeing no reason to share her personal interests with the public, Elaine sometimes made preposterous statements to those trying to delve into her private life. She once told columnist Earl Wilson that her measurements were "24-35-127½." She told another Hollywood reporter her favorite color was "puce."

Through a decade of performing sketches with Mike Nichols, and subsequent years of acting, writing, and directing, Elaine May brought a new type of comedy to American audiences — a comedy more psychological, social and cultural. Her work in films continues (a collaboration with Marlo Thomas is in the works), and she does not regard her position with indifference.

"It's odd to think that you are going to impose or inflict something you have in your head on a large number of people and get paid for it, too," she says.

Erma Bombeck

Art Buchwald has said of Erma Bombeck: "She hits the funnybone every time."

Erma Louise Fiste, later to become the most famous housewife in America, a best-selling author, television writer-performer, and playwright, was born in Dayton, Ohio, on February 21, 1927, the only child of Erma and Cassius Fiste.

"I knew what I wanted to do from the eighth grade on," she later said. Studying the work of Thurber and Benchley, she began by writing a humor column for her high school newspaper and working after school for the Dayton *Journal-Herald* as a copy girl. While majoring in English at the University of Dayton, Erma again contributed humor to the school paper and magazines, and worked part-time in writing-related jobs: editing a shoppers' newspaper, public relations, and advertising. After graduation, she married former sportswriter William Bombeck and returned to the *Journal-Herald* as a reporter. The dedicated young woman worked her way up from preparing radio listings and writing obituaries to becoming a feature writer for the women's section, and housekeeping columnist. ("I told people to clean their johns, lock them up, and send the kids to the gas station at the corner.")

When daughter Betsy was born a few years later, Erma quit work to devote herself to her daughter and, a little later, her two sons, Andrew and Matthew. In 1964, after ten years at home, Erma decided to resume her career. Motherhood and "putting on my first leotard" had gotten her to thinking funny again.

"I was 37," she has recalled, "too old for a paper route, too young for social security, and too tired for an affair."

Testing the waters, she began writing a humor column for a small weekly newspaper, the Kettering-Oakwood *Times*, for three dollars a week. Setting aside an hour or two in the mornings, she worked at a typewriter propped on the edge of her bed. Within a year, the *Journal-Herald* hired her to produce two columns titled *At Wit's End* every week, and syndication soon followed. She dealt with quotidian issues facing homemakers and mothers: losing weight, PTA meetings, sibling rivalry, chasing dustballs, and "car-pool crouch" disease.

"My type of humor is almost pure identification," she said at the time. "A housewife reads my column and says, 'But that's happened to ME!'"

Erma's first book, *At Wit's End* (a selection of her columns), was published in 1967. The book and the growing popularity of her column brought the housewife-turned-writer more speaking engagements around the country than she had time for. She declined with the explanation, "I can't be gone more than two days because that's all the underwear we have." Her next book, titled *Just Wait Till You Have Children of Your Own!* (1971) was written in collaboration with cartoonist Bil Keane and concerned the traumas of living with teenagers.

The Bombecks moved from Dayton, where her husband worked as an administrator in the public school system, to a suburb in Phoenix, where he became a high school principal. Erma made the transition easily and tapped out a third book, *I Lost Everything in the Post-Natal Depression*, with chapter headings like "We Have Measles — It Must Be Christmas" and "Put Down Your Brother, You Don't Know Where He's Been." Besides turning out *At Wit's End*, she wrote a monthly column for *Good Housekeeping* and numerous free-lance articles in other leading magazines.

Erma reflected upon the absurdities of suburban living in *The Grass Is Always Greener Over the Septic Tank*, and introduced her fans to Wanda the school bus driver, Ralph the Little League coach, and other typical characters. The book made the *New York Times* best seller list and was developed into a television movie starring Carol Burnett and Charles Grodin.

Erma's subsequent books have also been best sellers, often holding the number one position for months: *If Life Is a Bowl of Cherries — What Am I Doing in the Pits?*, *Aunt Erma's Cope Book*, and *Motherhood: The Second Oldest Profession*, which she energetically promoted on a twenty-three-city tour, maintaining that raising kids is never easy because "you don't know the results until years later."

In 1976, the amicable, green-eyed author made the jump to television, appearing twice every week on ABC's *Good Morning, America*. (When asked how she handles nervousness before going on, she replies, "I write ad-libs on my fingernails.")

Erma has always concentrated on writing about the family and community, leaving politics and world affairs to others. She has perfected the knack of humorously relating her first-hand experiences as bingo chairman, Girl Scout captain, and home room mother. There isn't a diet that she hasn't written about (her secret vice is pasta).

"I stick close to home . . . I know what my domain is."

Erma also stays physically close to the source of her material, writing all her columns, articles and books at home, within earshot of her pulsating washer and ringing doorbell. Mothers, grandmothers, and stepmothers everywhere want to hug her when she debunks a myth about motherhood by declaring, "The woman who says, 'My kids are all speaking to one another and they love us' is a psychopathic liar."

Erma Bombeck

They nod their heads knowingly when she writes about women who put off hysterectomies until their wax build-up is under control, or that after a friend's house was robbed, the police could not be convinced that the children's rooms had not been ransacked. They too hear a lot about "everybody else's mother," that mythical mama who adores unmade beds and live-in snakes, and they applaud the mother so fed up with four sons fighting about the ketchup, she gave each a large bottle of ketchup with his name on it.

Many times, Erma reinforces her readers' belief in themselves. In one column she challenged the so-called mathematical supremacy of men over women, noting that running a country with a national deficit of $200 billion is nothing for men to brag about.

"Can they multiply a pound of hamburger, divide it by six people and end up with a balanced meal?" she argued.

Though Erma has stated that she was turned off by the anger of the early days of the feminist movement ("I believe you can accomplish more with humor than with anger"), she is an ERA supporter because she's for equality for women — "without putting a time limit on it." She also wrote that she felt the movement neglected housewives whose work in raising a family was more important than many paying jobs. In addition to her work with various charities, in recent years she has spoken on behalf of battered wives and displaced homemakers. "Can you imagine what it would be like to have no place to run to if you'd been beaten?" she asks.

When asked by Joan Rivers on the *Tonight Show* what message she likes to give the thousands of graduates she addresses every year at commencement exercises, Erma allowed that since every graduate will not be a senator, rock star or notable personality, she tells them it is commendable "to be ordinary, to be a good friend." Erma's humor and advice are timeless and as a result she is attracting a second generation of followers and is especially delighted when she spots babies and toddlers at autograph sessions.

After dishing out advice all these years, Erma cracks that her own kids "still don't know how to change the toilet tissue." When asked what she seriously wishes most for her own children and grandchildren, she replies, "that they enjoy health, have enough faith to sustain them through the bad stuff, and don't sweat the small stuff."

Erma and Bill (now retired) enjoy their privacy in their adobe-style house near Phoenix. After thirty-five years of marriage, she says "he still breaks me up," and insists they both have adapted quite happily to their empty nest.

"It really means having the phone ring and it's for you . . . leftovers in the refrigerator that you can count on . . . hot water in the shower, ice cubes in the freezer, and gas in your car. It's like being reborn," she adds.

For years, Erma did her own housework, cooking and laundry, but as her career flourished, she employed a cleaning woman and a secretary to help handle the 200 letters that arrive each week along with the gifts of homebaked food and handicraft items.

Erma's familial humor has been a spectacular success — more than 12 million copies of her books have been sold; her thrice-weekly column is read by over 30 million people; she created, wrote and produced *Maggie*, a sitcom for ABC; she is writing her first Broadway play; and presented *Getting Through 1985 with Erma Bombeck*, an engagement calendar inscribed with her wry observations.

She's received the Mark Twain award for humor, National Headliner prize of Theta Sigma Phi, ten honorary doctorates, and was appointed to the President's National Advisory Committee for Women when it was formed in 1978. She was named by The World Almanac as one of the Twenty-five Most Influential Women in America in 1979, 1980, 1981, 1982, and 1984. Though deeply honored, Erma Bombeck humbly admits she's still the same woman who "can't get her one-size-fits-all panty hose past her knees."

Getting to the top meant weekends away from home on a circuit of endless lunches and interviews on obscure radio and television shows. Now that she has it made, Erma says she enjoys the freedom that money can bring. "But there's also something wonderful about the struggle to get there," she says. "The juices really flow when you're reaching for the next plateau."

She has pragmatic advice for would-be humorists: "Stop talking about it and write. Most people do not have the courage to find out how good or how bad they are. You have to put it on the line."

Besides the fame and monetary rewards over the years, Erma says she has especially cherished "the unexpected warmth of strangers who hug you in airports, write you personal accounts of their lives, and are happy for your success."

Her own mother, Erma Sr., and her three grown children have become accustomed to Erma's celebrity status. Erma, whose fantasies include being a prima ballerina and looking like Ann-Margret, seems happy enough with her thriving career and charter membership in Dust Anonymous. She expects to get five or six books out of each grandchild and says that her own child-raising experiences taught her that "a child needs your love the most when he deserves it the least."

The Bombecks' three children are, in Erma's words, "the most normal kids roaming the world today." Betsy sells computers in Los Angeles, Andrew is a teacher who did a stint in the Peace Corps, and Matt is an aspiring screenwriter who works part-time in a restaurant. She says they are her legacy: "The books come and go, but the kids. *That's* what I'm leaving."

Renee Taylor

"Our marriage exists for a higher purpose," Renee says, "to write comedy. We see our marriage as comedy, and we're observers of that comedy."

Renee Taylor and Joe Bologna are a husband-and-wife team who write, act, and direct. Besides a teenaged son Gabriel, who is also an actor, the twenty-year union has created numerous movies, plays and television scripts. Their first stage play, *Lovers and Other Strangers*, scored on Broadway in 1968, bringing the new team publicity and success. The film version earned the couple an Academy Award nomination in 1970. Since then, most of their work follows the same basic pattern of revealing the comical aspects of male-female relationships.

Renee Wexler was born in the late 1930s, grew up in the Bronx and attended the American Academy of Dramatic Arts. She started her acting career in improvisational revues Off Broadway in the mid-fifties. Soon she became a frequent guest on the *Jack Paar Show* and drifted into writing comedy. A few years later, a mutual friend introduced Renee (divorced from actor Frank Baxter) to director Joe Bologna, and they found they were compatible, right down to their off-beat humor. They married in 1965, holding their wedding reception on Merv Griffin's show.

They now commute between homes in New Jersey and Beverly Hills. ("One keeps us real, the other keeps us phoney," she quipped on the *David Letterman Show*.) As collaborators who draw on their own marital discord for material, each of the Bolognas has at one time said, "That's it. I'll never work with you again." But within minutes, they're wondering how they can use their argument in a scene.

"We can almost do the first line of a fight, then jump to the last line," Renee once said.

While they work exclusively together on scripts, Renee and Joe sometimes go their own ways as actors. Her acting credits include the films *Lovesick* with Dudley Moore, *Last of the Red Hot Lovers* with Alan Arkin, and *The Detective* with Frank Sinatra. In 1977, Renee played the lead part of Penny in the television pilot of *Good Penny* and also portrayed Annabelle Kearns, a psycho believing herself to be Mary Hartman on *Forever Fernwood*.

As an actor-writer-director (in Hollywood terms, a "hyphenate"), Renee is eligible to belong to her choice of the three branches of the Academy of Motion Picture Arts and Sciences. She carries a Writers membership card, as does her husband.

In 1971, Renee and Joe wrote the semiautobiographical screenplay for *Made for Each Other*, then starred in the film. The movie received good reviews, but didn't take off at the box office. Their 1973 television sitcom *Calucci's Department* ran for just one season. Their luck turned around and they won an Emmy award that year for the special *Acts of Love and Other Comedies* starring Marlo Thomas.

Together they wrote and starred in a two-character comedy about a wacky woman who holds the object of her affections hostage in her apartment. Titled *It Had to Be You*, the production had a short Broadway run in 1981, and later played at the Burt Reynolds Dinner Theatre in Florida, then in Los Angeles, with Renee and Joe again in the lead roles. Recently, their professional partnership was extended to include directing. The team wrote, directed, and starred together in a Home Box Office special titled *Bedrooms* with Jane Curtin, Louise Lasser, and Charles Grodin.

Renee says she and Joe have committed their thoughts to paper in many unusual settings over the years: "We wrote together in a synagogue . . . in a public school cafeteria . . . near a pool in Arizona . . . in our bedroom . . . in the double whirlpool. I wake him up in the middle of the night and say, 'How about this?'"

Theirs seems the perfect collaboration between two bright and hardworking people who just happen to love being married to each other. When asked what keeps them together, Renee (who has a penchant for health food) says, "Fidelity and pasta."

Gail Parent

Gail Parent, who received an Emmy award for television writing in 1972, has been called "a female pioneer in writing TV comedy" by *Newsweek*. She was born in New York City in 1940, and while quite young, wrote messages to other members of her family rather than confront them about problems. In high school, she became a fan of Mike Nichols and Elaine May, listening to their records for hours. While attending New York University, Gail met Kenny Solms, who also admired the comedy of Nichols and May. "So we started by repeating their routines and then evolving into our own," she later said.

Some of their sketch material was accepted for shows at Upstairs at the Downstairs and reviewed in the *New York Times*, thus giving the new writing team a foot in the door. Comedy albums followed graduation from college in 1962, the same year she married television producer Lair Parent. Joe Hamilton heard one of the recordings and liked it so much, he hired Gail as the first woman writer on the *Carol Burnett Show*.

She and Solms would offer premises for sketches to the head writer, and upon his approval, would write them. Once a week they met with other writers for a run-through of the entire show, then did any rewriting that was called for. The hilarious soap operas, "As the Stomach Turns," were their creation. Another specialty was writing political material. Their talent and hard work earned them the industry's highest award. Gail later wrote for other television comedy shows, including *Mary Hartman, Mary Hartman, The Mary Tyler Moore Show*, and specials. She has definite feelings about the makeup of those who write for laughs. "I find that all comedy writers are funny people," she has said. "If they *are* funny, they *write* funny."

During the early seventies, the vivacious brunette collaborated with Solms on two plays, the Broadway musical *Lorelei* and *Call Her Mom* (ABC-TV). With Andrew Smith she collaborated on the screenplay of *The Main Event* starring Barbra Streisand.

Her novels include *Sheila Levine Is Dead and Living in New York* (later adapted for both the movies and television), *David Meyer Is a Mother, The Best Laid Plans*, and *A Little Bit Married*, published in 1984 and slated to be made into a movie. *A Little Bit Married* is about a Long Island housewife who moves to Manhattan for the summer, leaving behind her straying husband and overweight daughter.

"I loved it," Carol Burnett said after reading it. "Now I know what happened to Marjorie Morningstar."

Gail's schedule can shift between hectic involvement in a movie production and working for months on a novel at home. The prolific writer insists that the actual process of writing is agonizing and lonely. Each new project begins tenuously and is pure drudgery until completed to her satisfaction.

"I have no imagination," she says. "My ideas come from reality."

The mother of two sons, Gail once attributed her sanity and even emotions to her offspring. "Having children has kept me very normal," she said, "because I haven't been able to celebrate joyously over something for a week . . . nor dwell on unhappiness when something has gone wrong."

Gail is an occasional guest on television talk shows where her bubbly personality belies the serious, disciplined woman who holes up for long periods of time to write. Wondering aloud on David Letterman's show about Nobel Prize winners who sell their sperm, Gail asked, "When there are new Nobel winners, does the old sperm get marked down?"

Anne Beatts

Anne Beatts (pronounced "Beets") has evolved from a self-described teenaged "misfit" to an Emmy-winning television writer and producer within a relatively short time. Often at odds with television's hierarchy, her tenacity is well known to those in the industry.

Born on February 25, 1947, in Buffalo, New York, Anne is the daughter of Patrick Murphy Threipland and Sheila Beatts. She attended McGill University in Montreal, Quebec, Canada.

"Luckily, things got much better," she said of her college years. "I found my fellow misfits on the school newspaper," she later said. "That was my first experience with writing."

After receiving a degree in English in 1966, Anne went to England to work in London as an advertising copywriter. Returning home a few years later, she moved to New York with her boyfriend Michel Choquette, a writer for *National Lampoon*. She began attending *Lampoon* dinners where her repartee soon convinced the others she'd be an asset. In 1970, Anne became the only woman on the writing staff and was a quick study as a political satirist.

"Humor for me is a weapon," she has said. "When you're not popular and you're standing on the sidelines, you develop a keen sense of observation. At some point, I learned those observations could be funny, and that being funny was a way of being popular."

After four years, the last of which was mostly spent writing for the *National Lampoon Radio Hour*, Anne left. With Deanne Stillman, she began coediting the book *Titters: The First Collection of Humor by Women* (1976).

Producer Lorne Michaels hired Anne for NBC's ninety-minute *Saturday Night Live* before it premiered on October 11, 1975. She later recalled that working on the show "was a combination summer camp and concentration camp." She installed a hospital bed in her office to make herself more comfortable during round-the-clock writing sessions.

"Anne was remarkably good under pressure," Michaels said after she left the show. "She had intelligence, wit and style. She also had a vulnerable side, which she hid less and less with people who appreciated her."

The "nerd" sketches, featuring snuffling, nearsighted Lisa Loopner

(Gilda Radner) were the creation of Anne and Rosie Shuster, another *SNL* writer. For her work on the show, Anne received an Emmy from the Academy of Television Arts and Sciences in both 1976 and 1977, and awards from the Writers Guild in 1976 and 1980.

After leaving *SNL*, Anne (along with Stillman and Judith Jacklin) wrote a movie script entitled *Where the Girls Are* but it was rejected. She wrote a television show based on *Titters*, and spent much of 1981 writing the screenplay for an updated version of Clare Boothe Luce's *The Women*. While her scripts made the rounds, an idea for a television pilot was germinating.

"At first the *Square Pegs* characters were little things moving around in my head saying funny lines to each other," she said. The script was drawn from her own teenage experiences in Somers, New York, and "based on me and my closest high school friend." Though she owns a 1959 Rambler and enjoys wearing fifties clothes and pointed sunglasses, Anne isn't the least bit nostalgic for her adolescence. But she does allow that most of the successful people she knows "were square pegs in high school."

Anne remembers herself as a flat-chested 12-year-old freshman. ("There I was in undershirts with everyone else in bras.") Though trying desperately to fit in, she ended up being "smart and smart-mouthed," and socially left out. "I remember a teacher saying to us that she was sick and tired of our blasé, cynical attitude."

The original *Square Pegs* pilot was one of fifty-five comedy scripts under development at CBS at that time. Of those, only three made it on TV. The high-powered writer-producer rented a luxurious house in West Hollywood. Her show, centering around two overly bright but socially ostracized high school freshmen, spindly Patty and overweight Lauren, was filmed at an abandoned school in Norwalk, a Los Angeles suburb. After its premiere episode in early 1983, *Square Pegs* was called "the sweetest surprise of the season" by *Time*. Anne became a rarity in Hollywood, one of the few female Hollywood producers to create a weekly series single-handedly and push it into prime time.

"Now, as the producer, the trick is to maintain a funny balance between control and, uhmm, *suicide*," she said. Anne had her differences with the television establishment and feuds ensued. Her determination to use certain lines in the show earned her a reputation of being hard to get along with.

"If you're a man in her position, people don't care if you're abrasive," cowriter Judith Jacklin said. "But if you're a woman, they say, 'She's bossy — what a bitch.'"

Anne has defended herself by recalling that during her childhood, verbal cuts among the little boys were considered normal, but when girls made similar remarks, they were being bitchy.

"Bitch is a word we've allowed to be held over our heads, to keep us from standing up," she said. "Sometimes the nicest thing you can do, for yourself or anyone else, is to be bitchy, because it means being real. Being nice all the time is about as natural and comfortable as a beauty pageant contestant's trick for keeping that perennial smile: Vaseline on the teeth."

Her *Square Pegs* (which some critics faulted for lacking form and structure) went into reruns but was not strong enough in the ratings to be brought back the following season. Anne immediately became involved in other projects, one of them a collaboration with Stillman and Jacklin on a book titled *Titters 101* (1984), which lists imaginary literary accomplishments of women.

Feeling outraged that women were portrayed on television as lovely but unintelligent, Anne has fought long and hard to present them in a better light through her humor. She has been called stubborn, determined, intense, and passionate about her material, but she doesn't give up. She feels women's humor is becoming more important because women have so much at stake. For her, comedy must have intelligence. Anne readily admits that she tries to convert people to her way of thinking. Getting the laugh is not enough: ". . . humor and message fit together for me," she says. "That's the only way I can work."

Chapter Eight
Rising Stars

Little by little, stand-up comedy has gained acceptance as a suitable occupation for a new generation of women. The future is bright for those coming out of colleges, offices, and kitchens to test their ability to make America laugh. Comedy workshops and showcases for fresh new talent have proliferated in cities and towns across the country; some of these establishments are chains or franchises. Major cities may boast a number of successful clubs that feature stand-up comics several nights a week. Neophytes have only to muster up enough courage to try out their material on "open mike" night, a regular evening set aside for amateurs. These auditions often run until three or four o'clock the following morning.

More than one-fourth of the stand-up comedy hopefuls today are women, so as a performer gains more exposure and a reputation, she is more likely to be spotted by talent scouts and offered work as a regular entertainer on the nightclub circuits or in television and films. Her achievements will in turn motivate other young women to consider comedy as a viable and rewarding career.

Topics for today's comedienne run the gamut from shaving her legs to getting elected for president of the United States. Her wit and spontaneity allow her to throw some light on the murky political and social issues confronting everyone. She may be ladylike, aggressive, poignant or raunchy, but one thing is certain — she is funny, and fans of both sexes are lining up to see her. Whether she gets her laughs by slipping in and out of characters as an impressionist, creates her humor improvisationally, or delivers a meticulously prepared monologue, the funny woman is on her way.

Geri Jewell

Young, blue-eyed comedienne Geri Jewell has carved out a career in show business despite enormous odds. She has cerebral palsy, a disorder of the nervous system characterized by the inability to fully control muscle movements. Born on September 13, 1956, in Buffalo, New York, and raised in southern California by loving parents, Geri underwent years of physical, occupational and speech therapy in order to talk, walk, and feed herself. She says her family had to dodge flying food at mealtimes and only the dog enjoyed sitting near her because he could catch what flew by.

Her lonely childhood was a succession of schools for the disabled and cruelties inflicted by other children. Yearning to be accepted, she quickly learned that humor about her affliction could be wielded as a weapon.

"I used comedy at school as a way of fitting in," she says. "I figured I'd get the first laugh out of it before anybody else had a chance to think of something . . . also . . . people would know it was CP I had, not mental retardation. . . ."

The dream of becoming an entertainer seemed unrealistic to everyone else, but Geri refused to listen to those who underestimated her potential. She got her first taste of performing at 14 when she wrote and costarred in a simple Christmas story at the school she was attending. More determined than ever, Geri wrote to Carol Burnett, asking if a girl with cerebral palsy could possibly become a comedienne. Carol promptly wrote back that God has a way of compensating for those who have been handicapped, and that Geri should get into some kind of acting as soon as possible. "I'd read that letter over and over again . . . this half-torn yellowing letter," she says. A few years later, the two began corresponding regularly.

Dramatics helped to make Geri's unhappy high school years more bearable and provided emotional release. She persuaded her family to let her study theater at a community college, but when put in charge of all the props for a play, she worked so hard that her grades suffered, and she was asked to leave. She was turned down for a job as a typist, a keypunch operator, and a waitress. ("They didn't like the way I tossed salad," she later joked.) She tried to join the Navy, but was told to try the Army. After a demeaning vocational training experience at a workshop near her home, she returned to school part-time.

Geri credits two teachers, Kaleta Brown and Dr. Jerry Hershey, for giving her the impetus to pursue her dream. John Holton, who drove the bus for the handicapped and overheard Geri cracking jokes all the time,

Geri Jewell

suggested she try her humor out at The Comedy Store in Los Angeles. Holton and his roommate Alex Valdez, a blind comic, helped her prepare for the audition.

"I knew I was finally home," she says of that night in 1978. From the moment she walked on stage in a T-shirt that read, "I'M NOT DRUNK—I HAVE CEREBRAL PALSY," to her closing joke, "Which one of you creeps took my handicapped parking space?" she was a hit. Within a short time, she was working at clubs and had enough confidence to leave her parents' home to start an independent life.

Geri's routines about her disability presented audiences with material entirely different from that of other comics. She good-naturedly told them of her difficulty in doing things most women take for granted, like putting on makeup and plucking her eyebrows. "I'm one of the few people who drive better than they walk," she'd tell them. "I've been pulled over once for speeding and four times for walking." Or: "I've had some really high scores bowling . . . only never in my lane."

Working the comedy clubs and doing shows for the handicapped gave Geri the confidence to talk her way onstage at the 1980 United Cerebral Palsy Telethon. That led to an invitation to perform at the Media Awards Banquet sponsored by the Committee for Employment of the Handicapped, where she met Norman Lear. "He came up, kissed me on the forehead, and said, 'I really love you.' That's all he said," Geri remembers.

A short time later, Lear arranged to have her written into NBC-TV's hit show *Facts of Life* (with Charlotte Rae), playing a visiting cousin in an episode entitled "Cousin Geri." The newcomer impressed everyone with her sense of timing and got along well with other cast members. She was invited back and now has her name on a parking space at Universal Studios.

"I was in seventh heaven," she said of her first appearance on *Facts of Life*. "I couldn't believe it."

After seeing Geri on television, Carol Burnett sent her a telegram: "Thank God and thank you that you made it, because you really got me off the hook! Love, Carol." Pleased that her encouragement helped, Carol said, ". . . Geri had to make it happen herself. . . . There's certainly no one else in the world like this kid!"

Since that time, Geri has performed in *The Righteous Apples* (PBS), *In Search Of*, *Livewire*, Lear's special *I Love Liberty*, a Dick Clark special, *20/20*, children's television, and many talk shows. She also appeared in the television movie *Two of a Kind* with George Burns and Robbie Benson.

In her free time, Geri likes to roller-skate and play Pac Man, which she considers great occupational and physical therapy because she has to use her hands. She often scores 30,000 points with a single quarter!

It takes great concentration to control her movements while performing, and if she is tired, she's apt to sway more. Audiences occasionally think she's making fun of the handicapped, and have to be set straight. On the street, she is still sometimes mistaken for being drunk, on drugs, or retarded.

"People talk to me like I'm 5 years old a lot," says the courageous young woman who has achieved a degree of success in the entertainment industry never before attained by a disabled person. The plucky comedienne, who is often asked for her autograph, is an inspration to other handicapped individuals who meet her at benefits and see her on television. Her book *Geri*, an autobiography written with Stewart Weiner, is sensitive, funny and full of love, and a film based on her life is in development.

"I have finally gained a true sense of confidence about myself," Geri says. "I've learned to love myself, and also how to love back. . . . Stand-up comedy has been great therapy for me."

Elayne Boosler

Elayne Boosler is credited with being a forerunner of the many women stand-ups today whose humor is spontaneous, topical, and not in the least bit self-degrading. The ex-singer from Brooklyn with a soft, friendly voice makes her savvy comments from a woman's point of view but doesn't coddle the men in the audience. A regular on the Las Vegas-Atlantic City circuit and frequent guest on television comedy shows, Elayne is a seasoned performer who can handle any situation on stage. She feels that a pat routine is now passé and "people lose interest if you don't relate to their situation."

When she started out, men in the audience were surprised to see a woman do anything on stage besides sing or strip. As an aspiring singer in 1973, 21-year-old Elayne worked as a hostess at a comedy club in New York's Hell's Kitchen section, going onstage to sing between comics. There she met comedian Andy Kaufman, who convinced her to try comedy. He coached her to relate to the audience by breaking down the "fourth wall" separating her from the audience.

> "I reached into my pocket for a pack of gum. Unwrapping a piece, I asked, 'Anybody want some?' They laughed, and I came down off the stage and began talking to people. 'I can tell by your eye shadow, you're from Brooklyn, right?' . . . 'Me too. My mother has plastic covers on all the furniture. Even the poodle. Looked like a barking hassock walking down the street.' Laughter. Andy had taught me a valuable lesson: the deeper the comedy came from within you, the funnier it was."

Elayne and Andy became inseparable and spent the next four years in Manhattan, talking about comedy and trying out different characters on the street, in restaurants, and porno shops. "We were broke, we were unknown, and we were happy. . . . Because we were so broke, we had to take any gig that came along," she once said.

In 1977 the couple broke up, each moving to California to go his or her own way, though in the years to follow, Andy would often show up in the audience at clubs where she was playing and join her onstage. Elayne was soon appearing on the *Tonight Show*, *Late Night with David Letterman*, *The Merv Griffin Show*, and TV specials. In 1983, she and Andy collaborated on the writing of his one-hour special on PBS and Elayne appeared as one of his guests. She had come a long way from the club dates in Mississippi and North Dakota, when male wits in the audience yelled, "Take if off, Elayne."

Much of the comedienne's smart material deals with the whimsies of single womanhood and brings laughs of recognition from both men and women. She tells them of dates so unintelligent they keep a bookmark in their *People* magazine: "Guys in Manhattan have the worst lines to try to meet you. It's not their fault—it's just an awkward situation. I'd be walking down the street in cut-offs, with a newspaper, cup of coffee and a dog. A guy would say, 'Hey, live around here?'"

And she thinks construction workers have more confidence than anyone else on earth: "They say to five thousand women a day, 'Ey, can I go witch you?' And they get rejected five thousand times, get a good night's sleep, and they're ready to start all over again.... I don't think they *could* go if somebody said 'yes,' because they're working!"

Elayne says its hard to have a personal life on the road because "it has to be with strangers." She worries about her biological clock ticking away while her friends are having babies by natural childbirth: "No drugs . . . until the kid's two and they can't take it anymore." She claims her parents don't understand what their children do.

"My brother's gay but my parents don't care as long as he marries a doctor, and as long as I don't ask for money, they don't care what I do," she says. "I love my parents and they're wonderful people, but they were strict, and I still look for ways to get even. When I got my own apartment for the very first time and they came to stay with me for the weekend, I made them stay in separate bedrooms."

About familial hang-ups, the comic says she knows that people say girls are looking for their fathers in a husband, but she sees no problem. "I can dig that. I can dig a man who gives me money and sleeps with my mother."

Getting her political licks in, she says, "President Reagan is a lot like E.T. He's cute, he's lovable, and he knows nothing about how Americans live."

Elayne is a natural comedienne who, within a few seconds of stepping on stage, starts getting laughs with her relaxed patter about whatever is on her mind. Hostile audiences are a thing of the past. She's paid her dues and will be around for a long time.

Diane Nichols

Diane is a pro at interacting with her audience. Striking a conversational note, she may take a poll of the make of cars they drive, then easily glide into jokes about her driving: "I hate driving a beat-up car because it always looks like you're leaving the scene of an accident," she says. "And every time I take a curve, my plastic Jesus clings to the dice."

Diane was born and raised in San Francisco. Her first stand-up routines were oral book reports to her classmates during the sixties.

"As a child, I was already looking sideways at situations," she says. "When they showed me my grandfather's grave, I asked 'If he's good, can he come out?' I was 4 years old."

For a period of eight months during her childhood, she was unable to walk because of an orthopedic dysfunction. "I remember coming home from the hospital after a long illness when I was 10," she says. "I had been scared I would never leave that place, nor ever walk again. I played my record player all day long and daydreamed about the future. Music's a memory you can take with you."

Voted "funniest in the class" in high school, and encouraged by her teachers, Diane wrote all the school's rally plays and sketches. Since deciding to become a stand-up comedienne in the late 1970s, the slim, attractive entertainer with an engaging smile has appeared at showcases across the country, from The Comedy Strip in Fort Lauderdale to her hangout, The Comedy Store in Los Angeles, where she now lives. Diane vividly remembers her audition at The Comedy Store, where newcomers breaking in get just six minutes to prove they're funny. If they don't make it, they have to wait three months before trying out again.

"I was still waiting to hear if I 'passed' to regular," she recalls. "Tom Dreesen came out in the hallway to talk to me. Those words he spoke to me over the mob of people stayed with me through some very rough sets over the next few months."

Besides her stints as a club performer, Diane offers her talents as a comedy writer, and presides as the mistress of ceremonies at local events such as the Los Angeles Policemen's Association Benefit and the Cerebral Palsy Telethon. She has dabbled in films, commercials, and the theater, and has racked up numerous television credits including the Letterman and Griffin shows, *Don Kirshner's Rock Concert*, the *Today Show*, and the cable news network special *Women in Comedy*.

"All women have one gorilla arm," she says. "That's the one we use to hold the purse and the kids, reach for the back zipper and protect the front seat. If we ever let it hang down, it would drag on the ground."

Diane's humor is middle-of-the-road and delivered in a friendly manner, though a cutting edge is still there. She attacks sexism in the workplace and offers a feminine perspective on the foibles of male-female relationships. Jokes about the handicapped, swearing, and ethnic jokes are taboo and she dislikes self-deprecating humor and double entendre jokes. "I talk about sex, but it's the way it affects real human beings," she claims.

According to *Variety*, Diane "quickly establishes a woman-to-woman rapport that draws appreciative chuckles from male eavesdroppers, too."

She talks about exercise classes, how men look in pajamas, and "guys who make love like they were the only ones in the room, which I think is a holdover from when they were."

The performer finds that men have no problem with laughing loudly or pounding the table if a joke strikes them funny. However, women can be near hysterics but not making a sound, a most frustrating situation for the comic on stage. Diane believes women have been taught to muffle their laughter.

Commiserating with women about blind dates, she says it's a hopeless situation because "We're all going out with the same guy.... This guy called me up, and said, 'Diane, I like a woman who can give me a real challenge.' I mailed him my bank statement. 'Call me back with the total.'"

The entertainer keeps in touch with reality by turning on the news and by not reading about the entertainment industry. To counteract stage jitters, she drinks a glass of wine in a club or says a little prayer before a television taping. Being a stand-up is seldom dull: "I was onstage once in Westwood when the place caught on fire. I thought the guy telling me to get off the stage was playing around with my act, so I ignored him — until I saw the smoke billowing out of the back."

One of the most exciting and challenging moments of her career was going on in front of Richard Pryor when the audience was chanting for *him*.

Diane feels that men are usually more helpful to women who are newcomers to doing stand-up. "If you are good and in control of your comedy, it threatens many male comedians," she says. "They consider stand-up, like baseball, a man's privilege."

She admires the comedy talents of Elayne Boosler (for her consistent, great material), Lotus Weinstock (brilliant, insightful, a privilege to know), and Jay Leno (the best material, attitude, delivery, etc.). She is hopeful that the many new comics coming out of clubs and workshops have a better chance to make it now that cable television is opening up new ground away from network pressures.

Diane Nichols

Diane's biggest laugh occurred one night when she asked a man in the audience his occupation: "Your gynecologist," he quipped. "Don't you recognize my hands?" (That got a laugh.) "No," she answered. "But I recognize the top of your head."

She got a standing ovation.

Whoopi Goldberg

When Whoopi Goldberg stepped into the spotlight on a New York stage in early 1984, theatergoers were in for a surprise. The black, spritelike comedy artist with dreadlocks and a toothsome smile showed them that she wasn't afraid to enter the "danger zone" of comedy. Her routines are devoid of impressions and one-liners, but consist entirely of exquisite characterizations into which she seems to disappear.

Whoopi, who says she's "half Jewish and half Catholic," claims she received her name by divine revelation: "One day I saw this burning bush and it said, 'Your name is boring, but have I got a name for you!'" (Her legal name has since been revealed as Caryn Johnson.) She was born "more or less and no one will ever know for sure" thirty-five years ago in the Chelsea district of New York City and raised by her mother, a teacher. The girl began performing at the age of 8 in the children's program of the Hudson Guild and the Helena Rubenstein Children's Theatre.

She "hung out with about ninety other hippies and took drugs" during the sixties and played small parts in *Pippin*, *Jesus Christ Superstar*, and *Hair*. Seeking a new direction to her life, she moved to the West Coast in 1975 and worked as a bank teller, bricklayer, and mortuary hairdresser before joining the improvisational company Spontaneous Combustion in San Diego. She teamed up with actor Don Victor to do improvisational skits in comedy clubs. Her partner couldn't make it for a job in San Francisco, so Whoopi went on alone, improvising monologues by three characters. "The audience went bananas," she later said. "It freaked me out. I had never contemplated being a solo performer."

In 1981, she joined the Blake Street Hawkeyes Theatre in Berkeley. After honing her style for a few years in San Francisco and San Diego, she returned to New York in 1984 with *The Spook Show* at the Economy Tires Theatre of Manhattan's Theatre Workshop. During the one-hour show, which was simultaneously translated for the hearing-impaired by a nearby interpreter, Whoopi took risks. At one point she competently handled a heckler while staying in the character of a thick-tongued crippled girl, a character who demanded empathy but never pity. She was next transformed into a California teenager who insists she's a surfer, not a Valley Girl, "because before there was a mall there was the ocean, OK?" She became a 9-year-old street urchin who covers her tight braids with a white skirt that she pretends is long blond hair: "I told my mother I don't want to be black no more. You have to have blond hair to be on *Love Boat*."

Nearly half the show was devoted to Fontaine, a tough-talking junkie with a Ph.D. in literature. Ridiculing a previous federal training program, he said, "Man, you could get a CETA job to learn how to part your hair." Fontaine convulsed the audiences with a story of a recent sojourn in Europe, and his en route fear of being sucked out of the plane if he flushed the toilet.

The show received favorable reviews, including one in the *New York Times*, and brought her to the attention of director Mike Nichols. Comparisons of Whoopi with Richard Pryor, another performer who forges ahead with hard-edged humor, were inevitable. Whoopi claims much of her material springs from everyday observances which she absorbs like a sponge. "I write in my head," she says. "Everywhere I go, I see incidents or I meet someone who sticks in my mind. And people tell me stories."

After her hometown success, the talented performer returned to Berkeley, California, with Alexandrea, her daughter from a brief marriage. On October 24, 1984, Whoopi opened at the Lyceum Theatre in New York in her one-woman show *Whoopi Goldberg*. In sketches combining comedy, political satire and drama, her six principal characters (basically the same as before) were presented on an empty stage with only a few props. Her monologue changed from one performance to the next, depending on her own mood and the audience's reactions. ("I like people to come without expectations, ready for a good time and to participate.") "I've never seen anyone like her," said Mike Nichols, who supervised the production. "Whoopi is one part Elaine May, one part Groucho, one part Ruth Draper, one part Richard Pryor, and five parts never before seen."

One of the most touching sketches featured a deformed girl whose dreams about wholeness are interpreted as Whoopi projects her inner beauty in a graceful dance. While the critics praised her talent ("One of the great actors of her generation," said *The Village Voice*), some of them called her character sketches manipulative. Whoopi responded by saying that while each of her characters experienced a moment of self-discovery, she wasn't trying to preach, but just trying to deliver comedy with a message. Full houses and enthusiastic crowds bolstered her confidence. "I'm very good," she stated, "and I'm gonna get better...."

During the show's run, Whoopi was a guest speaker one Sunday at New York's Cathedral of St. John the Divine. She addressed 7,000 worshippers from the pulpit, talking to them seriously about the nation's homeless and dispossessed. No stranger to poverty, she could by then afford to help out her friends who were having trouble paying the rent. In her leaner days, someone once sent her $300. ("I never knew who it was," she confided.)

Whoopi's show at the Lyceum closed in March of 1985. It was later made available to television audiences in a HBO special, *Whoopi*

Goldberg Direct From Broadway, also filmed at the Lyceum. Whoopi again returned to California to hang out with the Hawkeyes and subsidize their original musical performances of *Tokens*, with a cast of sixty. She says she depends on old friends to keep her ego in check: "This is where I know people will say, 'Hey, don't get Hollywood with me: I remember when I had to drive you to the welfare office.'"

One day she received a phone call from director Steven Spielberg, who had missed her show on stage. He asked her to do it for him and some friends. She was very flattered, and in addition to the original characters, threw in a parody of E.T. Among the people at that gathering was Alice Walker, author of the novel *The Color Purple*. After seeing her perform, Spielberg said, "I'm doing the movie version of *The Color Purple* and if you want to be Celie, she's yours." Whoopi was ecstatic. ("My teeth caught cold 'cause all I could do was grin.") She was subsequently nominated for an Academy Award as best actress for her performance in the award-winning film. The actress came out in defense of the movie after its release. "It irritates me to no end that some people are trying to turn this into a black film," she says. "It's about search of self."

The spirited performer lives in California with 12-year-old Alexandrea and two cats named Bud and Lou. She is determined to protect her privacy, but at the same time admits she gets a kick out of being recognized on the street. Currently at work on a second movie, she says she's ready for any challenge: "I used to *dream* about acting . . . and they handed it to me on a silver platter."

Jane Anderson

"I always loved costumes," says Jane, who has been "getting into" other characters since she was 4. "I would attend nursery school as Zorro, Davy Crockett, Superman, and once in a while as a kangaroo."

An intelligent and original talent, Jane can entertain an audience for an entire evening without uttering one joke about drugs or trendy sex. Sharp features and a straight haircut at first suggest a waif who needs protection, but the young woman's ability to transform her diminutive frame into historical personas like Mona Lisa (who reminisces with "Leo" da Vinci about their student activist days while posing for him) soon generates side-splitting laughter. Her comedic subtlety has been compared by some to that of Buster Keaton. According to *Variety*, Jane " . . . provides some touching sensitively observant truths."

Jane becomes "Shirley of Nazareth," who endures an excruciating

Jane Anderson

case of sibling rivalry with her older brother: "Yeah, he's my big brother
... the favored son." She says their Dad never liked her brother's buddies, the disciples. He called them "the bums." Shirley hates her job
washing feet and sees an opportunity to make some money from a best
seller about Him, written from a woman's perspective. Her agent says,
"Let me read it again. I'll get back to you."

    Autobiographical absurdities about growing up in a middle-class
American family also thread their way through Jane's performances.
Rubber-legged Baby Leslie, in a pink leotard and enormous diapers, is
a recurring character. Through Baby Leslie, Jane explores pop culture

and modern child-rearing methods. The babbling toddler on the potty hears her Mama brag, "If she took the SAT's now, she'd score over 600."

Jane was born in New Jersey but grew up during the sixties in Northern California. She happily remembers uncontrollable fits of laughter in church and Brownie camp skits which she says prepared her for show business. After moving to New York to pursue a theatrical career, she was offered a lead in David Mamet's Off Broadway hit *Sexual Perversity in Chicago*. Following the play's run, she found work in a succession of good-paying, though not creatively fulfilling, television commercials. "I always wanted to be a 'serious' actress," she admits. "But I'm five feet tall with a piccolo voice and a reluctance to cry in public. I finally realized I'd never play Medea, so I chose comedy instead."

With the full support of "family, shrink and friends," Jane began building a career. She remembers the first time she got up to do five minutes of material: "I heard the proverbial BIG SILENCE out there. I'll never forget the bus ride home and feeling all that flop sweat drying on my body underneath my dress. I was not too fond of myself that night!"

Jane paid her dues performing for "three bar stools and a grinning drunk," until she could book better club dates. Recalling one of those first jobs still makes her shudder: "It was a wretched little club run by a man named Rico who summoned me into the kitchen one night. 'Don't ever make fun of me, the club, my wife . . .,' he warned. I thought I'd end up in the East River."

Her confidence gradually increased and she hit a turning point in her career. "I got through my first forty-minute show and realized that I could indeed hold a stage alone and amuse people. No one could ever make me doubt that again."

Encouragement from other entertainers also helped to reinforce her self-worth as a comedy performer. "Victor Borge told me a story about how one of his records was played for catatonic, shell-shocked soldiers in a hospital," she says. "Nothing had helped them before, but that record made those men giggle their way back into consciousness. He affirmed my suspicion that comedy is pretty wonderful and powerful stuff."

Jane returned to her home state to be a regular on NBC's *Billy Crystal Comedy Hour* and perform her act, "From the Thighs of New York to the Heart of L.A.," at the Groundling Theatre in Los Angeles. Later in New York, the *Village Voice* found her act, "Back from the City of Angels — Jane Anderson," "scorchingly funny."

One of her most popular characters is a laid-back Joan of Arc who bums a cigarette from God, strikes a match on her suit of armor, and talks of her need to "explore her inner self" instead of leading armies into battle. She also portrays Madame Anna Svetlana, a cranky, arthritic Russian ballerina long past her prime, trying to teach a group of clumsy students. Another creation is a soap opera fan who confuses her own life with those of the television characters she watches every day. When she gets married, she insists that the show's theme music be played during the wedding ceremony. Jane sometimes reads news clippings aloud, then offers her own political assessment, à la Mort Sahl. In a clear, tuneful voice, she sings her renditions of "Look What They've Done to My Nose, Ma," and "My Mother, My Guilt."

"I always hire a piano player who also gives a good pre-show shoulder massage," she says of her secret for combatting nervousness.

Tiny Jane has another secret — her well-developed biceps: "I enjoy challenging unsuspecting souls to arm-wrestling contests."

When the comedienne-writer-actress is asked to describe herself, Jane thoughtfully says, "If Lily Tomlin and Woody Allen had a child...."

Jane's particular brand of humor is emotional and rather gentle as opposed to aggressive and punchy. Called 'Tomlinesque,' she admits Lily is a favorite. "Lily goes for characters instead of jokes," she explains. "And there is nothing malicious about her humor. She can make you love someone who is potentially pitiful. She has humanity."

Jane feels that her own considerable women's following is a result of her work being more emotional, though men are often equally moved by some of her pieces. She feels she can deal with any subject as long as it is presented with sympathy: "One of my characters is a 448-pound woman, but she has dignity. She controls the jokes. I'd never let an audience laugh *at* her."

The audience reaction the entertainer strives for most is what she calls the "Big Gasp." "You hear someone say 'Oh, my God,' because you've said something that hits them in the gut."

Jane hopes to eventually write novels and plays, and spend the twilight of her life painting eccentric water colors on a yacht sailing around the world. But that's light years away for this comedic sprite who is just beginning to enchant audiences with her warm humor.

Lotus Weinstock

Lotus is a West Coast stand-up comedienne who has secured a place for herself in the funny business, earning high marks from her peers and comedy club audiences. The performer with a mane of blonde curls says the name Lotus (formerly Marlena) represents her spiritual aspirations,

Weinstock her earthly. Lotus, the California cosmic; Weinstock, the Philadelphia Jewish.

"Lotus wants to be totally free; Weinstock will settle for a discount," she says.

Born in Philadelphia on January 29, 1943, Lotus was musically inclined, and at an early age began studying dance at the Philadelphia Academy of Music. She also loved to write poetry, and later on, songs.

After attending Emerson College in Boston as a theater arts major, she left to join a musical-comedy repertory company and appeared in dozens of productions. Her next challenge was New York City. There she studied dance and acting while working as a hostess at The Bitter End, where comedians such as Woody Allen were just getting started. With the help of Bill Cosby's manager, the spirited young woman soon hit the comedy trail as part of an act called The Turtles.

From that experience came the confidence to try to make it alone, and she began opening for the acts of folk singers, for whom she sometimes composed songs. She says she failed as a stand-up in Greenwich Village in the early sixties because audiences had difficulty in "accepting hip humor from a woman in pumps and a beehive."

Lotus moved to the West Coast where she met Lenny Bruce, who became her mentor and eventually her fiancé before he died in 1966. Under his tutelage, she rid her act of phony tricks and allowed the essence of her comedy to surface, generating thought as well as laughter wherever she performed.

She has spoken in favor of busing, but only if based on astrological signs: "Too many Geminis at one school? Bus them! Let them mingle with a Taurus or a Sagg! Get to know the other half of the zodiac!" Doing a freeze frame of Catherine Deneuve, she speaks with a heavy French accent. "Why do I have no wrinkles at 40? Because I never move a muscle in my face."

Lotus, who recently turned 40 herself, says she checked out a senior citizen driving course where "they teach you to drive with the steering wheel above your head, signal four blocks ahead of each turn, and come to a dead stop whenever any other car appears within a four-block radius." She says another requisite for growing older is "perfecting the one story you plan to tell over and over for the rest of your life."

Critics have been impressed by her fresh comedic approach. The *Village Voice* reported, "As her name suggests, Weinstock's style blends Jewish rue and sanity, with a Marin County spaciness in a comic rhythm." A review in the *Los Angeles Times* reported that "Weinstock's comedy questions and informs. She is a comedian with a sixth sense — a sense of humor, both humorist and humanist."

Her homebase in Los Angeles is The Comedy Store, where one-tenth of the comics are now female. Besides touring the circuit, she has appeared on *The Merv Griffin Show, Real People, First Annual Women's Comic Show* and her own television show, *28 Minutes of Reality with Lotus*, which brought her to the attention of Bill Dana. He persuaded her to compile some of her humor into book form, and in 1982, *The Lotus Position* (with an introduction by Phyllis Diller) was published. The author enthusiastically shares her views under such diverse headings as Fame, Health Food, Reincarnation, Fidelity, Gun Control, Psychic Phenomena, and Sex. She tries her best not to offend her mother's sensibilities, but when the inevitable word or phrase turns up, she throws in a footnote, **Sorry, Mom.*

The comedienne's split personality is put to the test in raising her daughter Lili—Lotus is serenely confident that the child is guided by the One Presence and Power, while Weinstock is a JAM (Jewish-American Mother) who constantly frets.

Even the message on her telephone answering machine reflects the chasm: "Lotus is here, but Weinstock is out pursuing her earthly goals. Please leave your number and we'll call back when we are at one. Beep. Beep."

Lotus is considered by friends and her sisters-in-comedy to be thoughtful, feminine, and a joy to know. She encourages those starting out and says her goal is to someday be able to say: "Fame and fortune didn't bring me happiness!"

Emily Levine

"Comedy is the core of everything I do," says the talented entertainer who is commanding attention in the mushrooming art of stand-up comedy, though her background certainly didn't prepare her for such a career: "We didn't have TV . . . go to Atlantic City or the Catskills, and I went to Radcliffe, where it was simply not a big career opportunity impressed upon you."

Noted for her precise delivery and willingness to show her own personality on stage, Emily looks at the perplexities of life with logical amusement, and has the knack of touching on painful subjects without alienating. Her feminist voicings and comic awareness of suburbia are guaranteed to get laughs (she explains a Total Woman course as "a revolutionary new idea whereby women give up their entire lives and can stay home and devote themselves to their husbands, whether they like them or not").

Emily Levine

Born in Nashville (circa 1948) and raised in New York, the petite
dark-haired entertainer who speaks French, German, and Italian says
that everything about her diverse career has been a fluke. An English
major at Radcliffe who later studied acting at Harvard, Emily went to
Italy where she dubbed spaghetti westerns for two years. Back home in
Brooklyn, she taught schizophrenic children and joined the comedy
group New York City Stickball Team after realizing that her natural bent
for comedy brought her laughs even when she was trying to be serious.
She had to settle for always being cast as "the girl" because she was the
only female in the group that did a spot on *The Ed Sullivan Show* before
finally disbanding.

Emily appeared in several Off-Broadway plays, but feeling that today's plays have no real parts for women, she decided to go it alone and wrote and performed in her own one-woman show, *Myself, Myself, I'll Do It Myself*, in 1975. She also presented a one-woman show, *Grounded*, at the Improvisation in New York, where "the response was very good."

Next offered a job at WNET as a comedy writer, she became an established writer and performer of an Emmy-winning series of commercial satire segments for WNET in New York, the script consultant for the TV series *Angie* and *The Associates*, and coauthor of a screenplay titled *The Fling*. "I sold my integrity for on-the-lot parking at Paramount," she often jokes.

Though successful in other areas of the humor business, Emily feels that stand-up is the most satisfying creative expression. In spite of difficult club owners and 3 a.m. time slots, she proved to herself that she could do it. "Nothing is stopping you," she said. "You're in charge . . . if you fail, it's your fault. If you don't, it's your credit. Stand-up is my center."

Emily has performed at clubs all over the country, where she gets laughs by needling the justice system (the slogan "use a gun, go to jail" isn't working when a criminal's lawyer gets him off because of dyslexia), the elderly ("Old people can be fun if they're not yours"), and religion ("There are even born-again bikers. They're the ones with the chains and tattoos that say 'Born Again to Lose'"). Fans of the popular sitcom *Barney Miller* and the talk shows hosted by Merv Griffin, Dick Cavett and David Letterman have also enjoyed her sharp witticisms.

Emily, who credits Lily Tomlin and the feminist movement for giving more women a creative outlet of expression through comedy, says performing at clubs makes her face reality: "The club scene breaks down the fantasy world. . . . You can look at yourself and at the audiences as well. . . . There's a tremendous give-and-take of energy between performer and audience . . . I love talking to an audience, touching it, in my way."

Judy Carter

Female magicians are a rarity, but Judy's unique combination of traditional wizardry and contemporary humor has impressed audiences everywhere she appears. She describes herself as "kind of like Gracie Allen doing magic tricks." A schoolteacher in the early seventies, the young woman with the infectious grin was initially surprised to find she could get hired doing a funny magic act.

The tricks are leftovers from a childhood where they seldom worked out "because I forgot to read the instructions." Her zany commentary on life is sharp and up-to-the-minute, as rave reviews prove: "Spaced out and wildly funny" (*Billboard*), "a real find" (*Variety*).

Judy's comedy and amazing illusions have scored with college students from California to New England to Florida. Though pleased with the collegiates' response to her act, she wishes there were more Mort Sahls and Dick Gregorys touring the campus circuit these days. "I loved those guys," she says.

Judy has appeared at Disneyworld, The Comedy Store and The Coconut Grove on the West Coast, played clubs from Montreal to New Orleans, been a regular on the Playboy Club circuit, and amused passengers on *Princess* cruises. She has shared billings with Robin Williams, Eartha Kitt and Blood, Sweat and Tears, among others.

Television viewers saw the wacky Houdini escape from a securely fastened Hefty bag in a covered garbage can. That feat on *The Mike Douglas Show* was followed by her first public escape from the "feminine bondage" of dress shields, in which she risked chafed underarms. Plans for future great escapes from a garbage truck or from a giant Cuisinart are in the works.

In addition to numerous guest spots on the Douglas show, Judy has appeared on *The Merv Griffin Show* and *Dinah!*. She's the veteran of many television comedy specials, including *That Thing on ABC, Midnight Special, Comedy and Magic Special*, and *Zany Awards*.

Keeping topical requires comediennes to be adaptable. Her jokes about being Jimmy Carter's daughter fell by the wayside with Reagan's election, so she now makes observations about the Reagan family. According to Judy, who scribbles ideas on napkins or whatever else is handy, there's no shortage of material for routines around. "You just have to be able to see it," she claims.

One of her characters is "Sunshine Lefkowitz," an anti-establishment burnt-out child of the sixties, who spends her days as a hotdog vendor.

The good-natured performer has her share of hecklers who usually surface in the early morning hours. During one late show, a drunk ruined so many of her punchlines, she stopped the act and gave him lessons on how to be *really* obnoxious instead of just mumbling incoherently. Her worst experience occurred when she was opening act for Kenny Loggins at Sahara-Tahoe. The show was running late and the audience was in a surly mood. She dodged flying glasses when she came on stage but bravely continued her patter until a customer tossed a tablecloth over her head and caught it on fire. A security guard carried her offstage and stamped the fire out.

Judy feels more women than ever before are entering the field of comedy because they need to talk about themselves and the situations they find themselves in today, instead of the stereotyped positions seen on television. "Comediennes are strong positive women who need a place to talk about their lives," she says.

Dana Vance

Dana is a first-rate caricaturist who happened into comedy on her way to an acting career. Born in Steubenville, Ohio, Dana broke others up at an early age.

"I realized I was funny when both my parents would look at each other, then burst out laughing," she says. "I remember imitating friends of the family, and just loved to dress up like someone and perform for that person. They'd all just cry laughing."

The tall attractive girl with a gravelly voice wanted to be an actress (she performed in nearly a dozen Off-Broadway productions before fulfilling her aspiration of appearing on Broadway in *Teaneck Tanzi, the Venus Flytrap*). But along the way, Dana got sidetracked into comedy, which she found more rewarding. Using only a few props, but armed with accents and body language, she became adept at getting her share of laughs. She eventually became an improv instructor at New Playwright's Theatre and a member of the Red Shoes Walkin' Troupe in Washington, D.C. Dana's biggest problem has always been getting people in the business to accept the fact that an attractive woman can be funny. "I have to overdo a lot to show them that I can be funny, and I will go overboard sometimes."

In 1979, Dana teamed up with Jan Frederick Shiffman and appeared in *Grown-Ups*, a collection of two-character sketches which began as improvisations by the two partners. Tim Grundmann directed and provided background piano music for the act. The well-received show, which included jabs at TV exercise programs, adoption agencies, and supermarket pests prompted critics to compare the new team with Nichols and May.

Their next collaboration was *An Evening Without Liza*, a revue-style show (again written and directed by Tim Grundmann) that earned glowing reviews during its 1980 run in Philadelphia and Washington, D.C. Critics noted the two entertainers' outstanding rapport and their "deadly senses of timing and delivery." With Jan playing straight man most of the time, Dana was free to fly with her extensive repertoire of oddball characters, such as an indifferent pharmacist whose indifference

Dana Vance

changes to shock as a customer orders progressively larger condoms from the "Great Masters of Art: Italian Renaissance" series (one style featured all the ceiling paintings of the Sistine Chapel).

Another sketch dealt with opera abuse, beginning with the "junkies" getting "harmless" kicks from Mozart's *Magic Flute*, then Puccini ("I told you to watch out for that Italian stuff!" Jan the pusher sneers), and finally hitting bottom with Wagner's *Ring*. While doing the show in Philadelphia, Dana got her biggest laugh. "A guy laughed so hard with such a peculiar-sounding laugh," she recalls, "it was the first time I ever broke up on stage."

In her pursuit of a show-business career, Dana admits she has worked in some terrible places and has had to overcome a lot of rejection. "Every rejection feels like the worst, until the next one comes along, especially a comedic role that I know I can do better than anyone else," she says.

Embarking on a solo career in recent years, the buoyant entertainer has appeared in the Oscar-winning film *Terms of Endearment*, worked on children's television, and played the lead in an ABC pilot.

She sees humor as a necessary quantity in our trouble-laden world, and is happiest with herself when "I can use my sense of humor to pick people up when they are down."

Monica Piper

Monica (formerly May Lee Davis) plans on becoming a star, and if laughter from her audiences is a barometer, she is on her way. A few years ago, the diminutive young woman (five feet one, 101 pounds) was teaching English "at a tough school called Our Lady of Charles Manson Junior High." Realizing that she was doing five sets a day and holding her own against the hecklers, Monica turned in her chalk to become a singing waitress. Her funny patter between lyrics got a good response, so she began writing routines and trying them out. She was soon confident enough to audition at The Comedy Store in Los Angeles.

Since that day in 1980, Monica's been a professional funny woman who performs improvisational comedy in Chicago and on the West Coast, and headlines at clubs around the country. Her television credits include the *Mike Douglas Show, Merv Griffin Show*, and *P.M. Magazine*. She worked in front of 30,000 people on Comedy Celebration Day in San Francisco's Golden Gate Park ("The closest thing I'll ever feel to being a rock star").

Born in New York City, Monica learned to ham it up from her show business father who did a lip-sync routine to records. When company came over, father and daughter performed their lip-syncing act to "Anything You Can Do, I Can Do Better" from *Annie Get Your Gun*. "I knew very early that I made people laugh," Monica says, "and that meant approval."

It was in an English class her junior year of high school that she blurted out her first spontaneous joke. The teacher was notorious for his surprise quizzes, which he referred to as "my little quizzies." Handing them out one day, he commented how easy they were. Monica didn't agree. "I looked at it and said, 'If these are your little quizzies, I'd hate to see your little testies.' I got applause. Then I was sent to the principal's office, but even he couldn't keep a straight face."

Monica, who likes the visual comedy of the late Joan Davis in *I Married Joan*, blossomed into a very physical comic who uses her body to act things out. Her new career presented problems she'd never had as an English teacher. "In the early days, I was often expected to share a room on the road with the middle or opening act (usually men) and this was difficult — especially sharing a bathroom."

Once told she would follow the dancing in Kamloops, B.C., Canada, the apprentice comic assumed she was appearing at a disco. However, it was a run-down hotel and all the dancing was done by a woman named Blaze. ("An aging stripper with two different sized pasties — the reason for this remains a mystery — I'd have seen a doctor.")

She went onstage to face 200 men in trucker hats yelling, "Take it off, eh?" Using every heckler line she'd ever heard, she got through the set. "The password here was ABUSE," she recalls. "We abused each other for forty minutes. The weird part was the owner, a guy named Bert, said they loved me. The *worst* part was spending the night in a room next to the ice machines, with velvet paintings and cockroaches for diversion. . . . After a six-hour layover in Vancouver the next day, I finally arrived back in L.A. and kissed the ground at LAX."

Monica's coworkers in comedy have been helpful in sharing tips about new clubs, television auditions, or even enhancing a joke by giving her a better tag line. Comic Robert Wuhl originally contacted Merv Griffin's staff about her. A strong believer in astrology, she will not showcase for anything important on a full moon night, and often consults her best friend, an astrologer, before setting up an important audition. Though often told she is "very feminine" for a comedienne, Monica doesn't restrict her humor to women.

"The subjects I find funny are universal," she says. "Things we do as humans that are funny. If the material is just plain funny *and* clean, it works better. I'm not a prude — I just know what works for me. I make a few menstruation references but nothing graphic."

One of her bits offers advice for women stopped for speeding:

> "I'm sorry, Officer. I was rushing home to my heating pad."
> "Why?"
> "Are you married?"
> "Yeah . . . why?"
> "Does your wife ever get cramps?"
> "Yeah . . . Yeah, BEAT IT! BEAT IT! GET OUTTA HERE! I DON'T WANTA TALK TO YOU!"

Monica Piper

"The men laugh just as hard as the women at that one," Monica says.

She tries out new material on "the only true judge — an audience," which she says can vary from town to town. In Houston, for instance, she finds the women take longer to warm up to her and decide it's okay to laugh.

"To include them in the act without alienating the men, I compare men and women in a funny way and eventually they realize I'm talking for them, not just myself. After the show, women often tell me they really related to what I was saying."

Bubbly Monica considers her sense of humor her finest asset, and the best way to approach any situation. Her "sound relationship with a man and two dogs, and a few dear friendships outside of show business" help to bolster her ego in a business so filled with rejection. She is hooked on comedy and plans to act, write, do funny commercials, and perform her comedy routines on all the top television shows. "I'm full of confidence and optimism," she says. "I think I'll live a longer, healthier life that way."

Maureen Murphy

Maureen says, "I was always told to be a good listener. Women have always been more concerned with being feminine and letting men get the laughs."

In 1974, she was young Daphne Davis from Australia, where she once tried to entertain an audience of drunk aborigines. Much of the pixie blonde's material deals with experiences of single life down under. She asks the audience if they saw her in the Australian science fiction movie *The Day The Sheep Stood Still.*

Since her arrival here, Maureen has earned a solid reputation as a comedy artist, appearing in Las Vegas's posh showrooms and enjoying the position as the only female comic (besides Joan Rivers) to be regularly invited on the *Tonight Show.* She works very hard before those appearances and has said on national television that show business is all she has and is therefore very important to her. "You sweat over the jokes," she says. "Then you do it and your material is gone, so it's like you're starting again."

Her mock-genteel manner allows her to get risqué without offending anyone. Much of Maureen's humor is about the differences between Australian and American men, and brings laughs from men in the audiences as well as women. She draws material from her firsthand experiences in California singles' bars: "One man called me up and said, 'Would you like to have dinner before I take you back to my apartment?' I said, 'That would be lovely.' He said, 'I'll pick you up about nine—you should have finished eating by then.'"

Maureen often includes in her nightclub act her four perfectly executed impressions of Bette Davis, Marlene Dietrich, Katy Hepburn, and Mae West (with a little W.C. Fields added). In one sketch, she does a woman smoking the ashes of her cremated husband, saying, "That's the best he's made me feel in years." Maureen is also an astute observer of

American politics: "A woman president would be great because she would save the country money, because she would make half of what a man president makes."

Pudgy

Beverly Wines was called Pudgy by her father and the moniker stuck. Though she has trimmed down in recent years, the funny woman known as Pudgy still packs them in on the nightclub circuit, where her fans happily submit themselves to the sharp tongue of the queen of put-down comedy, a "Don Rickles in drag." Pudgy is a pro at working an audience, going from table to table zinging the patrons, never forgetting a name. Phyllis Diller is one of her fans, saying, "She's really a pro, she's marvelous."

The comedienne was born circa 1945 and raised in Chicago. She graduated from Steinmetz High School and got her first taste of show business when she played a small role in a hometown production of *Bye Bye Birdie*. When the play closed, she worked at odd jobs during the day, making the rounds of Chicago's Rush Street piano bars at night, gradually perfecting her verbal darts. She says she developed her incredible memory working as a waitress.

Pudgy married her manager Mike Cardella in 1979, and the following year, gave birth to son Michael. When the baby was one month old, he joined his parents on tour. Besides being a popular draw at clubs from coast to coast, the comic has appeared on Showtime cable television. She feels that more women are deciding to get into the humor business since Joan Rivers instilled some glamour into it. Interspersing her act with singing, she has dropped the "fat jokes" about herself, and concentrates on a casual repartee with her audience: "What I do now isn't really putting people down. It's more exaggerating things and having fun."

Funny Ladies

The Funny Ladies are four zany and talented young women who belong to the First Amendment, a comedy and improvisational company that was moved from Berkeley to New York City in 1975 by its founder Barbara Contardi. In September of 1981, theater critic Jan Hoffman of

Funny Ladies (clockwise from top: Jane Brucker, Pat Baily, Nancy Lombardo, Kim Sykes).

The Village Voice wrote that the Funny Ladies "project a collective warmth, political savvy, and a friendly, beguiling sense of humor ..."

Jane Brucker, Kim Sykes, Nancy Lombardo, and Pat Baily have worked together for more than five years and are the perpetrators of bright, instantaneous creations. They build provocative and hilarious skits from tidbits thrown at them from the audience, which seldom stumps them. A color, name, object, town, musical style or film genre sends them off on a spontaneous give-and-take, with no cheating. Transforming themselves into posturing, kooky characters, they whip up vignettes that include impromptu musical renditions and even an occasional pratfall.

This interaction demands full attention from those in the audience who watch as the names of four playwrights and the word "food" beget a skit about the culinary penchants of Chekov, O'Neill, Shakespeare, and Williams. The Funny Ladies are involved in humor that tends to be more political and cultural than sex-and-drug oriented. From literati to gynecology, popes to politicians, the four performers expertly deliver their parodies, impersonations, and send-ups with an intense concentration needed to jump in without losing a beat.

"You have to be a very secure person to be able to come out and say whatever's in your subconscious," director Contardi says. "The toughest thing about teaching improv is teaching people not to think. . . . You have to learn to let go, and say whatever comes to mind. Once you stop and think, you've lost it."

Mistress of ceremonies and the strongest singer of the group is curvaceous, dark-haired Jane Brucker, whose confidence as a comedienne comes across. She has been cowriter and performer on the *New National Lampoon Radio Hour* and for the ½ *Hour Comedy Hour*. Her writing and cartoons have been published in *The National Lampoon* and *High Times*. She teaches improvisational workshops when she's not performing.

Kim Sykes, a native of New Orleans, did stage work and hosted a children's television show before moving to New York. Her theatrical talents, besides being a Funny Lady, include directing, lighting, filming, stage managing and commercial modeling. (She has appeared in *Ebony* magazine and other publications.) Kim is a vivacious performer whose portrayals range from naive gentility to street-tough belligerence.

Nancy Lombardo, mime extraordinaire, can also duplicate dialects with ease. She's worked in numerous summer stock productions, once understudying Maureen O'Sullivan in *Anastasia*. She was colyricist and vocalist for *Ladies in Lingerie*, performed by the Joeffrey II Ballet, and has appeared in New York clubs and on national television shows.

Pat Baily made her dancing debut at the age of 3, and later was a member of the Norfolk Civic Ballet Company for several years. She worked as a model and studied acting before becoming a comedienne whose forte is characterizations.

These four energetic clowns work beautifully together to produce laughs and keep their fans thinking. Their humor has continued to find receptive audiences on the New York scene.

Sandra Bernhard

A guest on both the Letterman and Carson shows, Sandra Bernhard claims that most comediennes are really serious: "It's usually serious things that drive people to be funny."

The aggressive entertainer was born circa 1955 in Flint, Michigan, "the youngest of four intense children." Her father was a proctologist and her mother an artist. After graduation from high school, she put in eight months at a kibbutz in Israel before becoming a Beverly Hills manicurist-pedicurist in 1974. She began developing her comedy routine and appearing at small showcases like The Comedy Store in Los Angeles. In 1978, she left her job to make comedy a full-time career. "I just want to become famous so I can have a nervous breakdown," she says.

Sandra told Johnny Carson she was self-conscious about her looks until *Newsweek* reported that she resembled an "Assyrian priestess." She is thin, with auburn hair and Mick Jagger lips. ("You just don't see lips like this on a white woman.")

Her club act is a potpourri of parodies (Tina Turner, Jackie Kennedy, Diana Ross), fantasies, singing or reciting old pop tunes, and talking about her childhood and the family maid, Marie: "She used to come over and make tuna salad and we'd watch *Let's Make a Deal* while my mom cleaned the house."

She likes to shock her audiences by coming on to a male customer, then suddenly turning venomous toward him. "I do a lot of sexuality until I get scared of myself," she admits.

She says 11-year-old models should "take off their makeup, go home, and get into their jammies." For self-protection, she advises women to wear "a live German shepherd around your neck."

Sandra landed the role of Masha, the rich neurotic groupie in *The King of Comedy* (with Robert DeNiro and Jerry Lewis). Her portrayal was well-received by critics ("a comic triumph," said one) and gave her career a boost. Actually, that was her third movie. She claims the first was never released and she was completely cut out of the second. Following *The King of Comedy*, she played a photographer in both *Paparazzi* and *Perfect*, with John Travolta. Someday she hopes to film a story she wrote about a female astronaut who meets up with aliens.

The caustic comic, once considered "too weird" by some comedy clubs, says she was influenced by Bette Midler and Carol Channing, whom she saw in *Hello, Dolly* when she was 8. She admires "people who take chances," and strives to be both raw and vulnerable. Always loose on stage, but not always funny, Sandra claims people are nevertheless fascinated by her. "I create a spark that nobody else does."

Marsha Warfield

Marsha Warfield won the 1979 San Francisco International Stand-up Comedy Competition, after a month-long series of appearances. That milestone led to guest shots on television comedy shows and specials with Richard Pryor, Alan King and Mac Davis, and a starring part in *That Thing on ABC*. She credits Pryor for encouraging her along the way.

Marsha's inquiring mind seeks answers to questions most people never think to ask. She wonders what restaurants do with frog *arms*, for example. "Are there black people in Iowa?" she inquires. "And if so, why?"

Marsha was born in Chicago in the mid-fifties and grew up on the tough South Side. She married and entered a succession of dead-end jobs after high school. Deciding to try her luck at a local talent showcase, she chickened out at the last minute, but a friend pushed her onstage, and "I was hooked," she later said. Already separated from her husband, she headed for Los Angeles where she worked for an answering service and hung around The Comedy Store, eventually shedding her stagefright: "It's like talking to friends in my living room, and for once they shut up and listen. . . ."

The up-and-coming entertainer knew Moms Mabley only from her records and seeing her on television. She admired Moms' honesty about sex, and her courage in doing political material about Fidel Castro, Lyndon Johnson, and others. Marsha regrets not ever having the chance to meet her idol. "I thought about getting a job as her chauffeur or secretary so I could somehow . . . soak up some of the knowledge she had," she says.

Marsha's own X-rated club routines deal with the oddities of male-female relationships: "It's a point of view . . . what it is really like to be a woman," she has said. "It's basically what women talk about when we're by ourselves. I use a lot of euphemisms because I don't want to offend. I try to be honest and at the same time not to offend so there's very little profanity. But I don't pull any punches, either."

High-Heeled Women

Four attractive women with vibrant personalities make up the troupe called The High-Heeled Women. Young Mary Fulham, Arleen Sorkin, Cassandra Danz and Tracey Berg meld their talents into highly physical and hilarious takeoffs on Busby Berkeley extravaganzas that they create, choreograph, and set to their own music and lyrics.

They can poke fun at snobbish wealthy women, plug an autobiography titled *Hooked on Speed* (the addiction is jogging), do a satire on a career woman's mothering urges or on a *Carrie*-type movie, all with spontaneous enthusiasm. Impersonations range from Eleanor Roosevelt to Phil Donahue to Joan Rivers. In the few years they've been together, the foursome whose goal it is to "put drapes up all over the Third World," has attracted a following in the New York area.

The ensemble's signature song is "For White Girls Who Have Considered Analysis When Electrolysis Is Enough." A review in *Variety* stated that their "wickedly funny airtight act . . . seems ready for Atlantic City, Vegas and beyond."

The High-Heeled Women were featured in a screwball exercise book *Plain Jane Works Out* (Bantam) which spoofs Jane Fonda's best seller. Photographs are included of the four contortionists, in baggy exercise attire, clumsily demonstrating for readers the way to a lithe and gorgeous body.

References

Chapter One: The Early Days

Lotta Crabtree
Cahn, William and Rhoda Cahn. *The Great American Comedy Scene*. New York: Monarch, 1978.
Hartnoll, Phyllis, ed. *Oxford Companion to the Theatre*. Oxford, England: Oxford University Press, 1983.
Interview with Gladys Hansen, city historian, San Francisco Public Library, Oct. 30, 1984.
Sicherman, Barbara and Carol Hurd Green, eds., with Ilene Kantrov and Harriette Walker. *Notable American Women — The Modern Period*. Cambridge: Belknap Press of Harvard University Press, 1980.
Young, William C. *Famous Actors and Actresses on the American Stage*. New York: R.R. Bowker, 1975.

May Irwin
Blum, Daniel. *Great Stars of the American Stage*. New York: Greenburg Publishers, 1952.
Gilbert, Douglas. *American Vaudeville*. New York: Dover Publications, 1968.
Hartnoll, Phyllis, ed. *Oxford Companion to the Theatre*. Oxford, England: Oxford University Press, 1983.
James, Edward T., ed. *Notable American Women — 1607–1950*. Cambridge: Belknap Press of Harvard University Press, 1971.
Kerr, Walter. *The Silent Clowns*. New York: Alfred A. Knopf, 1979.
Lahue, Kalton and Samuel Gill. *Clown Princes and Court Jesters*. New York: A.S. Barnes, 1970.
O'Neill, Lois Decker. *The Women's Book of World Records and Achievements*. Garden City, N.Y.: Anchor Books, 1979.
Spitzer, Marian. *The Palace*. New York: Atheneum, 1969.

Marie Dressler
Baxter, John. *Hollywood in the Thirties*. New York: Paperback Library, 1970.
Cahn, William and Rhoda Cahn. *The Great American Comedy Scene*. New York: Monarch, 1978.
Hartnoll, Phyllis, ed. *Oxford Companion to the Theatre*. Oxford, England: Oxford University Press, 1983.
Kerr, Walter. *The Silent Clowns*. New York: Alfred A. Knopf, 1979.
Lahue, Kalton and Samuel Gill. *Clown Princes and Court Jesters*. New York: A.S. Barnes, 1970.
Robertson, Patrick. *Movie Facts and Feats*. New York: Sterling Publishing Co., Inc., 1980.
Slide, Anthony. *The Vaudevillians*. Westport, Ct.: Arlington House, 1981.
Spitzer, Marian. *The Palace*. New York: Atheneum, 1969.

Trixie Friganza
Hartnoll, Phyllis, ed. *Oxford Companion to the Theatre*. Oxford, England: Oxford University Press, 1983.
Lahue, Kalton and Samuel Gill. *Clown Princes and Court Jesters*. New York: A.S. Barnes, 1970.
Samuels, Charles and Louise Samuels. *Once Upon a Stage*. New York: Dodd, Mead, 1974.
Slide, Anthony. *The Vaudevillians*. Westport, Ct.: Arlington House, 1981.

Irene Franklin
Gilbert, Douglas. *American Vaudeville*. New York: Dover Publications, 1968.
Hartnoll, Phyllis, ed. *Oxford Companion to the Theatre*. Oxford, England: Oxford University Press, 1983.
Slide, Anthony. *The Vaudevillians*. Westport, Ct.: Arlington House, 1981.

Ruth Draper
The Art of Ruth Draper (record album). Spoken Arts, 1960–61.
Ciardi, John. "The Genius of Ruth Draper." *Saturday Review*, Oct. 14, 1961.
Hartnoll, Phyllis, ed. *Oxford Companion to the Theatre*. Oxford, England: Oxford University Press, 1983.
Sicherman, Barbara and Carol Hurd Green, eds., with Ilene Kantrov and Harriette Walker. *Notable American Women — The Modern Period*. Cambridge: Belknap Press of Harvard University Press, 1980.

Ray Dooley
Hartnoll, Phyllis, ed. *Oxford Companion to the Theatre*. Oxford, England: Oxford University Press, 1983.
Saxon, Wolfgang. "Ray Dooley, Vaudeville Star and Comedienne, Dies at 93." *New York Times*, Jan. 28, 1984.

Charlotte Greenwood
Blum, Daniel. *Great Stars of the American Stage*. New York: Greenburg Publishers, 1952.
Franklin, Joe. *Joe Franklin's Encyclopedia of Comedians*. Secaucus, N.J.: Citadel Press, 1979.
Hartnoll, Phyllis, ed. *Oxford Companion to the Theatre*. Oxford, England: Oxford University Press, 1983.
James, Edward T., ed. *Notable American Women — 1607–1950*. Cambridge: Belknap Press of Harvard University Press, 1971.

Mabel Normand
Cahn, William and Rhoda Cahn. *The Great American Comedy Scene*. New York: Monarch, 1978.
Kerr, Walter. *The Silent Clowns*. New York: Alfred A. Knopf, 1979.
Lahue, Kalton C. and Terry Brewer. *Kops and Custards (The Legend of Keystone Films)*. Norman, Ok.: University of Oklahoma Press, 1968.
Lahue, Kalton and Samuel Gill. *Clown Princes and Court Jesters*. New York: A.S. Barnes, 1970.
Robinson, David. *Hollywood in the Twenties*. New York: Paperback Lib., 1970.

Belle Baker
Franklin, Joe. *Joe Franklin's Encyclopedia of Comedians*. Secaucus, N.J.: Citadel Press, 1979.

Hartnoll, Phyllis, ed. *Oxford Companion to the Theatre*. Oxford, England: Oxford University Press, 1983.
Spitzer, Marian. *The Palace*. New York: Atheneum, 1969.

Carole Lombard
Platt, Frank. *Great Stars of Hollywood's Golden Age*. Toronto: New American Library, 1966.
Robertson, Patrick. *Movie Facts and Feats*. New York: Sterling Publishing, 1980.
Sicherman, Barbara and Carol Hurd Green, eds., with Ilene Kantrov and Harriette Walker. *Notable American Women — The Modern Period*. Cambridge: Belknap Press of Harvard University Press, 1980.
Thomson, David. *A Biographical Dictionary of Film*. New York: William Morrow, 1976.

Chapter Two: Vaudeville Legends

Sophie Tucker
Current Biography, 1945.
Gilbert, Douglas. *American Vaudeville*. New York: Dover Publications, 1968.
O'Neill, Lois Decker. *The Women's Book of World Records and Achievements*. Garden City, New York: Anchor Books, 1979.
Samuels, Charles and Louise Samuels. *Once Upon a Stage*. New York: Dodd, Mead, 1974.
Slide, Anthony. *The Vaudevillians*. Westport, Ct.: Arlington House, 1981.
Spitzer, Marian. *The Palace*. New York: Atheneum, 1969.
Tucker, Sophie. *Some of These Days*. New York: Doubleday, 1945.

Fanny Brice
Cahn, William and Rhoda Cahn. *The Great American Comedy Scene*. New York: Monarch, 1978.
Current Biography, 1946.
Farnsworth, Marjorie. *The Ziegfeld Follies*. New York: Bonanza Books, 1956.
Franklin, Joe. *Joe Franklin's Encyclopedia of Comedians*. Secaucus, N.J.: Citadel Press, 1979.
Green, Stanley. *The World of Musical Comedy*. Cranbury, N.Y.: A.S. Barnes, 1968.
New York Times, May 29, 1951.
Samuels, Charles and Louise Samuels. *Once Upon a Stage*. New York: Dodd, Mead, 1974.
Slide, Anthony. *The Vaudevillians*. Westport, Ct.: Arlington House, 1981.
Wertheim, Arthur Frank. *Radio Comedy*. New York: Oxford University Press, 1979.

Mae West
Chandler, Charlotte. "The Outrageous Mae West." *Ms.* magazine, February, 1984.
Eells, George and Stanley Musgrove. *Mae West*. London: Robson Books, 1984.
Encyclopaedia Brittanica Book of the Year, 1981.
Franklin, Joe. *Joe Franklin's Encyclopedia of Comedians*. Secaucus, N.J.: Citadel Press, 1979.

Lapham, Lewis. "Let Me Tell You about Mae West." *Saturday Evening Post*, Nov. 14, 1964.
Mordden, Ethan. *The Hollywood Musical*. New York: St. Martin's Press, 1981.
Nash, Jay Robert. *Zanies*. Piscataway, N.J.: New Century Publishers, 1982.
O'Neill, Lois Decker. *Women's Book of World Records and Achievements*. Garden City, N.Y.: Anchor Books, 1979.
Robertson, Patrick. *Movie Facts and Feats*. New York: Sterling Publishing, 1980.
Slide, Anthony. *The Vaudevillians*. Westport, Ct.: Arlington House, 1981.
West, Mae. *Goodness Had Nothing to Do with It*. Englewood Cliffs, N.J.: Prentice-Hall, 1959.
Young, William C. *Famous Actors and Actresses of the American Stage*. New York: R.R. Bowker, 1975.

Bea Lillie
Current Biography, 1945.
Green, Stanley. *The World of Musical Comedy*. New York: Grosset & Dunlap, 1960.
Life, Nov. 10, 1958, pp. 18–19.
Lillie, Beatrice, aided and abetted by John Philip, written with James Brough. *Every Other Inch a Lady*. Garden City, N.Y.: Doubleday, 1972.
Short, Ernest. *Fifty Years of Vaudeville*. London: Eyre & Spottiswoode, 1946.
"Talk of the Town." *New Yorker*, Nov. 11, 1952.

Chapter Three: Funny Women of Radio

Gracie Allen
Burns, George. *The Third Time Around*. New York: Putnam, 1980.
Current Biography, 1940.
Mordden, Ethan. *The Hollywood Musical*. New York: St. Martin's Press, 1981.
New York Times, Aug. 29, 1964, pp. 1, 22.
Slide, Anthony. *The Vaudevillians*. Westport, Ct.: Arlington House, 1981.
Steinem, Gloria. "Here's Gloria and George Burns." *Ms.* magazine, February, 1983.
Terrace, Vincent. *Radio's Golden Years*. New York and San Diego: A.S. Barnes, 1981.
Wertheim, Arthur Frank. *Radio Comedy*. New York: Oxford Press, 1979.

Gertrude Berg
Franklin, Joe. *Joe Franklin's Encyclopedia of Comedians*. Secaucus, N.J.: Citadel Press, 1979.
Lahue, Kalton and Samuel Gill. *Clown Princes and Court Jesters*. New York: A.S. Barnes, 1970.
MacDonald, J. Fred. *Don't Touch That Dial*. Chicago: Nelson Hall, 1979.
Obituary. *New York Times*, Sept. 15, 1966.
Settel, Irving. *A Pictorial History of Radio*. New York: Citadel Press, 1960.
Terrace, Vincent. *Radio's Golden Years*. New York and San Diego: A.S. Barnes, 1981.

Marian Jordan
Dunning, John. *Tune in Yesterday*. Englewood Cliffs, N.J.: Prentice-Hall, 1976.

MacDonald, J. Fred. *Don't Touch That Dial: Radio Programming in American Life, 1920–1960*. Chicago: Nelson-Hall, 1979.
Terrace, Vincent. *Radio's Golden Years*. New York: A.S. Barnes, 1981.
Wertheim, Arthur Frank. *Radio Comedy*. New York: Oxford University Press, 1979.

Bernadine Flynn
MacDonald, J. Fred. *Don't Touch That Dial: Radio Programming in American Life, 1920–1960*. Chicago: Nelson-Hall, 1979.
Terrace, Vincent. *Radio's Golden Years*. New York: A.S. Barnes, 1981.
Wertheim, Arthur Frank. *Radio Comedy*. New York: Oxford University Press, 1979.

Jane Ace
Current Biography, 1948.
Terrace, Vincent. *Radio's Golden Years*. New York: A.S. Barnes, 1981.
Wertheim, Arthur Frank. *Radio Comedy*. New York: Oxford University Press, 1979.

Portland Hoffa
Franklin, Joe. *Joe Franklin's Encyclopedia of Comedians*. Secaucus, N.J.: Citadel Press, 1979.
Terrace, Vincent. *Radio's Golden Years*. New York: A.S. Barnes, 1981.

Minerva Pious
Franklin, Joe. *Joe Franklin's Encyclopedia of Comedians*. Secaucus, N.J.: Citadel Press, 1979.
Terrace, Vincent. *Radio's Golden Years*. New York: A.S. Barnes, 1981.

Mary Livingstone
"Milestones." *Time Magazine*, July 11, 1983.
Terrace, Vincent. *Radio's Golden Years*. New York: A.S. Barnes, 1981.

Hattie McDaniel
Current Biography, 1940.
Logan, Rayford W. and Michael R. Winston, eds. *Dictionary of American Negro Biography*. New York: W.W. Norton, 1982.
Terrace, Vincent. *Radio's Golden Years*. New York: A.S. Barnes, 1981.

Joan Davis
Franklin, Joe. *Joe Franklin's Encyclopedia of Comedians*. Secaucus, N.J.: Citadel Press, 1979.
Higham, Charles and Joel Greenberg. *Hollywood in the Forties*. New York: Paperback Library, 1968.
Obituary. *New York Times*, May 24, 1961.
Mitz, Rick. *Great TV Sitcom Book*. New York: Putnam, 1983.
Terrace, Vincent. *Radio's Golden Years*. New York and San Diego: A.S. Barnes, 1981.

Eve Arden
Current Biography, 1953.

Franklin, Joe. *Joe Franklin's Encyclopedia of Comedians.* Secaucus, N.J.: Citadel Press, 1979.
Mitz, Rick. *Great TV Sitcom Book.* New York: Putnam, 1983.
Terrace, Vincent. *Radio's Golden Years.* New York: A.S. Barnes, 1981.

Minnie Pearl
Aston-Wash, Barbara. "The World's Glad She Stopped to Say How-Dee." *The Knoxville News Sentinel,* Feb. 29, 1976.
Blackwell, Earl. *Celebrity Register.* New York: Simon and Schuster, 1973.
Correspondence with Minnie Pearl, March 20, 1984.
O'Neill, Lois Decker. *The Women's Book of World Records and Achievements.* Garden City, N.Y.: Anchor Books, 1979.
Tassin, Myron and Jerry Henderson. *Fifty Years at the Grand Ole Opry.* Gretna, La.: Pelican, 1975.

Ann Sothern
Current Biography, 1956.
MacDonald, J. Fred. *Don't Touch That Dial.* Chicago: Nelson Hall, 1979.
Mitz, Rick. *Great TV Sitcom Book.* New York: Putnam, 1983.

Marie Wilson
Mitz, Rick. *Great TV Sitcom Book.* New York: Putnam, 1983.
"Name Dropping." *Sunshine,* Nov. 11, 1984.
Obituary. "Marie Wilson, TV's 'Irma,' Dies at 56." *New York Times,* Nov. 24, 1972.

Judy Canova
Daley, Suzanne. Obituary. *New York Times,* August 7, 1983.
Higham, Charles and Joel Greenberg. *Hollywood in the Forties.* New York: Paperback Library, 1968.
Scheuer, Steven H. *Movies on TV.* New York: Bantam, 1981.

Chapter Four: Early Stand-Up Comics

Moms Mabley
Cahn, William and Rhoda Cahn. *The Great American Comedy Scene.* New York: Monarch, 1978.
Current Biography, 1975.
Fox, Ted. *Showtime at the Apollo.* New York: Holt, Rinehart and Winston, 1983.
Foxx, Redd and Norma Miller. *The Redd Foxx Encyclopedia of Black Humor.* Pasadena, Ca.: Ward Ritchie Press, 1977.
Obituary. *New York Times,* May 24, 1975.
Scheuer, Steven H., ed. *Movies on TV.* New York: Bantam, 1981.

Jean Carroll
Bernel, Albert. *Farce — A History from Aristophanes to Woody Allen.* New York: Simon and Schuster, 1982.
Slide, Anthony. *The Vaudevillians.* Westport, Ct.: Arlington House, 1981.
Smith, Bill. *The Vaudevillians.* New York: Macmillan, 1976.

Sally Marr
Goldman, Albert, from the journalism of Lawrence Schiller. *Ladies and Gentlemen, Lenny Bruce.* New York: Random House, 1971.
Scheuer, Steven H. *Movies on TV.* New York: Bantam, 1981.
Who Was Who On Screen, 3rd ed. New York: R.R. Bowker, 1983.

Phyllis Diller
Blackwell, Earl. *Celebrity Register.* New York: Simon and Schuster, 1973.
Diller, Phyllis. Interview, March 15, 1984.
"Diller Still a Dilly of a Comedienne." *Fort Lauderdale News/Sun Sentinel,* Feb. 24, 1984.
Entertainment Tonight, syndicated television series, March 3, 1984.
Payton, Sandy. WIOD Radio, Miami, Florida. Open phone interview with Phyllis Diller, Feb. 20, 1984.
"Phyllis Diller Fast and Funny As Ever." *The Miami Herald,* Feb. 24, 1984.
"Phyllis Diller: My Daily Prayer." *Movie Digest,* vol. 1, no. 3, May, 1972.
Phyllis Diller's Housekeeping Hints. New York: Doubleday, 1966.
"Say You're Sorry." *The Miami Herald,* Nov. 23, 1983.
Smith, Ronald L. "The Writing Life." *Writer's Digest,* November, 1982.
Television Academy Hall of Fame. NBC Special, March 4, 1984.
"V. Pres. Bush, Joan Rivers, Mickey Mantle, Jamie Farr Donate to Auction." *Putnam County Sentinel,* Ottawa, Ohio, Feb. 23, 1984.
"Vital Stats." *Sunshine,* Feb. 5, 1984.

Totie Fields
Encyclopaedia Britannica Book of the Year, 1979.
Franklin, Joe. *Joe Franklin's Encyclopedia of Comedians.* Secaucus, N.J.: Citadel Press, 1979.
"Milestones." *Time Magazine,* August 14, 1978.
Obituary. *New York Times,* August 3, 1978.

Chapter Five: Funny Women of Television

Imogene Coca
"Back Together Again." "TV-Radio," *Newsweek,* Aug. 5, 1957.
Caesar, Sid. *Tonight Show,* June 2, 1984.
Current Biography, 1951.
Freeman Presents. Turner Broadcasting Company. Television interview with Sid Caesar, March 9, 1984.
"Imogene." *Fort Lauderdale News/Sun Sentinel,* July 1, 1984.
"Last Time Together for a Great Pair." *Life,* June 21, 1954.
New York World Telegram, March 9, 1954.
Sennett, Ted. *Your Show of Shows.* New York: Collier Books, 1977.
Wilk, Max. *The Golden Age of Television.* New York: Delacorte Press, 1976.

Lucille Ball
"Ask Her Anything About Desi Sr., Divorce, Drugs, Gay Rights—Lucy Ball Hasn't Become Bashful at 68." *People Weekly,* Feb. 11, 1980.
"Broadcasting Museum Opens 'Lucy' Exhibit." *Miami Herald,* April 6, 1984.

Colombo, John Robert. *Popcorn in Paradise.* New York: Holt, Rinehart and
    Winston, 1979.
Current Biography, 1978.
"Henna Is the Color of Lucy's Success." *Fort Lauderdale News,* April 5, 1984.
Smith, Tim. "Lovable Lucy." *Fort Lauderdale News,* Aug. 7, 1983.
Wilk, Max. *The Golden Age of Television.* New York: Delacorte, 1976.

Martha Raye
Allen, Steve. *More Funny People.* New York: Stein & Day, 1982.
Biographical material from Ruth Webb Entertainment Talent Agency, Los
    Angeles, California.
Franklin, Joe. *Joe Franklin's Encyclopedia of Comedians.* Secaucus,
    N.J.:Citadel Press, 1979.
Higham, Charles and Joel Greenburg. *Hollywood in the Forties.* New York:
    Paperback Library, 1970.
Katz, Ephraim. *Film Encyclopedia.* New York: Crowell Publishing, 1969.
Mordden, Ethan. *The Hollywood Musical.* New York: St. Martin's Press, 1981.
Variety biographies.

Carol Burnett
Anderson, Christopher P. *Book of People.* New York: G.P. Putnam's Sons, 1981.
Biographical material from Rick Ingersol, ICPR Public Relations, Los Angeles,
    California.
Burke, Tom. "The Thespian Inside the Clown." *Cosmopolitan,* April, 1980.
Current Biography, 1962.
Dworkin, Susan. "Carol Burnett — Getting on with It." *Ms.* magazine, Sept.,
    1983.
Freeman Reports. Interview, Nov. 21, 1984.
Stanford, Herb. *Ladies and Gentlemen, The Garry Moore Show.* New York:
    Stein & Day, 1976.

Mary Tyler Moore
Alexander, Ron. "Mary Tyler Moore: A Late-night Cult." *New York Times,*
    April 9, 1984.
Amory, Cleveland. *Animail.* New York: Windmill Books & E.P. Dutton, 1976.
Current Biography, 1971.
Fury, Kathleen D. "Farewell, Mary Richards." *Ladies Home Journal,* March,
    1977.
"Mary Tyler Moore Looking for Laughs." *Ft. Lauderdale News,* May 31, 1984.
"Mary Tyler Moore Is in Good Shape." *McCall's,* Jan., 1983.
"Moore Set to Star in CBS Sitcom." *Fort Lauderdale News/Sun Sentinel,* Feb. 14,
    1985.
"MTM's Heart Is in Comedy." *USA Today,* June 5, 1984.
"Name Dropping." *Sunshine,* April 1, 1984.
"Newsmakers." *Fort Lauderdale News/Sun Sentinel,* June 23, 1985.
"Rhoda and Mary, Love and Laughs." *Time,* Oct. 28, 1974.
"Shine On, Val and Mare." *Newsweek,* Dec. 9, 1985.

Chapter Six: Familiar Faces

Joan Rivers
Adler, Jerry and Pamela Abramson. "Joan Rivers Gets Even with Laugh." *Newsweek*, Oct. 10, 1983.
Bark, Ed. "Can We Talk? Joan Rivers in Dallas Is Just to Die For." *Dallas Morning News*, Dec. 9, 1983.
Brenner, David. *Soft Pretzels with Mustard*. New York: Arbor House, 1983.
Clarke, Gerald. "Barbs for the Queen (and Others)." *Time*, April 11, 1984.
Collins, Nancy. "Funniest Lady." *People Weekly*, April 25, 1984.
Current Biography, 1970.
Entertainment Tonight, Feb. 11, 1984.
Hollywood's Private Home Movies, Nov. 11, 1983.
"I Was Losing My Best Friend—Everything." *People Weekly*, Dec. 10, 1984.
"People, etcetera." *Tropic Magazine*, Aug. 7, 1983.
Prial, Frank J. "For the 'Tonight Show,' Joan Rivers Is the Next Best Thing to Johnny Carson." *The New York Times*, July 31, 1983.
"Rivers Sole Carson Fill-in." *Miami Herald*, July 20, 1984.
Tonight Show broadcasts, Joan Rivers, host.

Kaye Ballard
Blackwell, Earl. *Celebrity Register*. New York: Simon and Schuster, 1973.
Franklin, Joe. *Joe Franklin's Encyclopedia of Comedians*. Secaucus, N.J.: Citadel Press, 1979.
Kuchwara, Michael. "Ma Teaches Survival, Ballard Style." *Ft. Lauderdale News/Sun Sentinel*, Friday, March 9, 1984.

Ruth Buzzi
Blackwell, Earl. *Celebrity Register*. New York: Simon and Schuster, 1973.
Laugh-In television shows.

Lily Tomlin
Allen, Steve. *Funny People*. New York: Stein & Day, 1981.
Anderson, Christopher P. *Book of People*. New York: G.P. Putnam's Sons, 1981.
Bennetts, Leslie. "Behind Lily Tomlin, There's Another Star." *New York Times*, Oct. 4, 1985.
Bernikow, Louise. "Women Comedians." *Mademoiselle*, Dec., 1981.
Burke, Tom. "Lily Tomlin—The Incredible Thinking Woman." *Cosmopolitan*, April, 1981.
Cahn, William and Rhoda Cahn. *The Great American Comedy Scene*. New York: Monarch, 1978.
Current Biography, 1973.
Judge, Diane. "Talking with Lily Tomlin." *Redbook*, January, 1981.
Kroll, Jack. "Divinely Human Comedy." *Newsweek*, Sept. 23, 1985.
"*Laugh-In* Crew Reunites to Celebrate Syndication." *Fort Lauderdale News*, Sept. 15, 1983.
Matthews, Jack. "'All of Me': 2 Fine Comics in 1 Body." *USA Today*, Sept. 21, 1984.
O'Neill, Lois Decker. *Women's Book of World Records and Achievements*. Garden City, N.Y.: Anchor Books, 1979.

Wagner, Jane. "Lily Tomlin's Memoirs of an Usherette." *The Movies*, July, 1983.

Fannie Flagg
Celebrities — Where Are They Now? Television Show, May 10, 1984.
"Fannie Flagg Develops a Game Plan for Acting." *Miami Herald*, March 14, 1984.
"Fannie Flagg Unfurls in All Directions." *People Weekly*, Nov. 23, 1981.
"Flagg 'em Down." "Showtime," *Ft. Lauderdale News*, April 20, 1984.
"Newsmakers." *Fort Lauderdale News*, Dec. 4, 1984.

Bette Midler
Anderson, Christopher P. *Book of People*. New York: G.P. Putnam's Sons, 1981.
"Back to Press." *Publishers Weekly*, Oct. 14, 1983.
Blackwell, Earl. *Celebrity Register*. New York: Simon and Schuster, 1973.
Bricker, Rebecca. "Take One." *People Weekly*, April 9, 1984.
Current Biography, 1973. Pp. 294–296.
"Name Dropping." *Sunshine*, Feb., 1984.
"No Frills." Cinemax TV, Oct. 14, 1983.
"People." *USA Today*, April 25, 1984.
Steinem, Gloria. "Our Best Bette." *Ms.* magazine, Dec., 1983.
Thornton, Linda R. "Divine Reception." *Miami Herald*, Oct. 9, 1983.

Goldie Hawn
Current Biography, 1971.
Darnton, Nina. "Miss Hawn Goes to Washington." *New York Times*, Dec. 23, 1984.
Franklin, Joe. *Joe Franklin's Encyclopedia of Comedians*. Secaucus, N.J.: Citadel Press, 1979.
"Goldie Hawn's Heartbreak Choice: Marriage or Career." *Ladies Home Journal*, January, 1982.
"Goldie the Riveter." *Newsweek*, April 23, 1984.
Haddad-Garcia, George. "Goldie Hawn Has the Last Laugh." *The Saturday Evening Post*, May/June, 1981.
Miller, Edwin. "Pure Goldie." *Seventeen*, May, 1981.
"People." *Time*, Dec. 2, 1985.
"Take One." *People's Weekly*, Nov. 21, 1983.
Watson, Linda E. "Pure Goldie!" *Teen Magazine*, July, 1983.
White, Timothy. "Prime Goldie — If You Think You Know Her, Think Again." *Rolling Stone*, March 5, 1981.

LaWanda Page
"Family." *Jet*, March 20, 1980.
"Gary Coleman: Are Black TV Stars Underpaid?" *Jet*, Dec. 10, 1981.
Mitz, Rick. *Great TV Sitcom Book*. New York: Putnam, 1983.

Gilda Radner
Collier, Denise and Kathleen Beckett. *Spare Ribs*. New York: St. Martin's Press, 1980.
Current Biography, 1980.
David Letterman Show. Late 1983.
Fort Lauderdale News, Dec. 20, 1983.

Miller, Edwin. "Gilda Update." *Seventeen*, Jan., 1981.
The New Show (Jan. 20, 1984). Gilda appeared as a ventriloquist with her dog Sparkles.
Stone, Elizabeth. "Gilda Radner: Goodbye, Roseanne, Hello, Broadway." *New York Times Magazine*, Nov. 9, 1980.
"Wilder, Radner Wed in France." *USA Today*, Sept. 19, 1984.

Jane Curtin
David Susskind Show. PBS, Jan. 18, 1985.
"Real Women Make a TV Comeback, Thanks to Susan Saint James and Jane Curtin in *Kate & Allie*." *People Weekly*, May 7, 1984.
Scheuer, Steven. *Movies on TV*. New York: Bantam, 1982.
"A Sitcom in Which Father Knows Nothing." *USA Today*, Feb. 10, 1984.
Who's Who in America, 1978–79.

Catherine O'Hara
Brown, Ian. "The Comic Triumph of *SCTV*." *Maclean's*, Dec. 27, 1982.
"Buffoons with Bite—SCTV is Vidiot's Delight." *Life*, October, 1982.
Hirschberg, Lynn. "Catherine O'Hara Needs a Rest." *Rolling Stone*, Sept. 15, 1983.
"Midnight Laughs in a New Key." *Newsweek*, March 30, 1981.
The New Show, March 2, 1984.
Wolcott, James. "Little Big Man." *New York*, Jan. 10, 1983.

Andrea Martin
Brown, Ian. "The Comic Triumph of *SCTV*." *Maclean's*, Dec. 27, 1982.
Collier, Denise, and Kathleen Beckett. *Spare Ribs*. New York: St. Martin's Press, 1980.
Stivers, Cyndi. "Buffoons with Bite." *Life*, October, 1982.
"20 Questions." *Playboy*, May, 1982.
Wolcott, James. "Little Big Man." *New York*, Jan. 10, 1983.

Mary Gross
Anderson, Jon. "Second City Pays Off for 'Ditsy' Mary Gross." *Chicago Tribune*, March 11, 1982.
Bianculli, David. "Not-Ready-for-Prime-Time Comedy Alive and Funny." Knight-Ridder Newspapers, Oct. 12, 1981.
Interview with Mary Gross, March 15, 1984.
Kogan, Rick. "Second City's 60th Shines." *Chicago Sun-Times*, Oct. 13, 1980.
St. Edmund, Bury. "Well, I'm Off to the Thirty Years' War." *Chicago Reader*, 1982.
"Second City, Chi." *Variety*, Oct. 22, 1980.

Chapter Seven: Writers and Directors

Selma Diamond
Ace, Goodman. "I Love Lucy Stone." *Saturday Review*, Jan. 17, 1953.
"The Current Cinema." *New Yorker*, July 25, 1983.
Metz, Robert. *The Tonight Show*. Playboy Press Book, New York: 1980.
Obituary. *Fort Lauderdale News*, May 15, 1985.

Obituary. *New York Times*, May 14, 1985.
"Selma Diamond: She Makes Paar Laugh." *Look*, April 10, 1962.
Tonight Show, Nov. 20, 1984.
"Watch the Windows." *Newsweek*, August 28, 1961.

Lucille Kallen
Contemporary Authors, vol. 102. Detroit, Mich.: Gale Research.
Sennett, Ted. *Your Show of Shows*. New York: Collier, 1977.
Wilk, Max. *Golden Age of Television*. New York: Delacorte, 1976.

Anne Meara
David Susskind Show. PBS, Jan. 18, 1985.
Kanner, Bernice. "Two for the Radio." On Madison Avenue, *New York*, April 11, 1983.
Murphy, Mary. "Without Blue Nun or Stiller." *TV Guide*, March 15, 1980.
"Newsmakers." *Ft. Lauderdale News*, Tuesday, Dec. 27, 1983.
"Role Takes Meara Back to Her Roots." *Fort Lauderdale News*, April 6, 1984.

Elaine May
Anderson, Christopher P. *The Book of People*. New York: G.P. Putnam's Sons, 1981.
Cahn, William and Rhoda Cahn. *The Great American Comedy Scene*. New York: Monarch, 1978.
Current Biography, 1961.
Gelb, Barbara, "Mike Nichols: The Director's Art." *The New York Times Magazine*, May 27, 1984.
Probst, Leonard. *Off Camera*. New York: Stein and Day, 1975.
"Vital Stats-Marlo Thomas." *Sunshine*, Feb. 24, 1984.

Erma Bombeck
Bailey, Eileen. "Bombeck on Bombeck." *Family Circle*, Jan. 3, 1984.
Bombeck, Erma. *If Life Is a Bowl of Cherries – What Am I Doing in the Pits?* New York: McGraw-Hill, 1971.
————. Interview, March 20, 1984.
————. *Motherhood – The Second Oldest Profession*. New York: McGraw-Hill, 1983.
Current Biography, 1979.
Good Morning, America television shows.
Publishers Weekly, June, 1984.
Tonight Show television shows.

Renee Taylor
David Letterman Show, April 17, 1984.
Kelleher, Terry. "'It Had to Be You' Is a Funny, Though Far-fetched Proposition." *The Miami Herald*, Jan. 16, 1984.
Wallace, David. "Joe Bologna Gets Laughs in *My Favorite Year*, but He Says the Real Comedy Is His Marriage." *People Weekly*, Nov. 8, 1982.
Whitaker, Charles. "Married Actors Turn Even Fights into Playtime." *Miami Herald*, Jan. 18, 1984.
Wiley, Mason. "Academy Awards – Among the Voters." *New York Times*, April 8, 1984.

Gail Parent
Beckett, Kathleen and Denise Collier. *Spare Ribs*. New York: St. Martin's Press, 1980.
Contemporary Authors, Volume 101. Detroit, Mich.: Gale Research.
David Letterman Show, May 10, 1984.
"36th Annual Awards." *Newsletter — Writers Guild of America West*, May, 1984.

Anne Beatts
Beatts, Anne. "Women, Friendship and Bitchiness." *Vogue*, August, 1981.
Beckett, Kathleen and Denise Collier. *Spare Ribs*. New York: St. Martin's Press, 1980.
Contemporary Authors, Volume 102. Detroit, Mich.: Gale Research.
Hammer, Joshua. "Anne Beatts." *People Weekly*, March 14, 1983.
Hirschberg, Lynn. "The Grody Bunch." *Rolling Stone*, April 14, 1983.

Chapter Eight: Rising Stars

Geri Jewell
Biographical material from G & L Management, Los Angeles.
Christy, Marian. "Humor Takes Edge Off of Handicap for 'Facts' Comic." *Fort Lauderdale News*, May 27, 1984.
Jewell, Geri. *Geri*. New York: William Morrow, 1984.
Kluge, P.F. "I've Been Pulled Over Once for Speeding and Four Times for Walking." *TV Guide*, May 15, 1982.
Miller, Edwin. "Courage Has a Face." *Seventeen*, Sept., 1982.
"Personal Touch." *20/20*, television show, May 24, 1984.

Elayne Boosler
Boosler, Elayne. "Andy, a Farewell to Andy Kaufman — By One Who Shared the Ride." *Esquire*, Nov., 1984.
Klein, Stewart. "The Queens of Comedy." *Bazaar*, August, 1983.
David Letterman Show, Dec. 16, 1982.

Diane Nichols
Dorschner, John. "The Comedians." *Tropic Magazine, The Miami Herald*, Sept. 26, 1982.
Hurst, John V. "Comedy Act Matter of Style." *Sacramento Bee*, March 19, 1982.
Johnson, Tom. "Thirteen of L.A.'s Funniest Tell the Time the Joke Was on Them." *California Living*, Feb. 26, 1984.
Nichols, Diane. Interview, March 27, 1984.
Simon, Richard. "It's a Birthday Party of Unlimited Laughter." *Sacramento Union*, August 7, 1981.
Variety, Sept. 22, 1982.

Whoopi Goldberg
Gussow, Mel. "Whoopi as Actress, Clown and Social Critic." *New York Times*, Oct. 28, 1984.

Nemy, Enid. "Whoopi's Ready, but Is Broadway?" *New York Times*, Oct. 21, 1984.
Peisch, Jeffrey. "Full Houses, Tough Critics for Whoopi." *USA Today*, Nov. 7, 1984.
Steinbaum, Ellen. "Goldberg Variations." *American Way*, March 5, 1985.
"The 'Whoopi' Comedy Show." *Newsweek*, March 5, 1984.
"Whoopi Goldberg — In Performance." *Ms.* magazine, May, 1984.

Jane Anderson
Anderson, Jane. Interview, Feb. 20, 1984.
Christon, Lawrence. "The Comedy Column." *Los Angeles Times*, Oct. 10, 1982.
"Critic's Corner." *Santa Monica Evening Lookout*, July 9, 1982.
Davis, Curt. "Anderson Is a Funny Girl." *New York Post*, July 14, 1981.
Henry, Kevin. "Anderson Is a Comic Relief to a One-Person Show." *Daily News*, July 4, 1982.
Hoffman, Jan. "Women Comics Cut Loose." *The Village Voice*, Sept. 9–15, 1981.

Lotus Weinstock
McGuigan, Cathleen, and Janet Huck. "The New Queens of Comedy." *Newsweek*, April 30, 1984.
Nichols, Diane. Interview.
Weinstock, Lotus. *The Lotus Position*. New York: Bantam, 1982.

Emily Levine
Johnson, Tom. "These Up-and-Coming Comics May Have the Last Laugh." *Weekend Style*, Jan. 20, 1984.
"A Standout as a Stand-Up." Los Angeles *Herald Examiner*, March, 1980.
"Women Comedians." *Mademoiselle*, January, 1982.

Dana Vance
Adcock, Joe. "This One Sparkles . . . Even Without Liza." *Philadelphia Bulletin*, Feb. 7, 1980.
Collins, William. "Revue Gives the Joy of Laughing." *Philadelphia Inquirer*, Friday, Feb. 8, 1980.
Richards, David. "A Devilish Pair at New Playwrights' Theater." *Washington Star*, July 24, 1979.
Takiff, Jonathan. "*Evening Without Liza* Is Inspired Insanity." *Philadelphia Daily News*, Feb. 6, 1980.
Vance, Dana. Interview, Feb. 2, 1984.
Winters, Sharon. "Comedy Revue Sparkles." *The Villanovan*, Feb. 8, 1980.

Monica Piper
Piper, Monica. Interview, May 5, 1984.
"What's Up." *The Register*, June 3, 1983.

Maureen Murphy — High-Heeled Women
Berger, Phil. "The New Comediennes." *The New York Times Magazine*, July 29, 1984.
Bernikow, Louise. "Women Comedians." *Mademoiselle*, December, 1981.
Contardi, Barbara. Correspondence, June 4, 1984.

"High-Heeled Women." *Ms.* magazine, June, 1984.

Hoffman, Jan. "She Who Laughs Last." *The Village Voice*, Sept. 9–15, 1981.

Hutchings, David. "Ask No More for a Manicure by Sandra Bernhard — She's the New Queen of Comedy." *People Weekly*, March 7, 1983.

"The Jesters," television special.

Johnny Carson Show, March, 1984.

Levitt, David M. "Comic's Improv Group a Very Serious Business." *New Tribune*, Woodbridge, N.J., April 24, 1984.

"Lookout." *People Weekly*, March 3, 1980.

"Lookout." *People Weekly*, July 11, 1982.

"Lookout." *People Weekly*, May 28, 1984.

McGuigan, Cathleen, and Janet Huck. "The New Queens of Comedy." *Newsweek*, April 30, 1984.

Morgenstern, Debra. "Women Who Get the Last Laugh." *McCall's*, March, 1983.

"Sahara, Las Vegas." *Variety*, May 4, 1983.

Saturday Night Live, Paula Poundstone, Feb. 11, 1984.

Weisman Celia. "Performance: The Best Medicine; A New Comedy Roundup." *The Villager*, Oct. 29, 1981.

Wetschler, Ed. "Cues and Reviews." *Entertainment New York*, April 15, 1982.

"Who Will Succeed Moms Mabley as Top X-Rated Comedienne?" *Jet*, Nov. 15, 1979.

Index

D

Daley, Augustin 8
"Dame Illya Dillya" 90
Damsel in Distress 54
Dana, Bill 213
Dana, Charles 15
Dandridge, Ruby 65
Danny Kaye Show 61
Danz, Cassandra 227–228
Darling, Alice 59
Darling, Eddie 9
A Dash Through the Clouds 20
Davenport, Alice 19
David Frost Revue 179
David Letterman Show 163, 191, 193, 203
David Meyer Is a Mother 193
Davies, Marion 44
Davis, Benny 109
Davis, Bette 86, 116, 135, 146, 222
Davis, Joan (Madonna Josephine Davis) 66–67, 220
Davis, Mac 227
Davis, Madonna *see* Davis, Joan
Davis, May Lee (now Monica Piper) 219–222
Dayton *Journal-Herald* 186
Deacon, Richard 121
The Death Trail 5
The Decline and Fall of the Entire World as Seen . . . 136
DeMarco, Rita 84
DeMarco, Tony 84
Deneuve, Catherine 212
DeNiro, Robert 226
Derek, Bo 132
Desilu Productions 105, 106
The Detective 191
Detective School 158
De Tour 150
Devine, Andy 110
Diamond, Selma 176–178
Diamond Lil 40
Diamond Lil (1928) 38
Dick Cavett Show 141
Dick Van Dyke Show 121, 177
Dietrich, Marlene 40, 101, 222
Different Strokes 159
Diller, Phyllis 1, 2, 82, 86–94, 130,

213, 223
Diller, Sherwood 87
Dinah! 216
Dinah Shore Show 72, 114
Dinner at Eight (1933) 12
Diplomat Hotel (Hollywood, Florida) 133
"The Divine Miss M." 148
Dixey, Henry E. 12
"Do You Think I'm Sexy?" 112
Doctor Rhythm 44
Dollars 155
Dolman, Bob 169
Dolman, Jack 169
Domingo, Placido 118
Don Kirshner's Rock Concert 203
Donahue, Phil 228
Donovan, King 102
Donovan, Warde 90
Don't Just Stand There 121
"Don't Send Me Back to Petrograd" 33
Dooley, Ray (Rachel Rice Dooley) 2, 17
Dooley, Robert Rogers 17
Double or Nothing (1937) 110
The Doughgirls (1944) 68
Douglas, Mike 81
Dowling, Eddie 17
Down, Harrison 44
Down and Out in Beverly Hills 151
Downstairs at the Upstairs (New York) 148
A Dozen Socks 20
The Drag 38
Draper, Ruth 1, 3, 15–16, 45, 141, 207
Draper, Ruth Dana 15
Draper, Dr. William Henry 15
Dreesen, Tom 203
Dressler, Marie (Leila Koerber) 2, 9–12, 14
Drexler, Rosalyn 149
Dreyfus, Richard 152
Driscoll, Marian *see* Jordan, Marian
Driver, Frances 87
Driver, Perry 87
Duffy, Henry 68
Duffy's Tavern 63
Dumas, Helene 61
Dunaway, Faye 166

I